D0049378

BY KURT EICHENWALD

500 Days: Secrets and Lies in the Terror Wars

Conspiracy of Fools: A True Story

The Informant: A True Story

Serpent on the Rock

A Mind
Unraveled

A Mind
Unraveled

A MEMOIR

Kurt Eichenwald

BALLANTINE BOOKS

NEW YORK

Copyright © 2018 by Kurt Eichenwald

All rights reserved.

Published in the United States by Ballantine Books, an imprint of Random House,
a division of Penguin Random House LLC, New York.

BALLANTINE and the HOUSE colophon are registered trademarks of
Penguin Random House LLC.

LIBRARY OF CONGRESS CATALOGING-IN-PUBLICATION DATA
Names: Eichenwald, Kurt, author.
Title: A mind unraveled : a memoir / Kurt Eichenwald.
Description: First edition. | New York : Ballantine Books, [2018]
Identifiers: LCCN 2018018965 | ISBN 9780399593628 (hardcover) |
ISBN 9780399593635 (ebook)
Subjects: LCSH: Eichenwald, Kurt, 1961—Health. | Epileptics—
United States—Biography. | LCGFT: Autobiographies.
Classification: LCC RC372 .E33 2018 | DDC 616.85/30092 [B]—dc23
LC record available at https://lccn.loc.gov/2018018965

Printed in the United States of America on acid-free paper

randomhousebooks.com

2 4 6 8 9 7 5 3 1

First Edition

Book design by Jo Anne Metsch

For Dr. Allan Naarden, who saved me

You may encounter many defeats, but you must not be defeated. In fact, it may be necessary to encounter the defeats, so you can know who you are, what you can rise from, how you can still come out of it.

—MAYA ANGELOU

AUTHOR'S NOTE

This book may raise a few questions, the most obvious being: How can readers trust the recollections of someone whose memory has been impaired by decades of seizures? The answer is simple. Throughout most of my experiences, I kept diaries, notes, and tapes, largely because I found a benefit in recounting thoughts and feelings I shared with no one. I also retained medical documents, letters, and other contemporaneous papers. Later, I interviewed friends, family, doctors, and colleagues, who related their perspectives. While digging through old papers, I also discovered a box filled with tapes that were recorded in the 1980s by people who went through these events with me. Two of the speakers say I requested the recordings and promised not to listen to them for decades. I do not remember asking for them, but these proved invaluable, allowing me to gain insight into the experiences and emotions of friends and family that otherwise I never would have known. Passages from these old recordings are included after most chapters in this book.

I had never reviewed all of the diaries and recordings until undertaking this project, and the level of detail they contain astonished me. In them, I seemed driven to describe every sight, every sound. I commented on chair squeaks, expressions, tones of voice. Perhaps I needed to paint a mental image for my future reference, perhaps my medications led me to ramble, perhaps reciting obsessive detail was my way of finding control in an uncontrolled situation. Whatever the reason, these records helped me reconstruct events I don't remember.

Then there is the nature of memory. As anyone with recollection problems can attest, it is not like a bucket that is either filled with water or not. There are pieces and pathways—which even neuroscientists only vaguely understand—woven into the tapestry of brain function that dictate whether memories stay or fade.

Names, including those of people I have known for years, are hard to retrieve, which has led me to techniques that allow me to dodge saying them. I often rely on nicknames, such as calling my editors "Boss." If my wife, Theresa, and I run into acquaintances or friends, she will casually utter their names so I can hear them. There have also been times when names of objects have been hard to recollect. I once stared at a chair trying to connect a word to this wooden thing with four legs; eventually, I recalled a term, but I couldn't move the sound from my mind to my mouth. So I just pointed.

Inconsequential or stress-free occurrences often disappear, which can be saddening, since I often forget vacations or nice experiences with my family. Sometimes, though, I'm glad memories fade—for example, I forgot a dental surgery; I know it occurred only because Theresa told me when I found gizmos intended for me to use after the procedure. I watch reruns of my beloved *Law & Order* over and over without remembering who committed the crime. I sat three times through my favorite movie—*Memento*, about a man with severe memory problems—each time knowing only that I loved the film; otherwise, it was all new to me.

Recollections of traumatic or important or funny events tend to remain accessible; in fact, they are surprisingly vivid. Then there is a technique others with memory problems will understand: remembering to remember. If I experience a short-term event of little significance but that I know I want to recall, at times I am able to store the memory if I focus on retention. I cannot do that with everything since, if I did, I would be standing in silence endlessly, thinking about remembering.

My age at the time of an event also plays a role. The deterioration of my memory seems to have begun when I was nineteen, after the seizures escalated. So I have found that I recall events from when I was younger with little difficulty.

Another question: Why would someone with an impaired memory become a journalist? Parts of this book address that subject, but the basic answer is simple: I wanted to and could. People with memory problems find compensation tricks, and I am certain those made me a better journalist. Moreover, once I accepted the magnitude of my memory problems (it takes time to recognize how much you forget once you've forgotten it), I was already successful, and no one was challenging the accuracy of my work.

In writing about myself, however, the techniques I describe above have limits. Often there is an amnesia surrounding a seizure that leaves me incapable of remembering. For example, in 2018 I learned from a good friend of my mother's that many years ago, I was arrested by police who misinterpreted my post-seizure symptoms as inebriation. The friend says I was taken to jail and locked up in the drunk tank. Somehow my mother learned of my arrest and attempted, unsuccessfully, to persuade the officers by phone that I did not drink alcohol and must be in a post-seizure state. Fearing I would go for too long without my medication, she boarded a plane, flew to wherever I was, bailed me out, and then bawled out the police. She died in 2016 and never told me this story, most likely because she thought it would upset me. I remember nothing about it, although it is disturbing to discover I probably have an arrest record somewhere.

Seizures also made it difficult over the years for me to fully recall events that had occurred just hours before, impeding my ability to write down what had happened. In those instances, trying to remember was like watching a silent movie while wearing a blindfold that is periodically removed for a few seconds and then tied back on. In other words, there are blank spots. When necessary, I cite missing chunks of memory involving events I describe here. Sometimes, there are occurrences I remember, but I have no idea when they took place. Several appear in this book at the point I believe most accurate, but I note that I am not certain of the timing.

Obviously, I am not claiming the dialogue in this book is a verbatim transcript. Much of it I recounted in my diaries within days or hours of my experiences. Friends and family did the same for me over the years when I asked for their recollections. I believe that reconstructing the conversations from this source material provides a far more accurate portrayal of what happened than mere paraphrase would.

A final note: If you have epilepsy, this book does not foretell your future. Everyone's experiences differ, and many of mine occurred because of my own bad decisions. Moreover, a careful reading can help you avoid my past errors—I was told fictions about epilepsy that damaged me, and some doctors made mistakes an educated patient never would have allowed. So don't look on this story as representative of what could happen to you. Learn from my errors. This book can help you understand that, for most people, epilepsy does not have to block you from the life you desire. I believe the lessons in this book apply to people who face a range of traumas or difficulties, even those unrelated to health.

Do not judge doctors—particularly neurologists—by the arrogant, incompetent ones who treated me in the earliest years after my first major seizure; in the decades since, my neurologists have been unfailingly knowledgeable, caring, and humble. Medicine has also advanced dramatically in the development of new treatments for seizures. Far more options are available now than there were even just a few years ago. Perhaps most important, epilepsy specialists say there is a growing recognition of the failures by neurologists in the past to understand the psychosocial difficulties faced by people with this condition and the role the medical community can play in helping to address them.

Also, do not draw conclusions about the effectiveness or side effects of the anticonvulsants prescribed to me based on my experiences. Reactions to these medications vary, and mine are not a sign of whether one drug is bad or another good.

Finally, for some individuals I encountered, I will be using pseudonyms or not naming them at all. I am uncomfortable dragging people into my story without permission. I also will not use the real names of medical professionals whose inattentiveness and poor judgment caused so much unnecessary damage. They know who they are.

A Mind
Unraveled

PROLOGUE

Swarthmore, Pennsylvania

WINTER 1982

At first, I couldn't feel the cold.

It was as if I had fallen from the sky, with no memory of where I had been or how I returned. My mind was in disarray, unfocused, aware that there was pain but not quite comprehending that it was mine.

I vaguely remember thinking that a blur of white and dark had clouded my vision, but the impression made no sense. I drifted into the unconsciousness that always followed one of my epileptic seizures.

Time passed. Eventually, cold stabbed into my head, seeping down my back and eating at my skin. After a convulsion, injuries were mysteries to solve, enigmas that might tell me if I was safe: What had I wounded and how? In the past, I'd burned my arm horribly with boiling water. Other times, I emerged from seizures with broken ribs but no idea how they'd fractured.

This time, the pain was hard to place. I woke a bit more, terrified as I struggled to figure out where I was. Then I knew.

Snow. I was buried under snow.

A day would pass before I pieced together what happened. I had been returning from a night at the Swarthmore College library and took a shortcut toward my dorm. As I made my way along this out-of-the-way path, I collapsed in a convulsion, one of many I experienced over the years. I rolled down a small hill, hitting a tennis court fence. As I lay unconscious, a blizzard swept in, covering me in a shroud of white.

After I awakened, I struggled to dig myself out, repeatedly falling down the slope that I did not realize was there. My strength ebbed. I wanted sleep. Just a little bit. I would try to find my way out of the snow after I slept.

I'm going to die. If I don't get up, I'm going to die.

The thought should have roused me, but I drifted, almost resigned to my disjointed recognition that I would not survive.

A twinge of pain shot through my right hand. At some point, I had cut my palm. The sting stirred me, but not enough to shock me awake. Even in my fog of confusion, I knew I had found an answer. To shake off sleep, to save my life, I had to intentionally hurt myself.

I thrust my hand through the snow and scraped my palm across the ground. I remember crying as twigs or dirt poked into the cut, the pain somehow worse because it was self-inflicted. Still not enough. I slid my throbbing hand across the ground again. It was difficult to deliberately hurt myself, but the effort worked; my overwhelming desire to sleep gave way to a determination to survive. I crawled up the hill.

A light, shimmering in the distance. I saw it ahead of me, beautiful and flickering like nothing I had ever cast my eyes on. I would not realize until the next day that the vision was a lamppost, turned glorious and twinkling by the snow in my eyes and my nearsightedness; my glasses had come off during my seizure.

That distant light became everything to me. I knew I was far from its glow, alone in darkness, invisible to others. But light meant people. Light meant I might be seen. Still unable to stand, my clothes frozen against my body, I edged toward that beacon, shoving my hand through the snow to scrape my palm again whenever I drifted toward sleep.

Edging forward on my hands and knees exhausted me; it seemed to go on forever, though it probably took less than ten minutes. Finally, I arrived at the bottom of an outdoor stairway and pulled myself up the steps.

I reached a stone patio. Lights from a dormitory blazed around me; other students were inside, so close, standing behind windows. I tried to scream, but because of exhaustion or fear or the cold itself, my cries came out as hoarse whimpers. The warm, safe students I saw through those nearby panes of glass couldn't hear me.

I became aware of someone else outside, a hulking man walking quickly, probably to escape the bitter cold. I called, "Help!" as best I could. I have no idea how loud or how often I said the word before attracting his attention.

A man stood over me. Later, I learned he was a Swarthmore football player whom I barely knew. He scooped me off the ground and carried me into the warmth of the dorm.

The burly student put me down and said something, but I didn't understand him. I lay at the bottom of the stairs off the entryway. The indoor light caused my head to throb after so much time in darkness, and I was soaking wet. My pants were frozen, in part because I had lost control of my bladder. Other students appeared, but all I recall are looks of shock on their faces. Noises, voices, chaos.

My hands were raw with pain. I looked at them, and what I saw was unrecognizable—bloody, swollen deformities. Small cuts where frozen skin had torn apart ran red across my knuckles; these would become tiny hairline scars that forever remain as reminders of one of the more horrific nights of my life.

Terror welled up, spurred by the sight of my monstrous wounded hands. The last thing I remember is screaming.

■ ■ ■

I suffer from the scourge of Christ for my sins. I practice witchcraft, and thousands of my kind have been burned to death. I have been attacked by demons. I am sacred, capable of miracles. I am a seer, blessed by God and infused with the Holy Spirit. I am forbidden from becoming a Catholic priest. I should be institutionalized, chained to walls, as I prepare for my death. I see lights that are not there. I think of words I cannot say. My arm throws; my head jerks. I become aware I am someplace with no idea how I got there.

I have epilepsy, a condition recorded in every known civilization. Largely incurable and mostly untreatable until the early twentieth century, for thousands of years, it has been associated with religious fanaticism and cruelty. In my mother's lifetime, people prone to seizures were dumped into institutions with names like the Eastern Pennsylvania State Institution for the Feeble-Minded and Epileptic—a hospital of nightmares that finally closed in 1987, eight years after my diagnosis.

I experienced frequent convulsions and losses of consciousness from 1979 through 1991, from the ages of eighteen to thirty years old. With a handful of exceptions, only lesser seizures have continued since. I have lived most of my life knowing I could be seconds from falling to the ground, seizing, burning, freezing, or worse. Am I too near that window? Am I too high up? Is the oven open? I ask these questions every day. Yet even with my precautions, I have not been able to protect myself—when I was at my worst, I fell down stairs, broke bones, cut my face. I awoke on a subway platform as teenagers kicked me. I regained consciousness in blood-drenched sheets, uncertain if it was me who had bled. I was thrown out of school and lost jobs because of my epilepsy. For years, I believed that each day might be my last, that I would die from an accident or a seizure or by my own hand. I lived in a boundless minefield, never knowing if I was a step away from triggering an explosion.

And yet I found success, both professional and personal. I vowed not to let seizures interfere and compartmentalized—sometimes in an unhealthy way—the pains and fears from my day-to-day experiences.

Partly because of that, I resisted pursuing this book. I wrote about my night in the snow in 2005, but after finishing those pages, I thought, *Why bother?* I had faced terrible things and surmounted them. Plenty of people have done the same. As a reporter, my job is to write about others' lives, not my own. And did I really want to publicly expose my personal demons and ordeals? I feared, perhaps irrationally, if everyone knew what had happened, they might think less of me. So this potential book went into a virtual folder on my computer. Unaware that I had already shelved the project, my wife, Theresa, kept it alive by urging me to recount my story, assuring me that my fears about public reaction were misplaced. She told me that, as a physician, she knew others fighting traumas unrelated to epilepsy who could benefit by reading about how I managed my challenges. I always replied that of course my family thought it was a tale worth telling, but who else would care?

Still, the idea nagged at me. Was I failing to face the central challenge of my life? By mostly keeping quiet after having gained some prominence as an author and a journalist, was I tacitly saying that others with seizures should hide?

I knew that epilepsy is misunderstood because so many of us with the condition stay silent, fearful of the stigma that still attaches to the word. We distrust our own bodies and grapple with a terror of losing control of our brains. Then there is the psychosocial damage. Because of the fear seizures engender, people with epilepsy have been subjected frequently to discrimination. A look at online message boards shows postings from women who were told they would be disowned if they married an epileptic boyfriend, others fired from jobs or shunned by friends after a seizure. Until 1956, eighteen states allowed for forced sterilization of epileptic people, and marrying them was illegal in seventeen; Missouri kept its marriage ban on the books until 1980.

In 2014, I sought the advice of prominent people in the epilepsy community, who encouraged me to write this book. When I suggested my experiences might be unique and unfairly terrifying to others with seizures, I heard for the first time that no, the things I had confronted—even the worst of them—were not exclusive to me. On the contrary, I was told that the fact I believed I alone faced certain experiences underscored the need to drag epilepsy out of the shadows.

And so I write.

I write, though, without self-pity, and I cringe at praise for having dealt with these challenges. After my first few years of major seizures, I never asked, *Why me?* Why not me? Fortune dealt me some bad cards, as it has many others in many different ways, and so I played them. In fact, despite all that has happened, if I had the power to travel back in time and push a button that would stop me from ever having epilepsy, I wouldn't do it. Even knowing what lay ahead—those nightmares of confusion, injuries, and frequent fear of death—I would accept that fate. This book is my explanation why. In that answer lies what is, I believe, the secret of how to find happiness, how to recapture control, how to build a life worth living, even in the wake of significant trauma.

In a conversation with

DR. ALLAN NAARDEN, 1987

My then neurologist

If all you give a seizure patient is sympathy, then I'm not sure how much you're really helping them. That's not to say that you shouldn't sympathize with them. You have to. But you have to also really encourage them and act like a cheerleader. And maybe push them to be better than they otherwise would wind up being.

CHAPTER ONE

A Christmas tree sparkled silver in front of me. My frequent, sudden sleepiness returned as I wondered how long I had been standing there. Or had I been walking? I felt odd, in a way difficult to describe—not sure where I was, not fully connected to my thoughts.

I glanced around the room. Gold tinsel hung on the walls of a living room stuffed with older furniture. Windows peered at a neighbor's house wreathed with colored lights. Nighttime. I remembered—this was a party thrown by kids from my girlfriend's high school. Across the room, I saw Mari Cossaboom, whom I had been dating for more than a year, chatting with classmates. I strolled up to them, trying to conceal my confusion with a veneer of confidence.

It was 1978, Christmas vacation of my senior year in high school. My blank out didn't scare me; such episodes occurred sporadically, and family and friends greeted them with shrugs. Even my parents saw nothing amiss—lots of people stared, they assured me. But I wondered, Did they really? Did others just drift away and wander around in a daze?

At least I thought I wandered, because when I became aware of my surroundings after an episode, I believed I was someplace I hadn't been earlier. But a friend of mine who witnessed one of these waking trances said no, I hadn't moved. Once, I realized a classmate was in front of me, and I had no idea how he had appeared there. He asked what I was doing with my hand. I looked down and saw my fingers grasping my shirt. He told me I had been picking at it. I had no memory of doing so.

The staring spells had worsened the previous summer when I attended a Harvard University program for high school debaters. I found myself reconnecting to consciousness with a feeling of confusion far more often than in the past. When I returned home, I asked my mom to set up an appointment with my pediatrician. She agreed but again told me not to worry—everybody stared.

I described the problem to my physician but failed to mention the sleepiness or disassociation that followed a staring episode. I didn't consider those to be symptoms, much less important. He confidently told me I was fine; lack of sleep and too much coffee were the culprits. I accepted the diagnosis, cut back on caffeine, and tried to get more rest, at least as best a teenager could.

If someone had suggested these spells were seizures, I would have laughed it off, since I bought into the falsehoods about epilepsy. In the uninformed popular imagination, a seizure meant a body convulsed by violent spasms, frothing at the mouth and swallowing a tongue as emergency workers loaded the sufferer into an ambulance for a desperate rush to the hospital. My experiences were nothing like that.

It would be stretching things to say my parents should have known what was happening, but they were better versed in medical issues than most. My father, Heinz Eichenwald, was a world-renowned specialist in pediatric infectious disease, though he spent more time in academia than seeing patients. Growing up in Dallas, I felt proud of his influence on medicine. He seemed to be chairman of pediatrics departments everywhere—University of Texas Southwestern Medical School, Children's Medical Center, Parkland. For one month every year during the Vietnam War, he traveled to Saigon, where he helped run a children's hospital. He was close to Albert Sabin, the developer of the oral polio vaccine, whom I called Uncle Al, and a Nobel Prize winner even dropped by our house.

My mother, Elva Eichenwald, was a nurse who knew more practical medicine than my father. They had met at New York Hospital and married in 1951. My sister, Kathie, came along in 1955, followed three years later by my brother, Eric. In 1960, while pregnant with me, my mom was stuck with a used hypodermic needle and contracted hepatitis. Her doctors advised that the pregnancy might lead to death or complications and ordered her to bed. When I was born in 1961, doctors found me healthy, but my mother wondered decades later if hepatitis had played a role in causing my epilepsy.

Mine was a fortunate childhood. My family wasn't wealthy, but I knew we were well off. With property cheap in Texas, we lived in a sprawling ranch-style house, separated from the street by a five-hundred-foot gravel driveway. We spent no money on swimming pools or fancy cars or vacations; if we couldn't drive to our destination, we didn't go. Instead, my parents invested in our education. My brother and I attended St. Mark's School of Texas, a private school I adored. My mom told me that each morning in first grade when we drove onto campus, I leaned out the window yelling, "Hello! I'm here!" as if everyone were waiting for me. Eventually, our family's connection to St. Mark's grew closer when the school hired my mom as the nurse. She became a beloved fixture there—other students often told me they considered her a second mother.

Nothing occurred in my childhood to prepare me for struggles in life. Probably my most harrowing childhood experience took place when I was five and attending a summer day camp. After weeks of waiting, my turn arrived to ride everybody's favorite horse, Ginger. A counselor boosted me onto the saddle, and I rode the pinto out of the stables. We arrived at the edge of the trail when Ginger collapsed under me, dead. At day's end, the counselors assured an angry mob of my fellow kindergartners that I had not personally killed her.

My siblings struggled with my father's high expectations and dictates on their life choices, but I largely escaped scrutiny, since he considered me a happy-go-lucky intellectual lightweight. If my brother came close to falling off the high honor roll, my father would sound off, but my B and C grades barely got a glance. Strangely, I didn't care.

Life was mostly calm with a dash of adventure. My best friend often joined me on hikes along a nearby creek, where we kept our eyes open for the ever-present water moccasins. After short treks, we'd scamper onto a bridge and throw off our G.I. Joe action figures with parachutes attached. On longer journeys, we'd stop at a run-down deserted sugar shack we called "the haunted cabin" until the structure disappeared. Meanwhile, another friend and I spent weeks along a portion of the creek, cutting down tiny trees and roping them together into a clubhouse. We returned to the spot one day to build the roof, only to discover that our ersatz cabin had also vanished. I even enjoyed time alone, lying on the grass while staring at the sky or climbing through a drainage tunnel that ran beneath our driveway.

I always found hobbies, from making yarn pictures on wooden slabs to building glue-soaked model cars. When my neighborhood friend pursued magic, I joined him. The two of us started performing around Dallas; the pay was good, but we invested most of it back into the show.

I recognized my good fortune and appreciated it, largely because I was exposed to others who faced hard times. My parents volunteered at free clinics for the indigent, and we would assist some of their patients in need. We also sponsored two orphans who visited on weekends, with the younger boy sleeping in my room, where we stayed up talking or jumping on the beds. On Sunday evenings, when we drove them back to Buckner Children's Home, I always felt guilty that my life was so much easier than theirs.

My first taste of journalism came at fifteen, and I hated it. I joined the school newspaper, the *Remarker*, but my assigned stories—budget plans, a play, a speaker, blah blah blah—were beyond boring. I had no doubt that unless they were looking for their own names, my fellow students never read a word.

A turning point came in my junior year when I was working on a piece about parent-teacher night. Once again, I plunged into the pointless routine: Report on an event nobody cared about, write a story no one would read. I went through the motions by interviewing the head of the high school, Mike Shepperd. After wrapping up, I started loading my backpack.

"So, do you enjoy working for the paper?" Shepperd asked.

"No," I replied. "I'm thinking about quitting. I never write anything interesting."

"What do you want to write about?"

Laetrile. I wanted to work on a story about laetrile. This was a supposed miracle cancer treatment that had not been approved in the United States, but plenty of patients traveled to Mexico for the drug and swore it worked. I had first heard about it on *60 Minutes* a few years before and discussed it with my father. The controversy fascinated me.

"So write about it," Shepperd said.

The *Remarker* didn't allow for that, I replied. We covered school events, not national news.

Without another word, Shepperd called the *Remarker*'s faculty sponsor. "Andy, Kurt Eichenwald is in my office, and he wants to do an article about laetrile. He thinks no one will let him. Can he write it?"

A second passed, and Shepperd hung up. "Okay, so now you're assigned the article. No more excuses."

Weeks of reporting and writing followed; the article filled two inside pages of the paper. I was delighted and proud and even won a local journalism prize. As a reward, I suppose, I was named a contributing editor in my senior year. I didn't want to be a spoilsport and reject the position, but I had accomplished all I wanted to at the *Remarker*. So I accepted without enthusiasm and almost immediately distanced myself from the job. That was a flaw in my character—I could devote enormous energy to something that fascinated me, but once I finished, my interest flagged. My obsession with a single task could end as fast as a flip of a switch. A few months into my senior year, that trait became obvious to the paper's staff, who nicknamed me "the noncontributing editor."

That do-it-and-drop-it trait played a large role in my choice of colleges. After four years of high school debate spent whiling away weekends at tournaments, I suddenly and inexplicably lost all enthusiasm for public speaking. As a result, I eliminated schools with strong debate teams from my list of options, fearing I'd be pressured to join. My brother was a junior at Swarthmore College, a small liberal-arts school about eleven miles from Philadelphia that offered little in the way of debate. The school was reputed to be an academic hothouse, so given my middling grades, I assumed I would have no chance at admission.

When Swarthmore's acceptance letter arrived, I raced so recklessly up the driveway in my father's car that I almost crashed into a fence.

Weeks before graduation, my class performed Senior Follies, the annual song-and-skit roast that poked good-natured fun at St. Mark's, the teachers, and other students. This event was considered a big deal, and my classmates elected me producer. I spent months huddled with friends writing skits and song lyrics, planning choreography, and getting by with little sleep. My staring episodes escalated, and some teachers worried about my health. One day, Shepperd saw my haggard face and ordered me to skip the rest of my classes, go home, and get some sleep.

I had never been so exhausted as on the night of Senior Follies. I appeared in a few skits, including one where I caricatured a quirky science teacher. I was reciting a joke about a toy car when I suddenly felt confused. I had stopped speaking and couldn't recall my most recent words. These "sudden break" episodes had begun earlier that year, and though I considered them minor annoyances compared with the staring spells, I had no idea how long they lasted. All I knew this time was that one had occurred onstage.

Later that night, the class got together for an after-show party. As I nursed a beer, someone played a recording of the performance. Everybody listened, laughing, but I sank into uneasiness. Had I made a fool of myself when I drifted away? Had my classmates hidden their embarrassment? When they heard the odd pause, would they quiz me about it?

We reached my sketch, and I listened as my voice broke off midsentence. A second passed, and I started my lines again, repeating two words I had just said.

As my fellow drinkers—who had noticed nothing amiss—continued enjoying our jokes, I felt lost in wonder. Was that it? The sudden breaks were no big deal. But what about my staring spells? Friends told me they lasted ten to fifteen seconds. Did they? Maybe it just seemed that way.

Looking back, I realize that my thoughts about these experiences were irrational. The episodes embarrassed me, but I believed they were commonplace. I had scores of questions—Why was I so confused afterward? Why had I picked at my clothes? Why did I think I'd walked somewhere when I hadn't?—but never raised them with anyone. Had I mentioned them, any doctor would have known I was experiencing seizures. To this day I believe that had I not been so deep in denial, many of my traumatic experiences in the years that followed never would have occurred.

An audio letter from

MARI COSSABOOM, 1981

A longtime friend

In high school, you would have those staring seizures, the staring spells. I assume they're seizures now, but we didn't know then. It used to happen all the time. . . . I didn't worry about them because your parents didn't worry about them. Everyone always said that the reason those things were happening was because you were tired. And you have to admit, you were always exhausted, because you were always working on a million things at once. So I just accepted it—all your friends accepted it—as just something that happened sometimes.

CHAPTER TWO

A deceitful September lured back another summer day, stirring bees that drifted through an open window into my college dorm room. I watched them buzz about as I rocked in a glider chair squeezed between school-issued furniture and a cheap table. One of my new roommates, Carl Moor, sat at his desk with his back to me, brushing aside my questions with one-word responses that left little doubt of his uninterest in chatting.

Following a miserable summer, I had arrived a few weeks late to my first semester at Swarthmore. In July, I tore ligaments in my ankle, which required me to walk on crutches with a plaster cast. Then, the following month, I contracted paratyphoid fever—the less deadly bacterial brother of typhoid—and was laid up with a temperature that hit 106 degrees. I'd never experienced delirium before, but as fever cooked my brain, I enjoyed conversations with a friend who was not there and grew angry at nonexistent people fighting nearby. By the time I could get out of bed, I had dropped more than ten pounds.

By then, freshman orientation at Swarthmore had passed, classes were under way, and newly minted classmates had begun forming friendships. I arrived with clothes drooping on my body, crutches, a green pallor to my face, and the misunderstood, not-quite-correct story that I had contracted typhoid fever.

I had been assigned to a four-person suite in Wharton Hall, among the most popular and storied dormitories on campus. Built in 1903, it exuded quaint collegiate charm. Gargoyles depicting every season and the signs of the zodiac decorated eaves of the building. Wrapping around three sides of an expansive patio, Wharton featured some of Swarthmore's largest dorm rooms; ours included two bedrooms and a living area that easily accommodated four work desks, bookcases, the glider chair, stereo tables, and an ancient, disheveled couch.

Another roommate, Pat Cronin, had been a friend at St. Mark's. Fellow Swarthmore students lumped us together as "the Texans," a segregating designation I hated. Carl was a boyish quasi athlete from Chicago, and the fourth roommate, Franz Paasche—born in New York, raised in Canada, and educated at a Vermont boarding school—rapidly developed a reputation as the coolest kid on the hall.

In the first days after my arrival, Carl and Franz rarely spoke to me. Carl later told me that my appearance—particularly the sallow face and crutches—had put him off; that, combined with the dreaded "typhoid fever" label, led him to keep his distance. Franz correctly concluded I was decidedly uncool. With my limited ability to roam campus and most cliques already formed, Pat remained my only friend in those early days.

Then came the bees. After the first few drifted in, I lifted one of my crutches and pushed the rubber tip against one, crushing it into the wall. As more flew through the window, I realized that either there was a nest directly outside or something in the room had attracted a small swarm.

"Carl, we've got a bee problem."

He turned around from his desk and saw the buzzing intruders; again I lifted a crutch and flattened another bee into the floor.

"Give me the other one," Carl said, reaching for a crutch.

He closed the window, and for the next few minutes, Carl and I competed in an insect safari. Once, I threw a crutch javelin at a bee, missing my target but ratcheting up the mood of hilarity. Carl dashed about, squashing them on the floor and against walls. We laughed at the spectacle—me hopping on one leg, balancing myself as I whacked at bees, Carl with the other crutch trying to top my score in the killing spree. I lost the competition, but in that bee hunt, I won a friend. From then on, Carl would remain one of my closest buddies.

My strained relationship with Franz persisted—bee hunt or not, I remained uncool—but we became closer a few weeks later when he returned from a frat party feeling ill. He hadn't drunk much and worried he'd unknowingly downed punch made with grain alcohol. I took him to the men's room. Whatever he'd drunk came back for a repeat appearance, hitting the toilet, floor, and wall. When the heaves stopped, I put him to bed, then returned to the bathroom to mop up the mess. Apparently, cleaning other people's vomit passes for cool, and we, too, became good friends. In our conversations I learned he came from an amazing family—his great-grandfather General Kurt von Hammerstein-Equord had been part of a failed plot to kill Adolf Hitler, while this hero's daughter, Maria Paasche, gained fame for helping Jews escape Nazi Germany on her motorcycle. But my bond with Franz didn't fully form until spring vacation, when we traveled to his home in Toronto. He showed himself to be enormously thoughtful and kind; he, in turn, learned that I could be a lot of fun.

Carl, Franz, and I grew to have one of those cliché "three musketeers" friendships. All of us were comedians of sorts—Carl was the king of the one-liner—and we began to attract a circle of friends who hung out in our room chatting endlessly over slices of pizza, sat with us in the dining hall, or accompanied us to parties. We also talked politics. I especially remember debating an ardent Marxist, throwing him off guard with a handful of questions; his face drooped as he proclaimed sadly, "Everything I've believed is wrong." While his obvious feeling of devastation gave me a twinge of guilt, I realized I loved the intellectual swordsmanship, camaraderie, and challenging conversation that came with college life.

The roommates soon discovered coincidences between us that defied probability, particularly since we had been assigned to share a suite arbitrarily. Franz's grandfather Milton Levine had been one of my father's medical school professors, and the two remained lifelong friends. Carl's middle-school girlfriend in Chicago had attended high school in

Vermont with Franz, and even dated his roommate. We continued discovering unlikely overlaps in our lives for decades, well into our fifties.

Time passed, with Pat and I seeing less of each other as we drifted
toward different circles of friends. Carl, who shared my love of horse-
play, pitched ideas for occasional off-campus adventures that I gladly
joined. In one escapade, we hopped a bus to Atlantic City; we met the
casinos' age minimum of eighteen, but Franz, still seventeen, grumbled
about being left behind.

Our destination was Caesars Boardwalk Regency. As we entered
the cavernous casino, a security guard demanded identification—no
surprise, since Carl looked at most sixteen. Smells of alcohol and grill-
ing meat wafted through the room. Flashing lights, spinning wheels,
and ambling waitresses imbued the place with a relentless air of excitement. But when we passed the slot machines, I cringed at the sight of
haggard-looking elderly people feeding in coins they obviously could
not afford to lose as they searched for a big win that would never come.

Carl and I decided to limit ourselves to one hundred dollars in
losses and hit the two-dollar blackjack table. We had been doing well
when a man wearing a white suit and gold chains joined us.

"They call me The Idiot," he said out of nowhere. He told us he had
just lost a fortune playing high-limit blackjack. "Now I have to sit here
with you losers at the two-dollar table."

I'd never met a high-stakes gambler before—or even someone who
professed to be one—and, despite his self-identification as The Idiot,
I was entranced. The dealer slid another round of cards out of the
shoe. Carl and I had placed our chips in the betting box when The
Idiot spoke up to demean our decisions. He doled out advice; since
this was a man who really knew casinos, we did as we were told. And
we started to lose, lose, lose. As we approached our loss limit, we suddenly looked at each other in astonishment. I don't remember if we
said it aloud or just understood our shared thought.

Why are we listening to a guy who just lost a ton of money?

So we started to ignore The Idiot. His rants about our playing decisions continued even as we climbed back from the hole he dug for us.
I don't remember if we ended up winning anything, but I didn't care;
we had a blast.

Back at Swarthmore, the four roommates enjoyed ribbing one another in bull sessions about the merits of the places where we grew up—Pat and I in Texas, Carl in Chicago, and Franz in Canada—and the flaws of the others' old stomping grounds. In early November, when six American diplomats were rescued from Iran by the Canadian government and the Central Intelligence Agency—a caper later depicted in the movie *Argo*—someone ran a full-page advertisement in *The New York Times* blaring, "THANK YOU, CANADA." Franz posted it on our bulletin board. In response, I cut out a photo of the New York City Marathon and wrote a caption beneath it saying, *Millions of Canadians flee for America after a guard accidentally left open a gate.* That went on our front door. Later that week, the *Times* published an article about Albert Spaggiari, a French master thief who escaped from the police by calmly opening a window; smiling; saying, "Goodbye"; and leaping out, bouncing off a car before riding off on a waiting motorcycle. The roommates declared him our new hero. We clipped out the story and up it went next to the "THANK YOU, CANADA" ad.

That same month, Carl and I were goofing around in our dorm room. We had started periodically launching into fake fights for reasons only teenagers could understand. During one match, Carl took a swing at me, and I flew backward theatrically. I had not seen the wooden desk chair a few feet behind me and smashed my head on the seat. The next thing I remember, I was on a bed at the campus health center. A doctor diagnosed a concussion. Something about the way I hit my head led the medical team to give me a neck brace, which I was told to wear for a couple of weeks.

Afterward, friends noticed that I periodically zoned out. I experienced an embarrassing episode when I suddenly became aware I was sitting in the dining hall with wet pants and my lunch mates staring at me. Apparently, I had started to stare while holding a glass of soda; it had fallen onto my chair and shattered.

Shortly before Thanksgiving vacation, I woke up confused; my muscles and hand hurt, and my head ached. I was on the ground beside my bed. I remembered nothing about what had happened but assumed something had caused me to slide off the mattress, leaving me in this disconnected state.

Terrified, the next morning I called my mother to tell her I needed to see a doctor when I came home.

An audio diary from

ELVA EICHENWALD, 1982

My mother

I want to go back to the beginning, in the fall of 1979. Kurt called me one evening to tell me he wanted to see a doctor as soon as he came home for Thanksgiving break. He said something was wrong with him, that his stares were worse and something had happened in his sleep. I made an appointment for him to see his pediatrician when he first came home from school. Just before he came home, the pediatrician's office called and canceled the appointment.

I was very confused at that time. I had not told Heinz about Kurt's fears, because he didn't deal well with family health problems, but once the pediatrician canceled, I felt I had to tell him. Heinz was very upset and tried to find a neurologist, but everyone he knew was out of town. I suggested a neurologist I met through St. Mark's, but Heinz turned that down because he didn't know the man. He then said there was somebody at the medical school who was supposedly pretty good. Thus began our trials and tribulations with Charles Nicholson.

CHAPTER THREE

In a dreary hospital hallway, I glanced at plastic chairs decorated with gloomy colors that would never be found in a box of crayons, much less in nature. My mother sat beside me, and I studied her face. Her look of fear crushed me. Whatever was happening with me, I felt terrible for the distress it caused her.

We were waiting for technicians to perform a CAT scan. After hearing about my strange experiences at school, my father, insisting only academic doctors could be trusted, arranged for me to consult a neurologist who worked under him at the medical school. Family medical decisions were always dictated by him, so his choice of a physician was the final word.

The doctor, Charles Nicholson, rarely saw patients, my father said, instead devoting himself to research. Years would pass before I realized why that made him a terrible choice. Nicholson was a pediatric neurologist who spent his time in the lab; I was over eighteen, an adult, and needed someone with hands-on clinical expertise. To this day, I believe Nicholson would have refused to be my doctor if my father hadn't been his boss.

The day so far had been a blur. Because of the episode at school, my parents had forbidden me from driving, so my mother brought me to my appointment. I had spent almost no time with Nicholson but already disliked him. He said little to me and ignored my mother. When he took my medical history, I mentioned the staring spells, which led to numerous questions about how I felt before and after those episodes. His inscrutable face flashed with recognition when I mentioned that I had been seen picking at my clothes while staring. Then we discussed my experience waking up on the floor next to my bed. All the while, he exhibited the bedside manner of a termite inspector.

He performed a neurological test, a process I would repeat dozens of times in the years that followed: Squeeze his fingers, push his outstretched hands, follow a light with my eyes. He knocked my knees with a hammer and squeezed around my neck.

After the examination, Nicholson sent my mother and me for more tests at Children's Medical Center. At the time, it didn't strike me as odd that I was an adult wandering the halls of a pediatric hospital in search of the lab for my next diagnostic test. We found the office for my EEG, a test that records electrical activity of the brain. The technician described how the exam worked and why it was used, then bound clumps of my hair with rubber bands to expose parts of my scalp. Afterward, he dabbed glue in each spot before attaching the electrodes. My mother thought I would be amused at my appearance and brought out a mirror. The sight horrified me. I snapped at her, and she apologized. We were both struggling our way through this, blindly trying to buck up the other.

Throughout the day, I took each step as if by rote. But when I saw my mother's face as we sat on the plastic chairs outside the CAT scan office, reality crashed down. A massive machine was about to take innumerable images of my brain. The doctor was looking for a tumor.

A tumor.

I hadn't considered this before but suddenly could think of nothing else. I might be dying. And I would find out soon.

The technician appeared and invited me in. A giant, donut-shaped machine stood to one side. Its size shocked me; I had thought it would be no bigger than an X-ray device. Minutes later, I was supine on a table, the top of my head facing the machine's massive hole. I may be mixing up my recollections—I have had many scans since then with different devices—but I believe this was the first time a technician infused a dye into me to make the pictures easier to read. He slid a needle into my arm, and the dye seeped in.

"You're going to taste something metallic," he said.

I waited. I wasn't tasting anything . . . Wait, yes I was. Perhaps, I mused, I now knew the flavor of a rust-covered lightning bolt. My face flushed.

The table quietly trundled back and forth through the donut hole as the technician adjusted my location under a red alignment laser. I stared at the white casing a foot or so from my face. I wondered if this was how it felt to be in a coffin.

The table moved out a little and then back in. A whirring sound started each time the table stopped.

"Just a minute," the technician called out.

Later, I would learn that CAT scan technicians always checked the images before ending the test. But in my feverish state of apprehension, I thought he had discovered something alarming. Soon, the moving table brought me out of the machine, and the technician said we had finished.

"Did you see anything?" I asked.

"You'll have to ask your doctor."

I'm dying. I was sure of it. I considered the technician's refusal to answer as confirmation that he had seen a tumor and wanted to leave the job of breaking the bad news to Nicholson.

That afternoon, I rejoined Nicholson, exhausted. My mother had accompanied me all day, and my father came down from his office to hear the verdict. I sat beside my mother in front of Nicholson's desk; my father leaned against the wall. The desk between my doctor and me gave me an uncomfortable sense of solitude, despite my parents' presence. I focused on Nicholson's flattened hair; the image of the villain from the 1930s film serial *The Perils of Pauline* flashed through my mind.

Stop it. I was taking out my fears on this man who, despite his disagreeable bearing, wanted to help. I picked at my head. The glue that had been used to attach the EEG electrodes stuck to my scalp like concrete. I felt certain I'd be walking around for days looking as though a drunken barber had taken a hatchet to my hair.

Nicholson said nothing as he flipped through each sheet of paper, examining all the test results. Then he put the file on his desk and looked at me.

"You have . . ."

A brain tumor.

". . . epilepsy."

A wave of relief swept over me. *Epilepsy. Not* cancer.

"Could that kill me?" I asked.

"No, it can't." His response was wrong; epilepsy can be fatal.

"So what does that mean?"

"It means you have seizures."

How is that an answer? I thought.

He told me that the staring spells were called petit mal seizures, and the symptoms I described from the night I awoke on the floor were common after a grand mal seizure.[*] I didn't know what that meant, and he explained it was the name used for general convulsions, which often strike when people sleep.

Nicholson turned to my father and began talking. I wanted this neurologist to explain our next steps, what the treatment was, whether the epilepsy might go away. Or would it get worse? Did epilepsy mean my brain needed surgical repair? I thought carefully, trying to arrange the words for my next question in a way that would force him to give more than flip answers.

Without looking at me, Nicholson told my father, "He's going to have to go on anticonvulsants."

"All right," my father replied. "Which are you going to prescribe?"

"I've seen success with Tegretol."

As their conversation rambled on, I imagined myself jumping on Nicholson's desk. *I'm right here!* I could scarcely believe he was ignoring me and that my father was allowing it to happen. When it seemed their conversation would not end soon, I interrupted.

"What is Tegretol?"

Nicholson shifted his gaze to me. "It's a medication that's been around for about a decade."

---

[*] In 2016, an international epilepsy group reclassified terminology for seizures since names like grand mal and petit mal did not capture all types of episodes. Because the words are relevant to my story, I will use the terms as they existed at the time of these events.

"Will it stop the seizures?"

"It should."

Don't yell at him. "I don't understand what that means. Will it stop the seizures?"

Nicholson looked annoyed. "Yes, it will stop the seizures." He hesitated. "Well, let me be specific. You might still have some staring spells until we get the medication adjusted."

I was about to ask another question when Nicholson cut me off. "Now, don't start feeling sorry for yourself," he said. "There are children dying from cancer, and they're a lot worse off than you. You're not going to die from seizures. Those kids could only wish they had epilepsy."

What? I had been diagnosed for maybe two minutes, I had asked a couple of questions, and now my neurologist was telling me I should feel lucky I didn't have cancer? Was I not allowed to ask about epilepsy because there were children with fatal diseases? But in my emotional condition, I didn't lash out at his comment. Instead, believing he was key to stopping the seizures, I accepted his implicit command to stay quiet.

Nicholson resumed speaking to my father. I looked at my mother and could see she was as intimidated as I was. She asked about medication side effects. Nicholson ignored her.

Finally, he turned to me again. "What do you want to do with your life?"

Were we about to start chitchatting? I still knew next to nothing about my diagnosis or treatment, and suddenly we were discussing my future? I had graduated from high school only five months ago.

"What do you mean?" I asked.

"What do you want to do for a living?"

"I don't know," I replied, still confused by his questions. "I've been thinking I might want to become a lawyer."

Nicholson eyed me evenly. "No, you can't do that," he said. "Seizures can be triggered by stress. You need to choose a career as stress free as possible."

"But—"

"I also think you need to reconsider attending Swarthmore," he said.

I had been about to ask, If the medication would control the seizures, why did I need to avoid a job that might trigger seizures?

"Swarthmore is tough," he continued. "It's not good for someone with epilepsy. You need to discuss with your parents whether it's wise to go back. You won't be able to keep up."

Each sentence was a kick in the gut. *Drop your plans; drop your school; leave your friends; prepare for failure. Oh, and the drugs will stop the seizures.* So many questions filled my head that I had no idea which to ask first.

"Also, don't tell anyone about your diagnosis," he said. "If people know you have epilepsy, they'll be afraid. Seizures are frightening. If you tell people, you might lose friends or jobs."

My chest tightened. "But what if I have a convulsion in front of someone?"

"That's why you're on the medicine, to stop that."

"Okay, but I've been having these staring spells forever. My roommates already know about that."

"Tell them not to tell anyone. And if you ever have to say something about this, call it a seizure disorder. Never say epilepsy. The word scares people. 'Seizure disorder' is less frightening."

I still didn't understand. If the anticonvulsants would stop the seizures, why were we talking about this? "But the medication—"

"Yes, that's critical. Never miss your medication."

"Why? What happens?"

"Just don't miss it."

Don't yell. "I understand I shouldn't miss it. But what happens if I miss it?"

"Don't even consider that. Don't miss it."

I thought for a second. "Okay, let's say I'm on an airplane, and it crashes into the ocean. I swim to a desert island. All my medication went down with the plane. What's going to happen?"

"You'd just have to find a way to get your medication."

I gave up. This doctor, I decided, took pleasure in confusing me. My father seemed untroubled; I figured he knew the answers to my questions. Maybe he would tell me later.

Nicholson instructed me to never use illegal drugs or over-the-counter medications that might be sedating and to limit myself to one drink of alcohol a day. Then, before I knew it, he ushered my mother and me away. I headed to the elevator baffled. He had failed to explain what caused the seizures, how the medication worked, or what side effects I might experience.

He had, however, convinced me that my life might be ruined by epilepsy. If I didn't hide, if I didn't lie, I would be tossed out of college, lose my friends, and spend the rest of my days alone in some low-stress job I hated. His words left me in shock, too emotionally over-whelmed to feel anything.

My mother and I reached the car, and I slid into the passenger seat. She said we needed to take my prescription to the pharmacy. I sat in silence, looking out the side window as trees and stores moved past. I thought I should be crying, but somehow I couldn't. I believed Nicholson. I believed I now had to live in secrecy and fear.

At home, I swallowed anticonvulsants for the first time, a ritual I would repeat almost every night for the rest of my life. *My daily dose of death*, I thought. I read the package insert that came with the medication, and the list of side effects sounded like the health nightmares suffered by a hopeless patient on a medical television show. Breathing problems, irregular heartbeat, confusion, life-threatening this, fatal that. The drug could cause serious diseases, particularly involving blood or skin, but I recognized none of the names. I didn't notice the black box, full-caps instructions at the top of the insert saying that, to ensure I didn't contract a dangerous condition called aplastic anemia, I needed comprehensive blood tests every week for three months and then monthly for at least two years. Nicholson either didn't know those instructions or, in the months that followed, ignored them.

My mother drove me to the Dallas Epilepsy Association, and the counselor there put me at ease. He answered my questions until I understood my condition and my medication. He explained that if I missed my Tegretol, I might have a seizure; if I stopped it altogether, I could end up hospitalized or even die. Eventually, I understood that the drug could help or hurt. Taken correctly, it might control seizures. Used irresponsibly, it could cause them. I couldn't help but wonder: *Why didn't Nicholson just tell me? Why did he play those cruel games?*

The counselor mentioned grand mal seizures, and I interrupted him. "I don't need to worry about those. My neurologist said I won't have them anymore."

"That's good," he replied, hesitation in his voice. "How did he determine that?"

"Because I'm going on the medication."

The counselor nodded silently. I wondered why he paused.

"Look at it this way," he said. "Even someone who's sure they'll never drive anywhere but down the block needs to know how to put on a seat belt. So let me talk to you about grand mal seizures, and then I can answer your questions."

He asked me about the night I woke up on the floor beside my bed, and I confessed that I didn't understand how Nicholson had concluded this was a grand mal seizure.

"Everything you're describing is what happens in a postictal state of a grand mal seizure," the counselor said. "That's the name for the period of time after a seizure when you can be awake, but the brain still hasn't recovered."

During convulsions, neurons—which control all action, thought, senses—fire out of control, he said. The brain protects itself by producing chemicals to inhibit those cells. Metaphorically, the brain was a burning house, and the inhibitors were firefighters spraying water on the flames. But just as a soaking wet house can't burn again until it dries, someone whose brain is filled with inhibitors won't feel or act normally until the chemical balance returns.

"And that made my hand hurt?" I asked.

"Not the seizure itself. You probably hit your hand during the seizure, though."

I still had doubts. "If I had a grand mal seizure, wouldn't it wake up my roommate?"

"It might. Sometimes grand mal seizures can be accompanied by loud noises. But other times they can be quiet."

The counselor also dispelled myths about convulsions. Tongue swallowing was an old wives' tale; if someone was lying faceup after a seizure, the tongue might flop backward, but elevating the head on a pillow or turning it to the side solved that problem. Putting spoons, pencils, or any hard object in the mouth was unnecessary and dangerous. That mistaken remedy for the tongue-swallowing myth likely resulted from seeing the well-trained place a wallet or soft bite stick between the teeth. People's jaws often clamp tight during a convulsion, and soft items could protect the tongue, lips, and cheeks from bad bites. If the mouth was already shut, it was too late to stop a bite, and prying open the jaw could fracture a bone. When the untrained used a spoon or another hard object, teeth could break.

Also, the counselor told me, no one should hold down a person experiencing a seizure; that could cause injury or intensify the convulsions. A seizure typically lasted a minute or two. If it continued more than four minutes, someone needed to summon medical help. Otherwise, there was no reason for an ambulance after a seizure; once emergency room doctors learned I had epilepsy, they would leave me to sleep it off and then send me home when I awoke. However, in case I ended up in the hospital, the counselor recommended I wear a medical-alert bracelet or necklace listing my name and diagnosis.

The bottom line, he said, was to tell friends and family to use common sense during a seizure—keep me from hitting solid objects, put something soft under my head to protect it, and let the episode run its course.

The conversation helped, but the meeting could have been more of a turning point had I not once again failed to ask important questions. I'd accepted Nicholson's depiction of my future and didn't want to hear the same dreary prognosis from this counselor. I left his office feeling better, but apprehensive about the lost opportunities that lay ahead for me. I tried to shake off the self-pity; after all, as Nicholson had said, children were dying of cancer.

Thanksgiving came and went. Normally I enjoyed the family dinner, but this time I remained lost in thought as I contemplated Nicholson's pitiless monologue. I couldn't let him be right. I liked school, enjoyed my friends, loved my life. Maybe if I tried hard, I thought, I could stay at Swarthmore. Maybe, if I stuck it out, I'd be able to handle any job after I graduated. From what Nicholson had said, it would be easy to stumble, to let years slip past as opportunities withered away because of my epilepsy.

While I still didn't understand the illogic of his statements—the medication would stop the seizures, but revealing the seizures could destroy everything—I set an inflexible goal for myself, one to use as the measure of whether my life was on track: I would graduate with my class. I would not let myself slide into a failure that forced me out of school. If I kept pace with my friends, I could be certain that the sentence Nicholson had handed down was wrong. I had to graduate with my class. This would be my emotional touchstone.

The first step, though, was to make sure no one would learn about my seizures. When I returned to school, I decided, I would sit down with my roommates and explain why they could never tell anyone about episodes they might witness or my diagnosis.

An audio letter from

CARL MOOR, 1986

My college roommate

You were very worried that people wouldn't hire you, that if people found this out about you that you would never get jobs or would never be treated the same. Wanting to be able to be treated the same was a big deal for you. So we had no trouble in agreeing to give you that secrecy. But that was—in the long run, that was detrimental and something I came to wish that we'd never started on.

CHAPTER FOUR

The sound of dishes smashing against the floor echoed through the Swarthmore dining hall. Shouts of panic, orders barked, thuds from a struggle. I had been eating with friends when the noise erupted from the entryway. Instinctively, I rushed toward the commotion along with others who wanted to find out what was happening.

At the bottom of a staircase lay a mob of students, arms grappling, legs akimbo. The people I recognized were upperclassmen; several played on Swarthmore's anemic football team. I couldn't make sense of the chaotic scene, so I asked someone what was going on.

He pointed into the mass of people. "That guy is having a seizure."

I went silent. Just weeks had passed since my diagnosis, and now, for the first time, I was seeing someone in convulsions. The mountain of students held down a kitchen worker, pinning the man's arms and legs. No, not a man, a teenager. His face was red, and he struggled to breathe as the weight of the would-be Good Samaritans crushed him against the floor. I panicked—the kid needed space, air. Weeks earlier, I wouldn't have known the danger he faced. But I'd learned a lot from the Epilepsy Association. These well-intentioned students were probably intensifying the seizure and could break the boy's bones or squeeze the life out of him.

Tentatively, I stepped toward the heap of bodies and saw a large redheaded man with a bushy mustache clutching the boy's left arm. "Excuse me," I said. "You're doing everything wrong."

Bushy Mustache ignored me as he shouted an order at another student. I stood silently for a second.

"Get off!" I suddenly shouted. "Let him go! You're making this worse!"

He whipped his head around, anger in his face. "Look, kid, I'm premed," he snapped. "What makes you think you know so much?"

I wanted to answer, *Because I have epilepsy.* But then all of the things Nicholson had warned about could come to pass—losing friends, school, everything. I had a choice: Save a stranger or protect myself. I turned from the hideous scene, walked away, then leaned against the stone wall, unable to shake the rush of guilt I felt. I looked back at the boy's face, contorted and flushed.

"I'm sorry," I whispered. "I'm so sorry."

I couldn't watch anymore. I headed upstairs toward the building's main exit, forgetting about the dishes I'd left on the dining table. I grabbed my jacket off a coat rod and pulled it tight around me before stepping outside. The sky was clear in a cold twilight as I trudged back to my dorm.

I thought about Nicholson's promise: I would never have a grand mal seizure again. He had been wrong. A few nights earlier, I had convulsed, this time in front of my roommates. None of them remembers the specifics of that seizure, but I know it left me devastated. Why would Nicholson have told me the convulsions were over if he wasn't sure?

Later that evening, Franz mentioned the kitchen worker's seizure. "It worried me," he said. "I thought it was you."

I tried to be casual about the whole thing—yeah, strange someone else at our tiny school had a seizure—but my unspoken thoughts were irrational. In an odd way, I thought the boy under that pile of bodies might have been me. Being forced to choose between two obligations—protecting the kitchen worker or myself—had kindled emotions I couldn't understand. Mortified by my weakness but too afraid to find out if the boy had survived, I needed to talk to someone. But with my thoughts irrational and my remorse tormenting me, who was there? My roommates had been supportive and sympathetic friends; I wasn't going to make them my counselors too. The only person who could understand what I needed to say, I realized, was me. I wouldn't need to confess my shame to others if I came to terms with the emotions on my own. I grabbed a blue spiral notebook and a black pen off my desk, then walked to the next room. I sat on my bed, flipped open the notebook, and wrote. I recounted the event. I wrote about Bushy Mustache.

Look, kid, I'm premed, I scrawled. *What makes you think you know so much?*

I dug my pen into the paper, gouging a hole as I reread the words. *What makes you think you know so much?*

A moment passed. *How can I be such a coward?* I wrote.

I ended there but returned to my notebook later that evening with a blue pen, this time to scribble two grammatically tortured sentences. *I don't know can handle this,* I wrote. *It's not right I lose much if people find out.*

Christmas vacation arrived, and I flew home to Dallas, eager to see Nicholson again. He was difficult to reach by phone, and even when we spoke, he just assured me I would be fine if I gave the medication more time. A face-to-face, I hoped, would give me the chance to find out why the convulsions hadn't stopped.

Once again, my mother drove me to his office, and with my father absent, Nicholson spoke only to me. I noticed his rudeness toward my mother; I wondered if women left him feeling threatened or if he was just contemptuous of them.

My appointment accomplished nothing. He performed another neurological exam—"Squeeze my fingers; push my hands"—but brushed aside my concerns. When I asked why the convulsions hadn't stopped, he questioned whether I had brought them on myself by ignoring the rules: "Are you drinking too much?" "Have you been using drugs?" "Did you miss your medicine? I told you not to miss your medicine."

I assured him that I had followed his instructions. I felt small, begging for an answer about why my health was not improving. Nicholson asked if I still experienced the petit mal seizures, and I told him yes. There was a lot I didn't know at the time: For one thing, his petit mal diagnosis was wrong.

Nicholson wondered if my Tegretol dosage needed to be increased and sent me for a blood test to check the amount of the drug circulating in my body. I handed the technician a form with check marks on preprinted entries, sat in a chair, and laid out my arm on a table. I winced, anticipating the sting, before she slid the small, thin needle into my skin. This was the first of hundreds of blood tests over the years; now they are so routine I can't remember if my fear of the needle was followed by any pain. I headed back to Nicholson, who said he would call me when he received the lab results. My visit ended. I knew nothing more than when I arrived.

Days later, my father returned from work with news that Nicholson had told him my drug levels were fine. I was stunned—why was *my* doctor talking to my father instead of to me?

I asked questions about the results. My father didn't know the answers, so I telephoned Nicholson; his secretary took a message, and he never called back. I urged my father to speak to Nicholson at work and tell him we needed to talk. After that prodding, my doctor finally contacted me. He assured me there were no problems; the lab tests showed the Tegretol had reached the minimum therapeutic level of five milligrams per liter. This made no sense to me. I still had seizures. Who cared what the blood levels showed if the problem hadn't stopped?

I asked if I might need more than the minimum level, but he insisted it was best to use as little as possible to avoid side effects. Over time, he promised, the seizures would be controlled. I could tell he was eager to end the conversation. The call lasted no more than a minute.

Looking back, I know I should have fired Nicholson, but at that point, I never considered switching doctors. The relationship between people with epilepsy and their neurologists is complex and, with the wrong doctor, can lend itself to abuse. The terrifying loss of control that accompanies convulsions leads to a sense of powerlessness, with the neurologist taking the role of the only possible savior. Other epilepsy patients I've spoken with experienced this same paralyzing, desperate dependence on their neurologists, a feeling that can override common sense or the courage to question decisions. Without that doctor, control can never be achieved, helplessness never defeated, life never stabilized.

So despite Nicholson's abrasiveness, I kept him as my doctor. Christmas vacation ended, and I returned to Swarthmore, as confused and frightened as ever.

The first thing I realized was that my left thigh ached. Then my groin and my lower back. The room light caused my head to feel as if an ice pick had plunged into my skull. The inside of my bottom lip throbbed with pain; I tongued it for the taste of blood. None, but I could tell I had bitten the meaty flesh.

I was waking from another convulsion, feeling as though I had just played ten consecutive games of basketball. While my memory of events before a seizure was always sketchy, sometimes I recalled seeing lights flash in the left side of my visual field. There were also instances when the world became amazingly vibrant. Whatever else happened before I lost consciousness was lost to the amnesia surrounding a convulsion. As a seizure began, my neurons fired in uncontrolled electrical bursts that swept across my brain. My muscles pulled tight as I fell to the floor in what is known as the tonic phase. My jaw closed so strongly that people could hear my teeth crunching even from the next room. A guttural noise from my throat made it sound as if my airway was obstructed; sometimes, I stopped breathing altogether. Then the clonic phase started, as the frenzied electrical impulses commanded my body to jerk. I assumed the pattern rarely changed, since afterward the same muscles always ached.

As I came to recognize I was awakening from a grand mal seizure, panic set in. I didn't know where I was, and I couldn't open my eyes without intensifying the headache. This pain, this fear, these seizures, had become part of my life every few weeks in the second semester of my freshman year. I knew I could be anywhere and often imagined the worst—on a street, a staircase, near a flame.

Then I heard a familiar voice.

"Remember me? Your old pal Hunk?"

Franz. Whenever I roused from a seizure, he and Carl had taken to reciting the scene from *The Wizard of Oz* where Dorothy's friends re-introduce themselves as she awakes in Kansas. It was goofy but incredibly important to me. This was their signal that I was safe or at least that I was around people who knew how to handle the situation.

Carl told me I was in our dorm room and recounted what he knew about everything I had done before the seizure began. My hand reached for my head; for reasons I never understood, I often feared it was bleeding. I struggled to speak without a stutter. Muscles in my throat also pulled tight, so my speech was unusually soft, with lots of delays. Still, when I finally could, I joked with them as I lay on the floor. It seemed humor was always the best way to communicate that I was all right.

The seizures mostly occurred after 9:00 P.M., so I rarely left our room that late unless accompanied by Carl, Franz, or Pat, becoming dependent on them in ways I now know were unfair. A few teenagers were dealing with a problem none of us should have faced alone. Still, they have assured me for decades that, at least during the first year and a half, the experience was not hard on them. Carl joked that the sei-zures gave him exercise, since he sometimes had to help me back to the room. But the three of them always communicated that they just con-sidered me a friend who needed help sometimes. "It was tremendously important for you," Franz recalled later, "to see that those of us who knew still loved you and that you weren't going to become a pariah."

In adhering to Nicholson's warnings, I left school administrators, the health center, and my professors in the dark. I told no friends about my epilepsy other than my roommates, and they honored my request that we keep it secret.

My father never wanted to discuss my health, and whenever I told my mother about another seizure, I heard her anguish as she tried to comfort me. She often suggested I come home until my health im-proved, but my goal of graduating with my class remained my benchmark, the proof that I could lead a full life. I feared that if I failed to reach this objective, I would become what Nicholson predicted—an *epileptic*, defined by my condition, rather than someone with broad interests and successes who happened to have seizures.

As a result, I made a foolish decision, one that I now attribute to being a young person overwhelmed by circumstance. While I could do little to control my health, I could take charge of my mother's pain—I stopped telling her the truth. In our conversations, I glossed over how bad the seizures were becoming, assuring her that, while I was still experiencing convulsions, I was fine. My brother, Eric, was in his senior year at Swarthmore; I hid my seizure frequency from him as well, knowing that whatever he knew would get back to my parents and set off an argument about my leaving school.

My roommates became expert in understanding my convulsions and could tell when one was approaching. I grew pasty-faced, a sheen of sweat beading on my skin as my lips dried. My facial muscles slackened; my speech slurred; sometimes, one of them told me, my eyes dilated. While I don't remember who came up with the idea, we began to refer to my seizures in the third person, naming them Michael. That allowed us to discuss seizures publicly without tipping anyone off. When Carl, Franz, or Pat saw signs of a problem emerging, they would tell me, "Michael is coming."

Creating Michael also brought me a strange sense of comfort. I knew he was not real, but still I found it consoling to think that the chaos during my seizures had nothing to do with me. When I awakened injured, I had no recollection of what had happened. Truthfully, since I was unconscious, I wasn't there. Michael was. Michael did it. I despised him for it.

Sometimes I wondered if creating a fictional person was a sign I was cracking up. But according to psychologists I've consulted in the decades since, nonexistent Michael was a powerful technique for dealing with trauma. So long as I knew Michael was imaginary, they said, I had created a self-protective device—a person I could hate for what was happening without directing animosity toward myself or my life.

Even so, after I regained consciousness, I always had to deal with whatever Michael had done. Once I awakened from what would prove to be a life-changing seizure, feeling cold on my back and hearing a man's voice. No one recited *The Wizard of Oz*; my roommates weren't there. Few things scared me more than being at the mercy of a stranger post-seizure. It might be anyone. Criminals or lunatics could have power over me.

This man sounded kind. I listened to him with my eyes closed, trying to avoid the light. Soon I figured out he was Allen Schneider, my professor from Introductory Psychology. That terrified me for a moment, because I thought I must have gone into convulsions in front of the class; Schneider was a beloved professor, and he taught in a lecture hall packed with students. But I heard no crowds, no panic. I was on a cold hallway floor. Schneider stayed with me as I recovered. Either someone called Carl, or he happened upon the scene, then took over. A day or so later, Schneider asked me to drop by his office.

"Are you all right?" he asked.

"Yeah. These happen sometimes."

"Do you have epilepsy?"

Don't use the word. Nicholson warned never to use the word.

"I have a seizure disorder," I replied.

We spoke for a few minutes as Schneider tried to assure himself I was receiving appropriate care. I asked him not to tell other professors or administrators what he had seen. He promised to respect my privacy.

"Do you know Al Bloom?" he asked.

I did. Bloom was a linguistics professor, and his class was tied with Schneider's as a freshman favorite. He had a family member with epilepsy, Schneider said, and it might be good for me to speak with him.

I never mentioned epilepsy. I said "seizure disorder."

I couldn't help feeling this was spiraling out of control. First Schneider, now Bloom? And Schneider said "epilepsy." I felt trapped; I appreciated his kindness, but I was balancing his advice against my neurologist's warnings to keep quiet.

"Would you like to meet Al?" Schneider asked.

No, I thought.

"Yes," I lied.

Days later, I walked across the campus, passing the library and arboretum before heading to the aptly named College Avenue. I had already spoken with Bloom, and he had invited me to his home for a chat with him and his wife, Peggi, the family member with epilepsy. I accepted despite my misgivings about ignoring Nicholson's instructions.

I strolled along a beautiful, treelined street before reaching the Blooms' house at the corner of Woodbrook Lane. Sunshine bathed the neighborhood in a cozy tranquility. I hesitated. Once we spoke, I wouldn't be able to stop the Blooms from telling others about me. For about the tenth time, I considered canceling our meeting.

Enough. I walked to the front door and knocked.

Al Bloom answered. A short man with glasses and a permanent smile, he gave me either a hug or a squeeze of the shoulder—I can't remember which, but I do recall the physical contact knocked down my defenses. He escorted me inside and introduced me to Peggi.

We sat in a living area, and Peggi asked about my health. I said that my convulsions were poorly controlled, but I was handling the problem and the psychological pressure well. I believed I was telling the truth; by that point, I was in denial about the impact of the seizures on my emotional well-being. I spent time laughing with friends, going to class, doing homework. Except for occasional convulsions, I was like everyone else, so I figured I must be fine.

Peggi told me about her epilepsy and her neurologist. Hearing from someone with the same condition, using words I had grown to know well, convinced me to let down my guard even more.

I mentioned my fears of telling the truth, of losing control of my life, of being abandoned by friends, the school, and future employers. Al Bloom took advantage of the opening, saying I had to deal with my health problem honestly. Wasting time wishing it away would delay my learning how to compensate. He explained that he had been diagnosed with hypoglycemia, meaning his blood sugar could crash to severely low levels after eating. So he ate hamburgers for breakfast, he told me, a high-protein meal that helped him avoid glucose problems.

Peggi spoke. "Are there things you're not letting yourself do?"

I could have listed so much—walking campus alone at night, using the health center, talking to my parents about how bad things were—but it didn't cross my mind to mention them.

"Well, I kind of wanted to try out for the spring musical," I said.

"Why don't you?"

The question shocked me. "What if I have a seizure onstage?"

"Then you do. But don't give up on something because you're afraid of someone seeing a seizure."

The words could have been the most important I had heard since my diagnosis, since they contradicted Nicholson's instructions to hide. But I had become too indoctrinated by his directives to understand the full import of Peggi's statement. I thought she was just telling me to audition for the show.

The conversation turned to grades. A seizure occasionally forced me to miss class, I explained. Even when things were fine, sometimes fear that I might be on the verge of a seizure interfered with my studies. My grades were good, but I worried epilepsy might prevent me from keeping up. Nicholson had warned me not to get stressed, because that could trigger a seizure. So when grade anxiety emerged, I became stressed about being stressed. It was a cycle I couldn't stop.

"Let me ask," Al said. "Are you planning to go to graduate school?"

Well, Nicholson told me law school is out, so . . .

"No," I replied.

"Then stop worrying about grades. I promise, after you graduate, no employer will ever ask what your grades were."

I was dumbstruck. Since high school, I'd believed grades dictated my future. Now this professor was saying I should ignore them?

"I can't just fail my courses," I said.

"I didn't tell you to fail," he said, speaking with renewed authority. "Just stop worrying about grades. Pay attention to what you're being taught. If you understand the material, then you're getting an education. You're learning how to think. That's why you're at Swarthmore."

Ignore my grades.

"So when my semester grades come out . . . ?"

"Don't check them."

"I won't know my GPA."

"So what?" He spoke in a caring tone. "If you understand the material, you won't fail. Beyond that, your grades don't matter."

We talked until I ran out of things I was willing to say. I headed out feeling stronger than I had in months. I was leaning toward auditioning for the musical. And I decided on my walk back to the dorm that I would never look at my grades again until the day I graduated.

An audio letter from

FRANZ PAASCHE, 1986

My college roommate

Humor was key. Absolutely key. I think you've been very lucky that you have such a good sense of humor, because I think that it's the one element that's made everybody be able to deal with this in some way or another. Without your sense of humor, I think the people around you would have had a tremendously difficult time dealing with this. It just breaks the tension.

It was also great to know that one can be a little bit irreverent about these kinds of things. You have to be irreverent, just in the way that anyone is irreverent, but we never took it too far. We never took it to the point of ridicule or belittling the condition. The humor was a part of it. It was a part of the bond that all of us had. Because we could be funny about it, we conquered it in a certain way.

CHAPTER FIVE

A rusty bridge on campus crossed high above a track for the commuter train that delivered passengers to and from Philadelphia. Swarthmore boasted a cabaret of hollies, magnolias, and hundreds of other botanical delights, so this homely spot on Fieldhouse Lane ranked as one of few locations that tour guides for prospective students made sure to avoid.

Every month or so, I trudged across the bridge toward the field house—a hefty detour, but the only place I felt comfortable calling Nicholson. The school prohibited telephones in dorm rooms, claiming that to do otherwise would violate the Quaker tradition of equality, since not everyone could afford the cost. So, whenever I needed to speak with my doctor, I could either use a public phone in a well-traveled spot like my dorm or find a place on campus that offered privacy.

In the first months after my diagnosis, I called from Parrish Hall, which housed some phone booths; I gave that up after another student stood outside the door, hearing my every word as she impatiently waited for me to hang up. I searched the school until I found the pay phone in the field house, outside a basketball court. Before sports practices, the building was mostly empty, and I could speak to Nicholson without fear of accidentally disclosing the seizures to someone passing by.

As I headed toward the gym on this day, I felt exhausted and battered. A particularly violent convulsion had struck the night before; it took longer than usual to recover from my confusion and grogginess, and I badly hurt my left arm.

I knew I had no choice but to notify Nicholson, a prospect I hated. His condescension and refusal to answer even basic questions always left me frustrated and miserable. As I trekked to the gym, I tried to steel myself in hopes of being able to walk away from the call without feeling devastated by what might be another pointless conversation.

Whenever we spoke, Nicholson delivered the same refrain: The Tegretol had reached the minimum therapeutic level, that was the best amount to avoid side effects, and eventually I would respond to the treatment. He had repeated this for about four months, with a growing tone of exasperation that I hadn't just accepted his assurances rather than phoning again. I once asked about the severity of the side effects that could come from increasing the Tegretol, suggesting I might prefer those to the seizures. He ignored me; I sensed he thought I was joking.

I opened the glass door of the field house and walked inside. After checking to make sure I was alone, I headed to the phone, then fumbled with the AT&T card my parents had given me for long-distance calls. I pushed what seemed to be dozens of numbers only to hear a woman's robotic voice tell me I had entered the wrong ones. Frustrated, I dialed again. This time the call went through.

As usual, Nicholson's assistant answered, and I explained that the convulsions were becoming worse. She put me on hold, and to my astonishment, Nicholson picked up.

"Hi, Kurt. What's happening?"

"I've been having more grand mal seizures. I had another one last night, and I'm feeling awful today."

"Okay, so what happened during that seizure?"

I wasn't sure how he expected me to answer that question.

"I don't know," I replied. "I wasn't there."

"Oh, don't be ridiculous! Of course you were there."

"That's not what I meant. I was unconscious. I don't know what happened."

"Yes, but that's not what you said. You said you weren't there. Why didn't you just say you were unconscious?"

What the fuck does this guy want from me? "I'm sorry," I replied, frightened he would hang up. "I said it the wrong way. I was there. I just don't know what happened."

"Did anyone witness it?"

"Yes, my roommates."

"Did you ask them to describe everything that happened?"

"No."

"How are you going to tell me what happened if you don't find out?"

I held back tears. Why was he always so abusive?

"I don't know," I sputtered. "I don't know what I'm supposed to ask. Isn't it enough just to tell you I had a grand mal seizure?"

"No, I need to know everything. What was the aura* like?"

"I don't remember. I know I've seen lights before, and my roommates say they can tell when a seizure is coming. But I usually don't remember what happened beforehand."

"You need to start asking."

"Asking what my aura was like?"

"Don't be ridiculous. Asking what happens during the seizure. I need to know specifics."

"All right," I promised. But we had been working together for months. Why, I wondered, had he never told me this before?

"Well, it sounds like the medication isn't working."

For the first time, I wanted to laugh. *No kidding.*

"I'm going to give you a prescription for Depakene and add it to your Tegretol."

Relief washed over me. Finally, he was doing something.

---

* An aura is a perceptual change that occurs prior to a seizure. It can manifest in many ways: the hallucination of lights, detecting an unpleasant smell that isn't there, a sense of déjà vu, confusion, and many other disturbances.

"What is it?" I asked.

"Another anticonvulsant. It was approved for epilepsy by the FDA a few years ago."

I wasn't sure how to feel about that. Wouldn't it be better to use a drug that had been shown to work for decades rather than a new one? No matter. I trusted Nicholson. I had no choice. There was no one else who might end my terror of losing control.

I never read the package insert for Depakene, and Nicholson explained nothing; I simply picked up the medicine at the drugstore and started swallowing the gelatinous orange capsules. My neurologist had told me to take the drug, I was desperate, so I followed his instructions. However, the 1980 edition of *Physicians' Desk Reference*—the book that every competent doctor keeps nearby to research any medication before prescribing it—shows that Nicholson had not made a good selection, at least based on the science known at the time. The primary use for Depakene listed in that year's *PDR* was to treat petit mal seizures, which Nicholson had incorrectly declared to be the cause of my staring spells. When used in conjunction with another drug, it could impede seizures localized on one side of the brain. But grand mal seizures involve both sides, and those were the episodes damaging my life.

Depakene carried warnings similar to the ones for Tegretol about possible impairment of blood cells. The manufacturer cautioned that it could trigger a dangerous dysfunction in platelets, the component that stops bleeding. Doctors needed to check a patient's platelet count and the length of time it took for bleeding to stop before prescribing the medication, the company specified; that way, changes would be evident in future tests. Nicholson followed none of the standard procedures.

If blood problems—apparent or suspected—emerged, the company directed doctors to stop use of the drug immediately. No one told me.

Despite the seizures, I tried—without complete success—never to miss class. But once on Depakene, at least for a while, I had no choice but to stay in my room. Moving made me sick. I spent hours lying on the wine-colored faux-leather couch in our living area. As long as I remained motionless, I felt fine. But if I shifted position, nausea overwhelmed me.

Yet even in this dreadful state where I could either stay still or feel the need to vomit, my spirits rose. By adding Depakene, Nicholson had finally acknowledged what I had known for so long: The minimum therapeutic dose of Tegretol hadn't worked.

I have no idea how long I lay on that sagging couch in total stillness. But I knew these side effects would pass. I just had to stick this out as the price for getting better.

After a few weeks, I suspected Nicholson's treatment decision had flopped again. The convulsions didn't decrease in number. My faith that he would ultimately find a way to stop them remained unshaken; still, I started wondering, given his failures so far, if maybe he had been wrong about my needing to hide my condition, to never utter the word "epilepsy." I had three caring confidants—my roommates—but I also had other kind friends. Maybe it was time to be more honest with them.

Then came a day I was walking through Parrish Hall. Between classes, there was always an urgent, ordered frenzy about the place. Amid the crowd, I saw a classmate headed toward me. She shared a freshman suite in our dorm, and we had become friends. I had developed a small crush on her but hadn't seen her in a while, so I was glad to have a chance to catch up.

"Hi!" I said.

She averted her eyes, maintaining an icy silence as she walked past. I was bewildered. Had I done something to offend her? I tried to recall the last time we had spoken. Nothing. I hadn't told anyone about my crush, hadn't acted on it, so that couldn't have been the reason.

Later, I found out she had learned about my convulsions and may have witnessed one; there had been no argument, nothing that might have ended our friendship. But she never spoke to me again. Nicholson, I decided, was right. I stopped questioning his insistence that I needed to keep my epilepsy secret.

In the spring, I ended my "late-night-gab-and-cram" sessions. I knew that lack of sleep triggered seizures. Procrastinating instead of studying for an exam or writing an essay was risky—what if a seizure struck the night before my work was due? At best, after hours of recovery, I'd arrive to class late, bedraggled, and unprepared. So I handled my homework in an un-college way: I did a little bit every day.

Despite my best intentions, sometimes circumstances required me to write a paper in the twenty-four hours after a seizure, and I soon noticed something odd.

My first college English paper, submitted before my diagnosis, had come back with so many red marks it appeared as if the professor had cleaned a slaughterhouse with it. *Your writing is grotesque*, he scrawled across the top. When I reread my work, I couldn't disagree.

I was terrified the first time I typed a paper at the computer lab shortly after a seizure. If my writing was atrocious when I was at my best, then this assignment was sure to be a disaster. I was exhausted, my brain swimming. My speech slurred, and I struggled with names. People stared at me as I pecked at a keyboard, looking so haggard that a few asked if I was all right. I nodded, hoping they would think I was nursing a hangover. I finished my essay on time and was delighted when it came back with an A, loaded with kudos about its insight. (Even though I was no longer paying attention to my semester grades, I couldn't avoid noticing the marks at the tops of my papers.) Then another paper was written soon after a seizure. Again, an A with effusive comments.

Eventually, I noticed a trend: Whenever I wrote within a day after a seizure, my work wowed my professors. If I typed papers while well and alert, my performance was nothing special. One day, I grew curious and reread one of my post-seizure essays that a professor had praised enthusiastically.

The paper left me speechless. *I wrote this?* It was … amazing. My sentence structure was perfect, my vocabulary top-notch. I had composed sentences I couldn't have spoken at the time. And my argument—where had those thoughts originated? As I read, I learned more about the subject than I thought I knew—from myself.

Michael is a genius! Could it be, I wondered, that convulsions triggered a creative part of my brain, temporarily allowing a *smarter* part of me to take control or simply making my thoughts clearer? Although I never found medical research about such changes, I did come across others with similar experiences—but more important, I saw the results in black and white. This was the first of many times I would marvel at the brain's power, elasticity, and secrets. I found it fascinating to read someone else's paper, written by me.

As the end of freshman year approached, I was proud that I had kept my months-old promises to the Blooms. My GPA was unknown to me. I had auditioned for the spring musical and was selected for the role of the romantic lead. Carl had also landed a part in the show, which delighted me; not only did I have a good friend to join in the fun, but if I had a seizure, at least someone there would know what to do.

After I was cast, I decided to tell the director about my seizures. After all, he had unknowingly assumed the risk of choosing a lead who might not be available on show night. He took my confession in stride and told me not to worry—he would be my understudy. I missed some rehearsals, but to my relief, I made it through every performance.

Because of my willingness to take a risk by appearing in the musical, I met Julia—a junior who appeared in the chorus—and soon faced a new problem: how to explain my condition to a girlfriend. Days passed as I worked to overcome my fear of rejection, until I finally admitted to myself that if I didn't tell her, a convulsion would.

One night, sitting on a curb and staring at my knees as I spoke, I rambled through an explanation of my epilepsy. She was supportive and asked only what she needed to do during a seizure. I explained the details—don't worry about tongue swallowing; no need for an ambulance unless the convulsions don't stop; don't hold me down; put something soft under my head and in my mouth if my jaw hasn't already clamped shut. Later, she spoke with Carl and Franz, who gave her more instructions based on their experiences. Nothing changed in our relationship; once Julia understood epilepsy, she treated it as an occasional nuisance, exactly as my roommates did.

I hadn't given much thought to my summer until weeks before the second semester ended. For years, I had worked at a day camp, but

I suddenly realized my uncontrolled epilepsy changed everything. I couldn't care for other people's children; they would be in the pool, on stairs, standing waist-high beside me. If I lost consciousness at a bad moment, I could hurt one of them. It didn't matter that my seizures mostly occurred at night. I wasn't going to take that risk.

Then reality struck. I couldn't drive. That hadn't posed a problem before. I had spent spring break with Franz at his home in Toronto, a city with public transportation. During Christmas, I had let friends cart me around Dallas. But summer? Three months without driving in a city where mass transit was a joke. Whatever job I got, I would need to commute every day. Unless someone drove me, my work would be dictated by the city's lousy bus routes.

My mother saved my summer and my morale by agreeing to serve as my chauffeur. I found a job as a "premium specialty ad sales representative," a hilarious name for telemarketers who sell pens, key chains, and Frisbees to companies that want their names and phone numbers on customer giveaways.

During training, I was told to ditch my real name on sales calls—too many syllables. If I announced myself as "Kurt Eichenwald," my spiel would be interrupted by the question "Who?" Instead, the boss told me to adopt an alias, one with first and last names of one syllable each. I thought for a minute, then made a choice I knew I wouldn't forget: Carl Moor. I took a desk, grabbed some phone books, and started cold-calling. After a few weeks, I decided to have some fun and pitch the Minnesota camp where Carl was working.

"What a coincidence!" the woman on the line bubbled after hearing my pseudonym. "We have a Carl Moor who works here."

"Well, he probably doesn't spell it the way I do. My first name starts with a C, and I don't have an e at the end of Moor."

"That *is* how he spells his name!"

"Huh," I replied trying to sound surprised. "Maybe we're related."

I told her what I supposedly looked like, delivering a dead-on description of Carl. She marveled; I sounded like Carl's twin! We agreed there was a chance this counselor of hers and I were distant relatives. We launched into a friendly "what a small world" conversation.

I sold her some Frisbees.

I was supposed to stick to a script but decided to treat potential customers like real human beings and engage them in conversation. This angered the supervisor, but there was not a lot he could say about it—although I worked part-time, I soon racked up the second-highest sales and the lowest number of packages rejected at time of delivery. My bosses surreptitiously recorded my calls, trying to learn my secret. Eventually, they gave up, unable to decipher the mystery behind my performance. The company president called me to his office to tell me of their eavesdropping and how they couldn't figure out why my sales were so strong. He asked me if I could think of an explanation.

"Yeah," I replied. "I don't lie."

And I tossed away the script, I explained. Listened to people, heard who they were and what they needed, spent time to earn their trust, and never ended the call so long as a prospect kept asking questions. The boss frowned; I don't know what he expected, but clearly he hoped I had divined some special trick that lured people into purchasing junk they didn't want. For decades afterward, I have told young reporters of my telemarketing days, explaining the lessons I learned about how to speak with people, a knack that paid dividends throughout my career.

Despite success at work, my summer was rough. I could no longer hide the severity of the convulsions from my parents. Once I woke in a hallway in our house, my mother kneeling beside me, stroking my cheek and assuring me I was all right. I tasted blood and, as always, reached to my head to check for an injury. A sticky ooze soaked the side of my face; I touched the back of my head and found it drenched. I panicked, struggling without success to scream for my mother to stop the gushing blood, not comprehending that she would have noticed a gaping wound. She had never seen me so distressed and struggled to understand me as I rubbed my head and the floor. I wiped my dripping hand across her face so she could finally see the blood. Then she understood.

"Your head isn't bleeding," she told me rapidly. "Listen to me. It's not bleeding. It isn't blood."

She explained repeatedly that the sticky liquid I felt was saliva. During the seizure, a froth had flowed from my mouth down the side of my face, forming a pool on the floor. Eventually, her explanation overcame my panic, and I calmed down.

That day, my mother confronted my father. The seizure she witnessed had been awful, she told him. Watching my body contort, listening as my teeth crunched, seeing blood in my mouth as I bit into my lip—and then afterward, my confusion and terror. I had been in a deep sleep for hours since then. This was far more serious than I had let on, she told him. She begged him to intervene with Nicholson or to find another doctor. He listened stone-faced. Throughout their marriage, my father demanded the last word on important decisions, dictated most parts of my mother's life, and often treated her like a fool. This was no different. He would not be doing anything, he told her. Nicholson was my doctor, and he was the best. And, he fumed, she needed to control herself.

"If you don't stop," he barked at her, "you're going to make Kurt think he's seriously ill!"

My father downplayed the seizures even when he witnessed them himself. While I'm not sure when it occurred, I know one time I fell into a grand mal seizure in front of my family, striking the playroom floor. My mother and my brother rushed to help me. My mother glanced up from me to my father, who sat near the ugly scene eating some watermelon.

"Look at this!" she shouted. "Look what's going on here!"

My father stayed silent and just kept munching.

That summer, I had one appointment with Nicholson but felt so concerned that he would abandon me if I angered him that I asked few questions. During the consultation, he told me that blood tests from earlier that week showed my Depakene levels were too low, so he increased my dosage. By that time, I had begun to take tentative steps toward admitting the truth: Nicholson had no idea what he was doing. He was a researcher, not someone who treated patients. He was so difficult with me, I thought, because I was interrupting his real job. When I called, I was delivering a new proclamation that he had failed. Was it that simple? I wondered. Were my seizures still uncontrolled because my neurologist's ego couldn't handle hearing that his treatment hadn't worked?

After a week of wrestling with these thoughts, I approached my father. I had been convinced that capable physicians worked only at medical schools and believed no other academic neurologist in Dallas would treat me without his approval. I found him in our bookcase-lined living room, sitting in his favorite chair, face pointed toward the ceiling as classical music swelled around the room. I parked myself on a couch beside him and began to discuss my concerns. I mentioned my epilepsy.

He interrupted. "You don't have epilepsy!" he snapped. "You have a seizure disorder!"

What? I was thunderstruck. My father, the world-renowned physician, had heard Nicholson's advice on how a euphemism could help hide my condition. Now, after all these months, he was grasping at the term to mask his dismay about the diagnosis. I realized the truth: Despite his training, my father feared the word "epilepsy." I didn't know if he was ashamed or ignorant or unwilling to face reality, but I knew I couldn't let this lie.

"Dad," I said, "epilepsy and a seizure disorder are the same thing."

"No they're not! Didn't you listen to what Nicholson said? You shouldn't say 'epilepsy.' It's not epilepsy."

"Then what is it?"

"It's a seizure disorder."

I paused. "Okay, so what does that mean? What do I have? How is it different than epilepsy?"

"It's different," he huffed. "And I don't want to talk about it anymore."

That clash was a turning point. For the first time, I realized my father was not fit to manage my medical care. But his denial hardened my belief that only Nicholson could save me; after all, how would I find another neurologist at a medical school without my father's help? Watching my mother's dismay—and knowing her solution was for me to come home, robbing me of the psychologically essential goal of graduating with my class—further convinced me to protect her. My brother was headed to Harvard Medical School, and I didn't want to trouble him. My sister lived in Los Angeles, and I kept her in the dark as well.

For years, I would think about that conversation with my father, as well as other instances where he refused to discuss what was happening, and the impact that had on my well-being. For a long time, I was furious at him; my wife never forgave him, even after his death, because she believes his failures contributed to long-term damage. Eventually, though, I made my peace with him. I realized, even though he was my father, even though he was this famous physician, he was as fallible as anyone. He had not intended to hurt me. He healed people for a living, but with his own family, he could not accept the helplessness he experienced as my seizures worsened, a feeling I shared.

DAD: *I went through a fairly long period of denial. I was thinking it was just a passing thing that you were going through and that even if you had seizures, they would probably get under control once the drug was found. That would be the end of it, and it'd probably burn out. I kept thinking that this was due to some injury that you'd had from falling and that it would heal and it would go away. And after that I was angry at a lot of people.*

KURT: *Who were you angry at?*

DAD: *I was angry at the doctors.*

KURT: *Were you angry at me?*

DAD: *Probably, yeah.*

KURT: *How come?*

DAD: *Subconsciously one knows it's not your fault that you have seizures, but you're still making life difficult for everybody and most of all for yourself. So I probably had some anger toward you also.*

KURT: *How about now? What's your attitude and your feeling about you, me, and this?*

DAD: *Well, right now I feel like, in a lot of ways, I failed you. I didn't handle the situation well. I've got all sorts of excuses I can make for myself. But they're just excuses.*

CHAPTER SIX

"I'll just wait until he's available."

I rubbed my face, then pulled on the metal cord running from the handset to the pay phone. It was my sophomore year, and I was in the field house calling Nicholson. I had stopped contacting him months before; the conversations had become too pointless and hurtful. The seizures had not abated, but chasing him down without success tore at me. Worse, after adjusting my medication, he treated me cruelly, continuing to throw me off guard with demands that I explain why I didn't know the answers to questions he'd never raised before.

But another grand mal seizure had struck the night before; nothing about it had been different, but I'd snapped. Perhaps the buildup of other terrifying complications in recent weeks had set me off. The latest was a white growth on the spot inside my lip that I often bit during convulsions. I had become skilled at denial, but I couldn't ignore the lump. I knew little about cancer except that it spread; maybe this thing was a malignancy. I researched "oral cancer" at the library and found a photograph that looked vaguely like what I saw in my mouth.

My decision to call Nicholson wasn't just about that growth, though. My resilience was faltering. The gambit of blaming my seizures on imaginary Michael had worn thin. These dreadful things were happening to me, not some fictional, faceless character. Also, I feared I was annoying my roommates with the detailed questions after seizures—where had I fallen, what did I look like beforehand, how was my body positioned during the episode?—a response to Nicholson having chastised me for not knowing everything that occurred in a convulsion.

And I was losing control of my secret: During one breakfast, a classmate joked that the audience at a concert was having "epileptic seizures"; another student laughed, looked at me, and said, "That couldn't be. Kurt wasn't there."

I stared at my bowl of cereal, silent and ashamed.

I needed help from someone. Anyone. The family dynamic and my own failings continued to block me from seeking another doctor. My girlfriend and I had broken up, mostly because our age difference prevented us from merging our social circles. My roommates handled the physical demands of my seizures with composure, but I tried to avoid putting my emotional health in their hands. Nicholson was all I had. As much as I hated him, I still thought he was the only person who could save me.

So I made my journey down to the field house, vowing to stay on the phone until we spoke. His assistant told me that he was in the lab but would call when he returned. I wasn't falling for that again. I would wait on the line for him, I told her.

"It could be ten minutes," she cautioned.

"That's fine," I said.

I heard a soft buzz after she pushed the HOLD button. There was no place to sit; the handset cord didn't stretch, so I couldn't rest on the floor. I leaned against the wall as time passed, alone in the cavernous building.

Five minutes.

Not much longer, I figured. I read the instructions on the phone about how to make different kinds of long-distance calls.

Ten minutes.

Okay, time's up. Nicholson will pick up any second now.

Fifteen minutes.

I guess his assistant underestimated how long it would take him to return to the office.

I heard the door to the field house open. A woman walked in. I hoped she didn't want to use the phone. She passed by and headed to the basketball court.

Twenty minutes.

I squeezed my forehead above the bridge of my nose, a nervous habit I had developed in the previous few months.

Twenty-five minutes.

My stomach knotted. I didn't know what to think.

Thirty minutes.

Something's wrong, I thought. Maybe Nicholson's assistant had neglected to tell him I was on hold. I could call back, but it took time to enter all the numbers to charge a long-distance call on my AT&T card. If I disconnected to redial, he might pick up the phone right after I hung up and wouldn't be available half a minute later when I called back. I just needed to wait.

Thirty-five minutes.

I wiped away tears. *I don't know what to do.* More students came into the building. I turned away from them. Was it time for sports teams to meet? I didn't know. They disappeared down a hallway.

Forty minutes.

I can't. I can't. I can't do this anymore. I can't.

Forty-five minutes.

Okay, I decided, *I'll call back.* I looked at my AT&T card and tried to memorize the number. It would take me only thirty seconds, just thirty seconds out of forty-five minutes. What was the chance Nicholson would pick up during those thirty seconds? I hesitated, made my decision, then pushed down the metal bar, disconnecting the call. I rushed to redial but forgot the AT&T number. It took two tries for the call to go through.

"Hi, it's Kurt Eichenwald. Is Dr. Nicholson back yet?"

"Oh, Kurt, I'm sorry. He's gone home for the day."

My mind went blank. "But . . . I was . . . When did he leave?"

"About thirty minutes ago."

I fell silent. Something shattered inside me, something that had held me together emotionally for a year, something that had kept me functioning. Then rage of an intensity beyond my experience rushed out in an uncontrollable explosion of anger, fear, hopelessness, and helplessness.

"*Fuck you!*" I yelled. "*And fuck him!*"

I pounded the handset against the receiver again and again, banging plastic on metal as deep, racking sobs shook my body. I screamed repeatedly, a wordless, guttural shriek of pain. *I can't live like this. I don't know where to go; I don't know what to do. I have no doctor. I'm alone.*

A man rushed toward me. I continued smashing the phone down, feeling lost, emotionally paralyzed, ravaged. The man touched my arm. I pushed him away. Then I ran. Still weeping, I hit the glass door of the gymnasium hard. It flew open with a bang as I raced into the street.

I ran going nowhere, going anywhere. I wanted to get away from me, from Nicholson, from Michael, from everything. I could not sprint fast enough to escape them all. I tripped on the grass next to Parrish Walk, tumbled across the asphalt, and stood. Someone called my name. I kept sprinting.

It seemed like I ran forever—across campus, into the village, down sidewalks, and back. I found myself at Al and Peggi Bloom's house. I pounded on the door, my face dripping from tears and sweat. When one of them answered, I lurched inside without waiting to be invited. I sat in the same chair I'd used months earlier and brought my hands to my face, sobbing, choking, and trying to talk at the same time.

I have almost no memory of that discussion, and the taped diary I made twenty-four hours later—a rambling tirade of pain and grief about the events of the previous day and year—reveals little of what occurred at the Blooms' house. What is clear is that they decided not just to counsel me but to intervene. Peggi promised to put me in contact with her Philadelphia neurologist.

Days passed before I spoke on the phone with Peggi's doctor. The contrast between him and Nicholson could not have been starker. Patience and compassion guided his words. I immediately overcame my fear of annoying—and then losing—my doctor and posed complicated questions I should have asked long before. The neurologist provided careful and comprehensive responses, although he expressed surprise that I knew so little about epilepsy. I mentioned that Nicholson had told me I suffered from petit mal episodes, but the Philadelphia doctor expressed doubt. Based on my answers to his questions, he said, it seemed more likely those spells were in a different category. I didn't know who was right, but I didn't care. What mattered was a neurologist was speaking to me without condemnation.

Then the bad news. He wasn't taking new patients and didn't believe he was the best doctor for me. Given the number of seizures I experienced, he said, I needed a physician with admitting privileges at a facility close to Swarthmore, not thirty minutes away in Philadelphia. While he didn't know any neurologists who practiced near the college, he assured me I shouldn't have trouble finding someone.

Given that my father had always chosen our physicians without consulting us, I had no idea how to track down a doctor. My first thought was to contact an epilepsy organization in the area and ask for a recommendation. At McCabe Library, I flipped through the local telephone book; the listings jumped from *Epicure* to *Episcopal Academy*—no epilepsy groups. Then I turned to the listings under *N* and found a handful of medical groups with names that began with variations of "neurological." I chose the closest one and wrote down the number.

Later that week, I called the nearby office of Dr. Milton Craddock. His staff told me that yes, he treated epilepsy and, after hearing details of my condition, scheduled me for the next day.

I took a cab to Craddock's office and found a seat in the waiting room. *A waiting room*. While under Nicholson's care, I had never seen a waiting room. He didn't have one; his office was off the hallway that led to a lab. A waiting room meant patients. Craddock treated people instead of conducting research.

The nurse called me into the exam room, where I saw a poster with a drawing of a brain. I was still studying the image when Craddock walked in. He was smiling, cheerful, the opposite of Nicholson in every way. He conducted the same neurological test—"squeeze my fingers; push my palms"—but explained what he was doing. He asked about my medical history but, unlike Peggi Bloom's neurologist, said nothing when I mentioned my supposed petit mal seizures. I couldn't remember the type of seizure Peggi's doctor had said was the more likely cause of my staring, but I figured if Craddock didn't care, neither did I.

He sent me to have my blood drawn to check medication levels. Then it was back to Craddock. He told me that he would be sending me for an EEG and a CAT scan. I liked him, and the more we talked, the more I trusted him. I decided to ask the most important question.

"Do you think you'll be able to get my seizures under control?"

He smiled broadly. "Of course!" he exclaimed.

I left Craddock relieved. He was supportive, exactly what I needed. I had found him on my own. I had taken control of my health. A renewed sense of strength surged within me.

A few days later, I returned to my room and, on a whiteboard on our front door, saw a message that Craddock had called. I quickly erased it, worried that my hall mates would wonder why a physician had telephoned. Then I walked to a nearby pay phone in our dorm; I no longer needed to sneak off to some secluded spot. There would be no pleading, no outbursts, no confrontations, just a quiet talk. Most likely no one would understand or care about the topic of conversation from hearing my side of it.

A woman answered, I identified myself, and soon Craddock was on the line. Relief washed over me as I realized I now had a doctor willing to speak to me.

"Kurt, your blood levels came back. It's no wonder the seizures haven't stopped. Your Tegretol level is just above the minimum, and your Depakene is only a little better."

I knew that already. "But doesn't the medication start working when it passes the minimum level?"

"No. The blood level is a range. Some people get better at the minimum. Some require the maximum. Think of it like alcohol. Some people get drunk off a single beer. Others can drink a case with no effect. There is no single right answer. It depends on the person."

That made sense. Anticonvulsants weren't like aspirin, with a recommended number of pills to take. I was about to ask a question, but Craddock answered it before I had the chance.

"We need to increase your dosage of both medications." He instructed me how much I should be taking each day and at what time.

He promised to send me new prescriptions, since the higher dose would cause me to run out of the drugs more quickly.

I hung up, ecstatic. Everything that had seemed so complicated and mysterious with Nicholson was now simple and clear with Craddock—my convulsions had not been controlled because my treatment was insufficient, because Nicholson was either too arrogant or too incompetent to recognize his error. This, I was sure, was the turning point; I was going to get better.

But I was wrong. While Craddock held himself out as a neurologist, he was not certified in the field. Other than epilepsy, he treated no purely neurological conditions, instead dealing with problems like schizophrenia, bipolar disorders, and other biologically based psychiatric conditions. I met other epilepsy patients he treated but have since learned we were a small part of his practice. His understanding of anticonvulsants and their dangers was shallow at best.

I could not have known at the time, but this friendly, supportive man whom I saw as my potential medical savior was instead, out of near-criminal incompetence, about to push me terrifyingly close to my own death.

DR. ALLAN NAARDEN, 2017

My former neurologist

Giving somebody false hope is worse than not giving them any hope at all, I think. You want to be honest with people even in small things because if you're not, then how will they believe you in anything that you say? The whole idea is the trust that you develop with your patient is something that's the responsibility of the doctor. It's as important as the medicine that you give somebody, if that's necessary.

CHAPTER SEVEN

Without warning, my muscles went limp, and I plunged down a flight of stairs. I was conscious, feeling every slam, every bump, every scrape, but I never flinched. It was as if I had suddenly become paralyzed. After crashing to the bottom, I was bruised and beaten but not in agony—nothing broken. Maybe, I figured, my inability to move had protected me as I tumbled.

These "drop attacks" had started a few weeks earlier in the second semester of sophomore year, and there was no hiding them from other students. Worse, the number of seizures was escalating. Every few days, I either toppled in one of the new episodes or awoke from convulsions. The falls occurred anytime; staying in my room at night accomplished nothing. Witnesses to my collapses marveled at how quickly I went from upright to crumpled on the ground. I frequently heard the words "You fell like a ton of bricks." One friend likened it to seeing a marionette tumble after someone cut its strings.

I phoned Craddock, desperate for an explanation. He told me I was describing "atonic seizures." Innocuous name, ghastly problem. Unlike convulsions, where muscles tighten before the body starts jerking, atonic seizures involve a sudden, complete loss of muscle tone. The episodes ended quickly and never involved loss of consciousness.

He could not be certain, he said, but the drop attacks may have started either as a result of my seizures being poorly treated for so long or because I needed more anticonvulsants.

A grand mal seizure, with all of its spasms and clenching, can appear petrifying and almost otherworldly. But for me, crashing to the ground without warning was far worse. Michael did not step in and take over my body as I blacked out; when I dropped, I was awake for the entire event. The experience of a convulsion was akin to waking up after a car accident, nursing wounds from a calamity I didn't remember. These new seizures were like driving down a busy highway knowing I would lose control of the car—maybe in a few hours, maybe in a few seconds—and then skid helplessly into a tree as metal crunched my body and glass cut my face.

I spent every moment looking around for dangerous objects I might hit in a fall—a rock, a pointed stick, a bench. Even so, I occasionally and foolishly disregarded threats, a carelessness I came to regret. Before the drop attacks started, my roommates—including Dave Robbins, who had taken Pat's place—had removed a couple of mirrors from the walls, placing them on two trunks to create a reflecting coffee table. Very cool, we thought. Unfortunately, the risk of this funky piece of do-it-yourself furniture escaped me. I recognized the danger only when I crumpled on top of the table, breaking the mirrors.

Craddock urged me to contact him if the seizures worsened, and after every few calls, he upped my anticonvulsant dosage. We fell into a cycle that showed no sign of ending: He increased my medication, more seizures occurred, and he bumped up the prescription again. He ordered the changes without checking my blood to determine the drug levels or possible problems. It never occurred to me that he should have.

When Nicholson diagnosed my epilepsy, he placed me on one Tegretol pill a day, gradually increased that by two more, then added Depakene. By the second semester of my sophomore year, Craddock had boosted my dosage from four to eleven pills a day.

Nausea and dizziness were my frequent companions. Sometimes I lay down on the grass because my head was spinning. My hands trembled. I often gasped, feeling as though I couldn't get enough air. Bruises that appeared after my seizures remained for a long time. If I rubbed my hands through my hair, a surprising amount came out. I assumed I was just going bald at a young age until I realized a large number of the follicles were falling from the sides and the back, not the typical pattern for male hair loss.

Each time a new symptom surfaced, I phoned Craddock and asked whether the drugs might be the cause. At least half a dozen times, he uttered the same reply: "I've never heard of that as a side effect of the medication."

Although it took years for me to grasp the magnitude of the problem, signs emerged that my memory was flagging. I didn't remember events that my friends told me I had attended. I struggled with people's names, even those of longtime friends. Once I looked at one of my roommates attempting without success to summon up the name "Franz."

Worse, I was increasingly forgetting to take my medication. That had rarely been a problem before, but now some mornings I woke feeling dreadful from having missed at least one of the sets of pills I was supposed to take three times daily. I tried to set up a system to give myself a visual cue that I had swallowed my medicine, but then forgot how the system worked. My roommates became angry at me when I missed my drugs; after all, they dealt with the consequences too. I promised to do better, but then forgot again. I could not understand what was happening.

I wish I could recount more of this terrible time, but with my deteriorating ability to recollect and my attempts to push aside troubling experiences, I made no tapes and turned my written diaries into bare-bones recitations of wounds: "Hurt my right hand, typing is hard." "Not possible but my forehead looks dented." "Woke up with mouth bleeding. Don't think anyone heard."

As I read these journals now, the most stunning aspect of them is not what I wrote but what I left out. I list my injuries with the matter-of-fact tone of a grocer taking inventory, but I never mention my emotional state or what happened each day. It's clear I dreaded pain, but otherwise I seem indifferent to my fate.

In fact, the only feelings I relate in these diaries involve concerns for my friends, particularly my roommates, and my guilt for the demands my health imposed on them. "How can you thank people who let you live your life?" I say nothing about fearing death but express concern that a fatal fall would traumatize Carl, Franz, and Dave. At the time, I didn't know that crashing into something was only one danger and that I could perish from a condition called SUDEP—Sudden Unexpected Death in Epilepsy.

I'd begun to be aware of my emotional shutdown during Christmas break. My father choked on a piece of roast beef at dinner, grabbed his throat, leapt out of his seat, and fell face-first onto the floor. As the rest of my family dashed about in panic, I calmly stepped past him—seeing his face dripping blood from the impact with the ground—and headed to the kitchen telephone. I figured he might be dying. I dialed 911.

"What's your emergency?"

"Yes," I said. "My father just choked on some food and is on the floor."

"Is he breathing?"

"I don't know," I replied. I glanced across the room and saw my mother helping him sit up.

"Oh, he's okay," I advised. "Never mind."

I hung up. Suddenly, I could see myself, cold-blooded and composed. Despite my father's failures, I knew I loved him. I understood my family's distress. But I felt nothing. Not fear, not love, not hate, not boredom. Nothing.

This probably isn't good, I thought coolly. *I'm broken.*

The explanation came to me as I stood by the phone. For so long, I had denied so much, hidden so much, lied so much, and been hurt so much that the person I had been was gone. I was a shell of my true self. Instinctive reactions to threats—fight or flight—remained, but I had subconsciously slammed most emotions, good and bad, into a psychological box. I didn't want to feel anguish, so I didn't feel anything. *I should speak to someone about this,* I thought, *maybe a counselor.* Then I walked toward my father, who was off the floor. My family headed back to our dinner, and I forgot all about being dead inside.

As the seizures increased in the second semester of my sophomore year, I decided Nicholson had allowed me freedoms that undermined my health. Shortly after my original diagnosis, he had told me I could have one glass of alcohol a day; in my sophomore year, I stopped drinking entirely. I decided to avoid booze after getting together with the woman who would become my new girlfriend, Joelle. The night we met, we shared some cheap whiskey, and later that night I had convulsions that were worse than usual. I didn't know if the alcohol had caused them, but I realized Nicholson's rules were irrational. Based on his directives, one beer was no worse than one glass of vodka—the concept made no sense. With Joelle, I attended more parties, and often someone pushed me to drink. Finally, to stop the pestering, I mixed glasses of seltzer and orange juice, leading fellow students to think I was downing screwdrivers.

Cutting out alcohol accomplished nothing. Almost every other day, I either experienced a convulsion or a drop attack or was recovering from one. Carl, Franz, Dave, and Joelle often helped me back to my room after some event. They knew that when I woke from a grand mal seizure, I feared what had happened while I was unconscious, so they patiently listened as I struggled to ask questions. Carl and Dave told frequent, often ribald jokes to make me smile. What they called "The Carl and Dave Show" was deemed a success if the first understandable words I said were "That's disgusting."

Injuries from my seizures made it difficult to walk the campus; I realized that Swarthmore was virtually inaccessible to the disabled, with only a few feeble attempts at aiding them. The campus had just two wheelchair ramps, each leading to staircases. One of the few wheelchair-accessible bathroom stalls could be reached only by passing through a narrow doorway.[*]

The school's inattention to accessibility made things hard for me. A year after it had happened, I recalled a difficult experience during this time on a recording. "After two consecutive seizures, I was going around the school, and I was just so torn up," I said. "I couldn't walk in certain places. So many of the doors were too heavy for me to open. There were so many stairs I had to climb and go down. I made them

---

[*] Such failures violated Section 504 of the Rehabilitation Act of 1973, but since my time there, Swarthmore has launched a major renovation and is now fully accessible to the disabled.

most of the time by clinging to the handrail because I was afraid I would fall."

Though I never learned how, my mother heard about the severe deterioration in my health. For all I know, I told her myself in one of my matter-of-fact, emotionless moments. Again she pleaded with me to come home, and again I refused. It made no sense for me to abandon Craddock; I liked him. I would not go near Nicholson, I said, nor would I allow my father to choose a new doctor. And I would not surrender the commitment to graduate with my class, a goal that grew in importance as my health worsened, since that would prove I had not let my life slip away.

Besides, apart from my seizures, I enjoyed college. I relished the camaraderie and the intellectual challenges. Even in the foggy aftermath of a convulsion, I found classes fascinating. I remember some hours after one episode, I was still recovering while my professor Kenneth Lieberthal led a discussion on Chinese politics. My thinking grew clearer as I focused on the debate. Then an insight struck me—some of Michael's brilliant analysis, I assumed. I decided to risk stuttering in front of the class, raised my hand, and explained my assessment. Lieberthal pointed at me excitedly and proclaimed, "Now you're thinking like someone in the Chinese government!" I had to suppress a smile: My brain was most attuned to the thought processes of Chinese politicians after a grand mal seizure?

I again decided to take the risk and auditioned for the new school musical. The danger of an onstage seizure was higher than in my freshman year—they were happening every few days. Carl and Franz, as well as a few other friends, also tried out. All of us were cast, me again as the romantic lead, Carl as the villain, and Franz as a boy who befriended a mute dancer. After the casting choices were posted, I sought out the director to tell him of the risk in selecting me for a lead role. Just like the director from the previous year, he told me he would be my understudy, although I learned years later that he was far more concerned about me—and my ability to perform in the show—than he let on. Some seizures kept me from rehearsals, but I performed all three nights. While onstage, I found that, as a result of my focusing so much on my performance, my usual stress about the possibility of a seizure faded away.

Inspired, I decided to try running the spring musical the next school year and proposed *Pippin*. I was the only applicant, so the drama board approved my idea.

Despite these small triumphs, my roommates began to discuss among themselves their concerns about my decline, conversations they did not disclose to me for years. They feared my falls. They knew convulsions had occurred in terrible places. One had battered me badly in the middle of a row of immovable metal-and-wood seats during a showing of the French thriller *Diva*.

Then there was the emergence of psychological issues that they sometimes observed. Despite subconscious efforts to bury my feelings, I experienced occasional severe emotional outbursts. Circumstances may have been the direct cause, but other factors likely played a role: The manufacturers of the drugs I swallowed in huge, unmonitored dosages warned that these mind-altering medications could lead to emotional upset, psychosis, and behavioral deterioration; Craddock never told me. Worse, a typical dose greatly increased the probability of suicidal thoughts; that was revealed in 2008 in an urgent alert from the Food and Drug Administration. Decades before, when I was taking eleven pills a day, no one knew such a side effect was possible.

I experienced one of my worst breakdowns in the second semester of my sophomore year. I was in the room with Dave when my head started swirling with fatalistic, morbid thoughts.

I'm dying. I want to get better. I want to die. I need to leave school. It's too hard. It's too hard. I want it to stop. Nicholson. He'll be right. I'll leave school. I'll lose everything. I'll be nothing. I'll be nothing. I'll be alone. No friends, no job. No education. I'll be alone. I can't be alone. I can't keep going. Please let me die.

Suddenly, I sobbed and gasped, near hysterics. Dave asked something, but he couldn't understand my response. I don't even know if I spoke words or just blubbered. Carl showed up. The two of them spoke to me, but I have no idea what they said.

Kill me, I thought. *I want to die.*

I cried uncontrollably for a long time.

Another problem was obvious even from a distance: I was rapidly losing weight. My jeans slipped past my hips, and my shirts became baggy. I needed new clothes and bought some at a secondhand store. I telephoned Craddock to ask if this might be related to the drugs; again he replied, "I've never heard of that as a side effect of the medication." Probably, he said, stress was causing me to drop so many pounds.

Carl and Franz were more concerned. Franz likened me to a skeleton and feared that when I fell, there was no fat to cushion the blow. My bones, he told Carl, would take all of the impact. That couldn't be safe.

In the final months of my sophomore year, I started planning for the summer. I ruled out Dallas—I wasn't going to spend another vacation dependent on others to drive me around. I also didn't want my mother to see how bad the seizures had become. Hearing about them was one thing. Watching them would intensify her effort to keep me home. And I didn't want to deal with my father's denial or risk him meddling in my medical care. For all I knew, I might find myself forced back to Nicholson's office. I needed to find a city with mass transit, good medical care, and a safe place to live.

Carl offered an answer: Go with him to Chicago. His family lived in a brownstone on the city's posh North Side, plenty of his friends resided nearby, and the "L"—Chicago's train system—was a short walk away. While he and I would be in the house for much of the summer by ourselves, it seemed perfect. All I needed was a job.

I had plenty of money from my telemarketing days, so I didn't need a salary, and an internship would build my résumé. Carl and I checked a book in Swarthmore's library that listed summer jobs for college students. He zeroed in on an entry for a group called the Better Government Association (BGA), which had a reputation in Chicago for teaming up with news reporters to expose government corruption. A few years earlier, the BGA had made a splash through a sting conducted with the *Chicago Sun-Times*, in which they purchased a rundown bar in the city's Old Town neighborhood, loaded the walls with hidden cameras, and then reopened as the Mirage Tavern. Months of filming caught a parade of city inspectors and other government employees seeking bribes. The BGA took some foolish risks—the tavern's matchbooks advertised "Beer, Grog, and Ale" with the first letter of each word highlighted, leaving "BGA" emblazoned on the covers.

But no one caught on. After the *Sun-Times* and the BGA revealed their deception, *60 Minutes* broadcast the story and set off a national sensation.

Carl and I were entranced by the idea of working for such a dynamic organization. We landed internships, so we were both destined for Chicago. Neither of us thought my seizures might cause a problem—we had dealt with them for more than a year, and Carl knew what to do. He was just looking forward to introducing me to his high school buddies and having a summer of fun.

Instead, the next few months would be the worst nightmare I could have imagined, one that inflicted traumatic damage on one of my best friends.

Sophomore year was the first year you started, outwardly for us, showing signs of great emotional strain. You always seemed very much together in the first year, but in the second semester of sophomore year, emotionally, you started falling apart sometimes. I remember once I was next door, and Dave Robbins knocked on the door and said, "Carl, you better come back to our room." I figured you would be having a seizure. But I came in, and you weren't having a seizure but were sobbing so hard that we couldn't get through to you. It just freaked us out. You were completely incoherent and impossible to talk to. I thought, This must be what a nervous breakdown is.

CHAPTER EIGHT

Over the two years we roomed together at Swarthmore, Carl never told his parents about my epilepsy. They knew nothing of the times he helped me back to our dorm after a seizure, of the nights he waited for me to awaken from a convulsion, of his support during my breakdowns. Since the Moors traveled to the school occasionally, he had concluded that his promise to keep my condition secret required him to leave them unaware.

That changed with my stay in their home over the summer after sophomore year. Shortly before my arrival at their three-story brownstone, Carl told his parents about my seizures. He was casual in the conversation and vague on details; he said I had epilepsy, that I took medication, that I sometimes experienced seizures. His nonchalance reflected his attitude that it was no big deal, but it left his parents unprepared for the spectacle they would witness in their soon-to-be houseguest.

The Moors are a loving family, and Carl's parents, Donell and Lynne, welcomed me with a generosity of spirit that spoke to their character. They joked and laughed in an easygoing style that put me at ease. Donell discussed music and the family, saying that Carl would have been the best piano player among the three Moor sons if he had tried. Lynne showed me a wall lined with picture frames, each holding dozens of family photographs, and told me some of the stories behind them. Later we were in the kitchen when she mentioned my slender build.

"How much do you weigh?" she asked.

"Last I checked, one hundred twenty-five pounds."

She laughed lovingly. "That's less than me!"

I couldn't bring myself to say that four months earlier, I had weighed more than 165 pounds. I had lost about a quarter of my body weight and had no idea why. Craddock's answer was still the same—"stress." That simplistic diagnosis seemed more ridiculous to me with each pound that melted away.

Carl told me that his parents knew about my epilepsy, and I worried about what they would think once they saw a seizure. I didn't have to wait long to find out. Within a week, I fell to the kitchen floor in convulsions. They watched, uncertain what to do, as Carl walked over to me, performed the usual routine—waiting for me to awaken, explaining to me where I was, telling jokes, moving me somewhere to sleep it off—and then returned to his parents. His father looked stunned and dismayed.

"We started talking, and I told him about what had been going on for the last couple of years and how sick you had been," Carl told me. "It brought tears to his eyes."

I resisted my mother's urgings to put myself in the hands of yet another neurologist while I was in Chicago but gave in after she used my own logic against me—I had insisted I wouldn't come to Dallas because I didn't want long-distance care. "Well," she said, "Craddock doesn't live in Chicago. You're relying on long-distance care."

I listened, annoyed. She had been getting more assertive and better at picking apart my rationalizations. Fine, I told her, I would see a Chicago neurologist. I figured the concession would make her happy but have no real bearing on my life. This physician would be involved in my care for only nine weeks; Craddock would still be in charge. I asked my father for a name, and he searched the academic world, locating someone at Northwestern University Medical School. When I called, I realized to my delight that my father had not portrayed my condition as particularly urgent; at first, they said the earliest appointment was four weeks down the road. Then someone canceled and they offered me a consultation in two weeks.

Two weeks. Fourteen days in which the clock on my life was ticking down toward zero. Unknown to me, as I quietly celebrated the short reprieve from visiting a new doctor, several critical body systems were failing. In less than twenty-five days, my death would be almost inevitable.

The Carbide & Carbon Building looms over North Michigan Avenue in Chicago, its thirty-seven floors sheathed in black granite, bronze trim, and a cap of twenty-four-karat gold. In city lore, the dazzling structure, built in 1929, was designed to resemble a massive champagne bottle as an homage to high society. Towering close to the Chicago River, the architectural masterpiece had become a popular site for some of the city's most prominent companies and organizations, including the Better Government Association.

On June 7, 1981, Carl and I walked through the building's two-story lobby for the first day of our internships. Soft indirect lighting illuminated the Belgian marble and sumptuous metalwork. As I stared at the art deco engravings on the bronze elevator doors, I wondered how an organization that depended largely on public contributions could afford such luxurious surroundings.

As the elevator whisked us to the seventeenth floor, I could scarcely control my excitement. This was a real office building, with real people in real jobs, the kind of place Nicholson had told me I would never be able to work. Yet even with my seizures still uncontrolled, here I was, ready to take on any assignment.

Arriving at suite 1710, I saw that the elegance downstairs belied the BGA's no-frills simplicity. Just offices and inexpensive furniture, with paper work piled high on desks. The organization appeared to have spared every expense. Someone ushered us into a conference room where a few other college students waited. We mumbled uncomfortably among ourselves until the arrival of John Laing, the organization's research coordinator. Laing's broad smile, friendly demeanor, and obvious respect for the students put us at ease. He reviewed the BGA's history and described investigations being conducted by the staff. One probe examined suspicious transactions by a Chicago alderman, a second looked into potential corruption involving a no-bid contract to run a music festival, and a third, called the Child Advocacy Project, reported on state foster care and daycare programs.

As Laing spoke, a slender man with a boyish face, sharp blue eyes, and prematurely gray hair stepped into the room. I recognized him as Terry Brunner, the group's executive director. Laing introduced Brunner, and for a few minutes, he spoke enthusiastically about the BGA and the contributions we could make as interns. His pep talk inspired me—already I was eager to find a phone and start tracking down corruption.

After the meeting, Laing assigned me to work with Linda Lipton, director of the Child Advocacy Project. I sat with her in her office, growing disappointed as she described the job. She had already issued a report, and from what I could tell, her work was winding down. Still, I shook off my doubts after Lipton gave me some assignments.

Later that day, Lipton asked for help. There was information she needed that required placing dozens of phone calls. Somewhere in the country there existed an organization called Quest that provided treatment for young alcohol abusers. The problem: She didn't know the group's full name or its location, and there were hundreds of entities with names that began with "Quest." I needed to call every one of them until I located the teen alcoholism center. The job sounded like it could take forever, but Lipton told me I had to finish in two weeks. This was real reporting, with a real deadline—I'd get right on it, I promised.

Before my first phone call, I thought about the assignment. Today, a Google search would find the information in seconds; without the Internet, the most apparent way to handle the job was to call information in every area code, ask the operator for each organization that included "Quest" as the first word of its name, and then dial all of them to ask about their business. Maybe the job would take forever after all.

Then it struck me. There might be a faster way. New York City was home to more businesses and charitable groups than anywhere in the country; no doubt many large organizations had names starting with "Quest." Perhaps, I thought, one of them might have leads on other entities with similar names. I dialed information in New York and told the operator I was trying to locate a group named Quest but didn't know its address. She checked and said there were many places in Manhattan with that name. At my request, she started reading me each address. When she recited a street I recognized, I asked for that company's phone number; given my unfamiliarity with New York, I figured any name I knew, like Fifth Avenue, must be an important address that attracted large companies. I wrote down the number, then dialed.

A woman answered.

"Hi, I'm calling from Chicago, and I'm trying to find a group called Quest that provides treatment for people with alcohol problems."

"That's not us." She told me her company's line of work.

"I figured it was unlikely you were the ones," I said. "But I was wondering, with a name like Quest, you must have a lot of people who call the wrong place."

She laughed. "Every day."

"Well, is there any chance someone has been asked about the company I'm looking for?"

A moment's hesitation. "You know what? Give me a minute."

She placed me on hold.

Soon after, I heard a click. "Found it," she said. She told me that a fellow receptionist had started keeping track of places named Quest whenever someone called the wrong number. "She's very obsessive."

The woman told me to try a midwestern city with a name I didn't recognize. I checked with a Chicago operator for the area code of that town, phoned information there, and got the number for Quest. One more call gave me the answer: This Quest, in the middle of nowhere, was the place Lipton wanted to find. I scribbled the details on my notepad, tore off the page, and walked to her office.

"Got it," I said as I stepped through the doorway.

She looked puzzled. "Got what?"

"Quest. The full name, address, and phone number."

I handed her the piece of paper with the information. She stared at it in disbelief. "That took five minutes. How did you do that?"

Stifling my excitement, I recounted the story, explaining how I decided that, rather than just dialing phone numbers all over the country, contacting a large company with the same name would give me a better chance of finding the right Quest.

"It worked," I said. "I was lucky."

She glanced at the paper. "That's not luck."

My success in tracking down Quest brought big rewards. John Laing heard about it and offered to let me expand my responsibilities. I began poring through documents obtained by staff investigators regarding Chicago medical facilities, then came across something odd. A small local hospital had pushed for years to open a rehabilitation unit for teenage alcoholics. The state balked at first but had recently given the program the go-ahead. As I read the regulations, I couldn't understand why. The hospital's occupancy rate was too low for expansion; every day, one out of every four beds went unused. Under state rules, hospitals needed an 85 percent occupancy rate before they could expand, and this place didn't come close. So why add beds if it couldn't fill the ones it had? I found a filing saying that patients in the alcoholism unit would receive five days of medical care but were required to stay at the hospital for thirty; the kids could have lived at Chicago's finest hotel for less. Then I noticed the key piece of information: The hospital would accept only teens whose families carried top-notch health insurance. Those policies paid for thirty days of treatment—the amount of time the hospital advised was required for a cure. So a hospital that didn't have enough patients had opened a unit where teenagers would be forced to remain for a month, all paid by insurance, and the state had approved the plan in violation of regulations. A BGA investigator needed to look into this, I decided.

I brought my findings to Laing, who found my information fascinating. Then he noticed the hospital owner's name; he was the father-in-law of a BGA investigator. I braced for Laing to tell me to stop reporting.

"Don't worry," he said. "That doesn't matter. Do you want to make this case your primary responsibility?"

Be the lead investigator on my own project? "Shouldn't it go to one of the staff guys?"

"You found it. Your investigation."

I beamed. "That would be great."

Laing spoke to Lipton. I was off the Child Advocacy Project and would instead be probing potential corruption involving a Chicago hospital.

Two days later, I arrived at work limping and looking haggard, my speech slurred. The previous night, I'd suffered major convulsions and injured myself in a fall. I did my best to avoid attention, smiling and waving when someone said hello. Sometime after noon, feeling clearer and in less pain, I joined Carl for a walk to a Michigan Avenue hot dog joint that had become a frequent lunch spot for interns. I made it through the day without attracting much attention.

Even though the seizures kept coming, I managed to avoid my usual fretting. I focused on work and my adventures in Chicago. Carl and I spent time with two of his high school friends, Joe Wein and Tom Eley, feasting on stuffed pizza, visiting comedy clubs, and sneaking off some afternoons to Wrigley Field's famous left-field bleachers for Cubs games. Carl told them about my seizure disorder, and following his example, they, too, treated it as unimportant.

Occasionally, they joined in trying to make their experiences with my seizures lighthearted events. Once, Joe, Carl, and I went for dinner at R.J. Grunts, a restaurant famous for its hamburgers and shakes. During the meal, I experienced a grand mal seizure. Carl and Joe moved the table to decrease the chance I would injure myself.

"That's when Joe and I came up with a famous line to tell the waitresses, who were pawing all over us while we were taking care of you: 'I just don't want to be alone tonight,'" Carl told me. "And Joe decided that being with you during a seizure was the greatest pickup opportunity ever."

The line never worked, but it did provide opportunities for laughs. I was so happy. I was living a normal life, excelling at a demanding job, and having fun despite frequent and often violent seizures.

I didn't tell anyone at work about my epilepsy, and it never occurred to me that I should. In my earliest days, I experienced no significant seizures at the office. I knew I was intellectually engaged and focused during work, leading me to wonder if boredom and inattentiveness might trigger convulsions. I also had some illogical thoughts—I pictured Swarthmore as the place where seizures occurred, and so I foolishly assumed I was safer anywhere else. It was wishful thinking, a way of staving off the fear that my investigative project would be taken away if my bosses learned of my epilepsy.

Reality intruded. The BGA sponsored an annual picnic for staff and interns. There was plenty to eat and a big softball game. At the time, I was trying to eat high-calorie, high-sugar food in a fruitless effort to stop my weight loss. For some reason, the smell of grilled meat left me nauseous, so I feasted on chocolate cake and brownies instead.

That's all I remember. Sometime during the picnic, I collapsed in a convulsion. Years later, a fellow intern told me that she and other students had been terrified as they watched my body clench and contort. Carl took control, telling everyone to stay calm. As I regained consciousness, he explained to me where I was and what had happened. Then he and a BGA investigator named Jack Doppelt helped me back to Carl's house.

After hours of sleep, I awoke deeply confused. Carl told me that I had convulsed during the BGA picnic. It took me time to understand, because at first, I couldn't remember the outing at all. Eventually, scattered memories of the picnic returned, and Carl's explanations got through to me. I was devastated. Until that moment, work had been a source of happiness for me. Now, I feared, it was over.

To my relief, no one from the BGA suggested I quit; they only asked about my well-being. But out of concern, Laing and Doppelt approached Carl. They asked how often the seizures occurred and how long this had been going on. With no secret to keep, Carl told the whole story.

"They couldn't believe it," Carl told me years later. "They couldn't believe that you, that anyone, could put up with all of that."

Two weeks after arriving in Chicago, I strolled the short distance from the Moors' house to the Fullerton Station of the "L." From there I took the Red Line downtown. I hesitated at the bottom of the stairs that led to State Street, waiting to be sure no one followed behind me, a precaution I had adopted when I realized I could kill people if I hit them while plunging down the steps during a drop attack.

As I walked toward Northwestern, I window-shopped, people watched, and lollygagged even though it was almost time for my first appointment with my Chicago neurologist, Dr. Matthew Strauss. I realized I was attempting to sabotage the consultation, dawdling in hopes he might cancel if I showed up late. *This is stupid*, I thought. I glanced again at the slip of paper with his address on it and picked up the pace.

Soon I was in Strauss's exam room. After some pleasantries, I instructed him on his role. My neurologist was in Pennsylvania, I said. Strauss would be my doctor for only a couple of months, just so there would be someone to write my prescriptions and to be available in case of an emergency. I didn't want multiple doctors offering different treatment plans. Craddock was in charge; Strauss would answer to him.

I realized my tone had been blunt, almost to the point of disrespectful, but I didn't care. If I offended him, so what?

Strauss ignored my combativeness. He told me that Craddock had sent my medical records and that he was willing to serve as a short-term stand-in. But, he insisted, he still needed to conduct basic exams. So same old, same old: "Push my hands. Squeeze my fingers. Follow my finger with your eyes . . ."

He stopped, then brought out a small penlight. "Follow the light with your eyes."

This is odd. No one had ever conducted the eye test twice. I watched the light until he reached the far side of my visual field; then I looked back at him, assuming we were done.

"No," he said. "Do it again. Don't stop looking at the light until I tell you to."

Once again, I moved my eyes from the far left, struggling not to blink. He held the light there longer than before. Then he moved it to the right. He kept it in place for several seconds at the farthest reaches of my vision.

He slid the penlight into his lab coat, then performed the test again, this time having me watch his finger. I already knew he must have discovered a problem.

"Have you ever been told you have nystagmus?" he asked.

Fear struck hard. *A new diagnosis?*

"No," I replied. "What's that?"

"Your eyes shake erratically, particularly when you're looking to either side."

"What does that mean?"

"It could mean a lot of things. It might just be a reaction to your medication. I'd need to run some more tests."

I shook my head. "No. No more tests."

I was tired of the poking and prodding; I wanted to be left alone. I had a job. I had a life. I was not going to become a professional patient. I promised that I would talk to Craddock about this eye problem when I returned to Swarthmore.

Strauss put up no argument. I was the patient; he couldn't order me around. "But you need to have this checked as soon as you get back to college," he said.

I agreed, but deep down I knew I would procrastinate.

My mother telephoned Strauss at his office later that day. "What do you suggest he should do?" she asked.

"It's not up to me," Strauss replied. "He's made it very clear that I'm just a consultant to Dr. Craddock while he's in Chicago."

"Forget that," my mother said. "How would you handle Kurt if he was your patient?"

Strauss was quick to answer. "I'd hospitalize him immediately."

ELVA EICHENWALD, 1982

He went to Chicago, and we begged him to come home, but he refused, saying that he could get just as good care in Chicago as he could in Dallas. I couldn't disagree with him. We hadn't been too successful with what we had tried to do. He saw a neurologist in Chicago and called and told us that he was going to maintain him on the medication and wouldn't see him again for five weeks. At this point, I became very angry, and Heinz became very angry and told him that he had to see him sooner, and the kid was just bogged down from dealing with a bunch of idiots, I think. I called Dr. Strauss, who told me that if he [Kurt] were his patient, he would hospitalize him. I asked him to please do that, and he told me he would, with Kurt's permission.

Kurt was angry, but he agreed to go to the hospital in Chicago in June of 1981. I went to Chicago, and I guess it was all still a pretty nonchalant thing, figuring we'd get a diagnosis and get him on medication. I was going up to stay with him while he was in the hospital and then go on to the East Coast to a seminar and to visit my mother. I never made that trip, not after everything went to hell in the hospital.

CHAPTER NINE

I arrived angry and numb in my room at Northwestern hospital, carrying a sports bag filled with neatly folded clothes. Usually, I would have just stuffed the shirts and pants into the duffel—a lazy trade-off of time for wrinkles—but my mother had packed for me.

She had telephoned me after speaking to Strauss, recounted their conversation, and announced she was flying to Chicago. I protested—going to the hospital would force me to abandon my job and might get me fired—but she brushed off my protests. She would be on the next flight, she told me. Then she doubled down, saying if I refused to check in to Northwestern, she would contact the BGA and tell them I was too sick to work. I was appalled—she was threatening to make me look like a child to my bosses. I considered calling my father to complain but thought better of it. I had never seen my mother act with such assertiveness, and I had no doubt my dad was already furious at her for leaving him alone in Dallas. He hated when she traveled without him, so I was sure he had already lost an argument.

I threw my bag on the hospital bed and greeted my roommate, an obese fortysomething man who stank of stale cigarettes. My mother walked in a minute later. We had arrived together, but she had stopped at the nurses' station while I stormed off. I didn't want to be here. I didn't need to be here. What was the point? More tests, more prodding, another false proclamation by a neurologist that he had divined the secret to stopping my seizures. I had learned to dread hope. As long as I didn't trick myself into thinking things could improve, no one could disappoint me. I had made that mistake too many times, falling for assurances that a new treatment would work; my emotional devastation always lasted for weeks when I realized they had lied. *Lied*, not made a mistake. If they didn't know whether a drug would stop the seizures, why didn't they say so? What arrogance drove these doctors to make promises they couldn't keep?

I glanced at the wall over my bed. A tongue depressor wrapped in gauze and surgical tape had been fastened there. *What the hell is that?* I dropped onto the mattress as my mother bustled around the room, unzipped the duffel bag, and unpacked my clothes into a small closet that resembled a gym locker.

"So, what are you in for?" Stale Cigarettes asked.

"I have no *fucking* idea," I snapped.

My mother turned to him. "I'm sorry. He's just upset."

Don't apologize for me! I thought. I stomped toward the closet to inspect how my mother had arranged my clothes. I wanted to cry but shook off the urge. I needed to feel anger, not self-pity.

A nurse with strawberry blond hair stepped into the room and smiled at me. She was stunning. As she introduced herself, I decided maybe it was time to behave myself.

She placed a hospital gown beside me. "You're going to need to change into this, Kurt."

"I can't just wear my regular clothes?" This was my first hospital stay; I didn't know the procedures.

"No," Strawberry Blonde replied. "The doctor is planning a number of tests and they need you in the gown."

With anybody else, I would have argued. But Strawberry Blonde? "Okay." I smiled.

"Also, never be in bed with the guardrails down. We don't want you falling onto the floor if you have a seizure."

I looked at the looping tubes of metal as she raised them on each side. "Won't I just end up getting wrapped up in them?"

She raised her index finger. "That's why we always do this."

Two white blankets appeared. She tightly wrapped them around both guardrails. I squeezed one; the padding was thick. Definitely, if I hit those during a grand mal seizure, I would be fine. *I should have thought of this years ago.*

I pointed at the wrapped tongue depressor taped to the wall. "What's that for?"

"It's a bite stick. If you have a seizure, it's better for you to bite gauze than your tongue."

"I bite my lip." *That sounded goofy.*

"Your lip, then. We don't want you getting hurt."

She ticked off a few more instructions, told me she would return soon, then whisked out the door toward some other lucky patient's room. *Doctors I hate. Nurses I like,* I thought.

I changed into the gown, feeling uncomfortably exposed. I climbed into bed and covered myself with the blanket. My mother told me she had some things to attend to but would be back in an hour. After she left, I glanced around the room. Drab, dreary place.

Stale Cigarettes spoke. "So you have seizures, huh?"

"Yeah."

"That sucks, man."

I nodded. "Yeah."

Since we were getting all disorder chummy, I asked why he was in the hospital. I recall thinking that, based on his size and smell, I could diagnose his problem myself.

A woman walked into the room rolling a cart loaded with tubes capped with different colored rubber stoppers. I'd seen those before, so I knew why she was there.

"The vampire arrives," I joked.

She prepared a needle. "Well, I'm not going to take all your blood."

She asked if I had a preference of which side to stick, and I told her to use the right. She wrapped a rubber tube around my upper arm. "Nice veins," she said just before she slid in the needle.

She filled a number of tubes, drawing more blood than anyone had before. I knew they didn't need such a large amount to measure drug levels.

"Why do they want so much? What are they checking?"

She tilted her head toward a form someone had filled out. "Pretty much everything."

Within the hour, Strawberry Blonde inserted an IV saline drip into a vein, telling me this was in case they needed to load my bloodstream with Valium, a treatment hospitals used to stop a seizure quickly. Once that was done, she told me someone would be coming to take me to the EEG lab. *Wonderful. Electrodes glued to my head again.*

It was worse. After an orderly brought me downstairs, the technician explained they would be using nasopharyngeal electrodes in addition to the usual scalp attachments. I had never heard of them.

"Let me show you," she said. She brought out two pieces of metal that looked like bent coat hangers. I ran a mental inventory, moving down my body; I couldn't imagine where these went.

"We put them up your nose, then slide them down closer to the lower side of your brain."

What? "How can something that big go up my nose?"

"We do it all the time. Don't worry."

About ten minutes later, the technician finished wiring me up. Inserting the nasopharyngeals had hurt. She'd slid them so far up my nose that I couldn't tell where the tips had ended up in my head. The rubber bands used to open up spots for the electrodes across my scalp pulled my hair. Then the technician brought out a block of wood wrapped in gauze and tape and told me to place it in my mouth. I didn't ask why; this was a crueler version of the bite stick hanging over my hospital bed.

I was thinking that this getup seemed like something out of a torture chamber when the technician spoke. "Okay," she said. "Now I want you to go to sleep."

I removed the block of wood from my mouth. "Are you kidding? How am I supposed to sleep like this? Everything hurts."

She told me she would give me a sedative and poured a capful of a pink liquid that she identified as chloral hydrate. I asked if the drug would cause problems with my anticonvulsants. After she assured me there would be no problem, I drank it. Then she put the wrapped block back in my mouth.

I woke later in my hospital room. No confusion, nothing injured; my speech was fine—definitely no seizures. I figured that the pink liquid either put me to sleep or just wiped out my memory of the EEG.

The next morning, Stale Cigarettes disappeared. I never saw him pack or leave. I looked around the room, uncertain about my surroundings. I was in the hospital, at Northwestern, but something seemed wrong. I knew I was supposed to be here but couldn't fathom why. Of course, there were the seizures. Had I been hospitalized for that? Wait. Did someone say something? It was a voice from far off, detached from my surroundings.

"What?"

"I asked if you're okay."

I turned my head and saw my mother in a chair.

"Yeah, I'm fine," I said. "I just woke up."

"Do you remember talking to me before?"

"No."

I closed my eyes. *Body assessment. Nothing hurts.* But things weren't right. *Very weak.* Better than after a grand mal seizure, worse than after a drop attack. Something had happened. I couldn't figure it out.

"When did that other guy leave?" I asked.

"About an hour ago."

"Is he gone for good?"

"Yes, he's been released by his doctor. He said to let you know he hopes you get better."

Okay. So, I guess I was asleep.

My mother walked to the guardrail by my bed. "You don't seem right. You don't remember talking to me this morning?"

"No. But I forget a lot of things."

"Do you think you had a seizure?"

"I don't know. Everything seems weird. But I don't feel the same way I usually do afterward."

"What's today's date?"

That's not fair. "I never know the date."

"What month is it?"

"June."

She questioned me until I asked her to stop. There was no reason to test my cognition and memory. Obviously, some sort of seizure had occurred. Maybe if I had been standing, it would have been a drop attack. I didn't know what one felt like if it happened while I was in bed.

We talked for about twenty minutes, and I described my investigation of the alcohol program. She pressed for details, never explaining that she was trying to help me regain the focus I lost post-seizure.

The door swung open, and Strawberry Blonde appeared.

"How are you feeling?" she asked.

"Fine." I wasn't lying. The confusion had mostly cleared up, though the strange feeling hadn't passed. I couldn't think of words that would properly explain what was wrong. "Fine" struck me as close to the right answer.

"They're taking you for a CAT scan today. Have you had one of those before?"

"Yes."

She made a few more comments and then was gone. I wondered if I should have answered, "I feel strange" just so she would have stayed longer to ask more questions. She was so cheery. I loved having her around.

Not a minute passed before a man in scrubs appeared and told me he was there to check my bleeding time.

"What's bleeding time?" I thought of a joke: Maybe if the technician were British, I could tell him the bleeding time. About 11:00 A.M.

"I make a couple of small cuts in your forearm and then time how long it takes for the bleeding to stop."

"Why do they want to know that?"

"I don't know. I just have an order to get it done."

"Will it leave a scar?"

"Maybe a hairline one, but nothing so bad you could see it without trying pretty hard."

He wrapped a blood pressure cuff around my upper arm and inflated it, then brought out a small device that looked like a white box.

"This is spring-loaded," he said. "The blades shoot out and retract very fast. It stings for a second."

He pushed the box into my inside forearm. I ignored the slight pain; I was distracted by how quickly the blades cut the skin. The technician clicked a stopwatch. I looked at the spot where he'd cut me. Two red slices, like squinting cat's eyes. He brought out something that resembled a flat, circular coffee filter and dabbed at the blood. I realized my mother was standing beside the bed across from the technician.

"Mom, this is nothing. You don't need to stand there."

"Humor me," she said.

I glanced back at the technician, who was still sopping up my blood. I couldn't think of anything to say.

"What's the usual bleeding time?" I asked after a moment.

"Most people tend to be around three to five minutes, although I've seen some go as long as nine," he said.

Silence again. We would be standing next to each other for five minutes? I inquired about his job, how he had chosen it, and anything else I could think of to pass the time.

Three minutes. Still bleeding.

At five minutes, he took out another coffee-filter dabber. To me, the bleeding seemed to have sped up. In fact, I couldn't remember ever bleeding so much from such small cuts.

By seven minutes, his casual demeanor turned serious. We were no longer chatting.

Nine minutes. The blood looked to me as if it was pumping out of my arm, not just seeping. He removed the pressure cuff.

Twelve minutes. "So am I your career record?" I asked.

"I think so," he replied, his tone signaling he was in no mood for jokes.

Fifteen minutes. He had used several dabbers. He brought out a gauze pad and pressed down on the cat's eyes. The cotton mesh was quickly sopped in red; he grabbed another and pressed again. Blood dripped down the sides of my arm. He threw the second pad on my rollaway table when it was soaked, then reached for a third one and pressed it down hard on the cuts.

At about eighteen minutes, he hit the nurse's call button.

A woman's voice came over a speaker. "Yes?"

The technician identified himself. "I need help down here."

"I guess this isn't going so well," I said. He didn't respond. A nurse appeared. It wasn't Strawberry Blonde. The technician told her I had been bleeding for close to twenty minutes.

I glanced at my mother's frightened face. Her fear struck me as odd. Why was she worried? I was just bleeding. It would be okay.

A few minutes passed before the nurse and the technician finally succeeded in stopping the flow, placed a thick pad of gauze on the cut marks, and wrapped it tight with surgical tape. The technician threw out the bloody mess, put away his equipment, and darted away without a word. The nurse asked a few questions, checking to see if I was frightened or confused about what had happened. I assured her I was fine. She told me she needed to change the bloody sheets. I stood and gave my mother a hug; I could tell she needed one. The nurse was fast, and in a flash, I was in a clean bed. She instructed me to click the call button if the bleeding resumed, then left.

That wasn't epilepsy, I thought.

I watched my mom and could tell she was trying not to cry. I felt nothing. I had shut down emotionally again. Nothing. Not scared, not sad, not concerned for my mom. Nothing.

Guess I've got some new disease, I thought casually. *I wonder what it is.*

A new doctor showed up and asked to speak to my mother in the hallway. There was lots of dashing in and out. I realized no one ever took me for my CAT scan. I'd have to talk to Strawberry Blonde about that.

My mother returned to the room trying to hide her tears. The new doctor followed her. He introduced himself, but I forgot his name almost as soon as he mentioned it.

You've got really thick eyebrows, I thought. *Should I tell you to trim them, or would that be rude?*

I heard him say something about hematology. I didn't know what that meant. "So what do I have?" I asked.

"Well, the white—"

"Stop, stop. Cut to the chase. What do I have?"

Dr. Eyebrows took a breath. "We don't know yet. Your blood looks very similar to what we see in leukemia. But it could be that your bone marrow is shutting down."

I thought bone marrow just sat there. I wasn't sure what he meant by "shutting down." It certainly didn't sound good.

"Okay," I said. "What makes you think that?"

The production of both white and red blood cells was very low, the doctor explained. My hemoglobin level was three.

"What is it supposed to be?"

"For someone your age, about fourteen or fifteen."

I tried to calculate fifteen divided by three. I couldn't.

My count of platelets, the cells in blood that make it clot, was also dangerously low, the doctor said, and the white cells being produced were all immature.

"Well, I can be immature, so I guess that makes sense."

Dr. Eyebrows spoke in a stern voice. "Kurt, you need to be serious. We have a lot of things to do, and we have to do them very quickly."

I nodded. "Okay, I'm sorry. So why is this happening?"

Before he answered, the doctor said, he needed a medical history. He focused on the last few months, telling me to describe every problem I'd experienced. I recounted the nausea, the dizziness, the weakness, the tremors, the weight loss, the bruises that wouldn't go away.

"Why didn't you call your doctor about this?" Dr. Eyebrows asked.

"I did."

Dr. Eyebrows hesitated. He clearly hadn't expected that answer. "What did he tell you?"

"That everything was caused by stress."

Another pause. "What did he say about your medication blood levels?"

"Nothing. He only checked my levels when I first saw him."

"Why didn't you have them checked again?"

"He never told me to. In fact, whenever I asked if the medication might be causing these problems, he told me no."

"He said no?"

"Well, not exactly. He told me that he'd never heard of anyone having those side effects from the medication before."

The doctor stopped speaking. His expression harbored some inner disquiet. I was ready to yell at him if he started being mean to me. What had I done? Why was he angry?

"Did anyone ever tell you that your medications could cause problems with your blood?" he asked. "Did anyone tell you there were symptoms you needed to look out for?"

"No. I remember when I went on Tegretol I read the package insert, and it mentioned something about blood, but I don't remember what it was. I never read the insert for Depakene."

"How long have you been on your current dosage?"

"I don't know. Maybe three to five months?"

The doctor seemed to calculate something in his head.

"Look, we're talking around everything," I said insistently. "Just tell me. Is the medication killing me?"

"It could be causing this problem."

I heard my mother choke back a sob.

"Which one, the Tegretol or the Depakene?" I asked.

"We don't know," the doctor said. "It could be either."

Okay. "So, what, am I allergic to both of them?"

"No. This is going to be hard for you to hear, but you're going to have to make a lot of decisions very quickly, so you need to understand what's happening."

"Okay, tell me."

"Both of your medications are at very toxic levels. They're not medicines anymore. They're poison. What your neurologist did is unforgivable. I'm sorry to be this blunt, but you have to know the truth. If we don't move quickly, you could die."

The news bounced off me, leaving no emotional impact other than satisfaction; I had *told* Craddock my weight loss wasn't from stress. *That stupid jerk,* I thought. I had been right. He had been wrong.

Confused by my blasé response, my mother asked if I understood what I had been told.

"I get it," I replied. "I mean, I don't know exactly what's happening, but it sounds like nobody else does either. Whatever it is, it is."

My fatalistic indifference disturbed my mother, but she realized that, for the moment, the doctors needed her help more than I needed emotional repair. She asked Dr. Eyebrows if they could speak in the hallway. There, the doctor raged about Craddock, tossing out words like "incompetent" and "malpractice." The records Craddock had sent to Strauss included only a single blood test—incomplete at that and taken during my first visit—and the medical team at Northwestern had assumed some office clerk had forgotten to ship the rest. Dr. Eyebrows said he had called Craddock's office seeking the other blood tests on an urgent basis but never heard back.

"We have no recent records," Dr. Eyebrows told my mother. "We're flying blind."

Nicholson. My mother said there was another neurologist, one in Dallas whom I hadn't seen in many months, but at least he would have old blood tests. That doctor had drawn blood on at least two occasions, maybe more, she said.

"Please call him and ask him to send the records immediately," Dr. Eyebrows said. "Anything we can get might help."

She poked her head into my room to check on me. Seeing I had fallen asleep, she walked to the nurses' station on my floor in search of a phone; the staff knew what was happening with me and offered my mother every support as they brought her to a desk where she could call Nicholson. The secretary answered, and my mother quickly explained the circumstances, stressing that she needed to speak to Nicholson urgently.

"Hold on," the secretary said.

For five minutes, my mother waited, tears streaming down her face, hoping that Nicholson would answer any second. Finally, he clicked onto the line. Speaking rapidly, my mother spelled out the dire prognosis and explained why the Northwestern doctors wanted my old blood records. Nicholson interrupted several times, demanding information he didn't need and she didn't know.

"All that matters right now is we need you to send Kurt's blood tests," she said.

There was a pause. "They're wrong," Nicholson said, referring to the Chicago doctors.

My mother thought she must have misheard him. "What?"

"They're wrong," Nicholson repeated. "It's a lab error."

She wanted to scream at him, to call him inhuman for arguing about medical tests he hadn't seen with a mother whose son could be dying. But the blood records came first. She asked for them again.

"I'll see what I have," Nicholson replied. "Call me back later."

Then he hung up.

Over the next hour, my mother met with other doctors to update them on Nicholson and find out if they had any more information about my condition. A hematologist—a doctor who specializes in diseases of the blood—told her that they would soon perform two tests, a bone marrow aspiration and a bone biopsy. She cried at the news; she knew both could be excruciating and worried that I wouldn't bear up under the onslaught of health problems.

She called Nicholson, but his assistant said he wasn't available. Thirty minutes later, she tried again. He had located the blood tests, he told her, but insisted again that the Northwestern doctors were wrong. My mother begged him again to just send the records. She told Nicholson that the doctors considered the situation an emergency, were about to perform the painful bone marrow test and bone biopsy, and were insisting that the old blood analyses might be helpful in reaching a diagnosis.

"All Kurt has to do is to grow up," Nicholson said to the mother of a dying son. "Maybe after he has a bone marrow aspiration, he'll grow up."

ELVA EICHENWALD, 1982

A couple of days after Kurt was admitted to the hospital, they came back with the fact that his bone marrow was suppressed, and I was scared. I was so scared. Kurt did not look well. He had lost so much weight. He did not behave right. He seemed to be not well. I was very afraid for him, of course, realizing that he could have leukemia, or bone cancer, or aplastic anemia, or a reaction to the drug, and I was alone. I was very alone in a strange city with people I didn't know.

[After the "Maybe Kurt will grow up" phone call with Nicholson] I never spoke to that man again. However, everything that he has caused us and all the pain and the misery, both to Kurt and to me—I will sometime; I will talk with him someday, because I think it's the only way I can be free from him.

I tried so hard to bear up under all of this. There were so many painful procedures that Kurt faced. When I could slip away, I spent a number of hours praying in the hospital chapel. I didn't want to lose my son.

CHAPTER TEN

A new team of doctors and nurses showed up in my room that same day. Their arrival surprised me—they were planning to do the next series of tests *here?* I had assumed orderlies would be wheeling me all over the hospital, from one lab to the next. Maybe they had decided to cut the travel time. *They really are rushing,* I thought.

"Hi, everybody," I said.

One doctor introduced himself while another person handed me a sheaf of papers to sign. Authorize this, informed consent that. The physician kept speaking as I scrawled my signature on each page, having no idea what permission I was granting. I didn't care. I heard the word "aspiration" and glanced up.

"I'm sorry, what are we talking about?" I asked.

He apologized. That meant a lot; no doctor had ever expressed regret to me for anything over the past two years. He started his explanation again—they were going to perform two tests, a bone marrow aspiration and a bone biopsy.

I knew the word "biopsy." "Is there a tumor?"

"Not that we know of."

Then why do it? I didn't care enough to ask.

"I want you to know, this is going to be painful," the doctor warned. I would have a lot of choices to make in the next twenty-four hours. That meant they had to avoid using a sedative that ran any risk of knocking me out or triggering a seizure. While they would use a local anesthetic, they had to keep the dosage minimal. My neurologist was calling the manufacturers of my anticonvulsant, the doctor explained, but no one knew what might happen when another drug was added to toxic levels of medications already causing significant problems.

I remembered a question I had forgotten to ask earlier. "How toxic am I on these medications?"

"I've been told the levels are very toxic."

"Okay. But what does that have to do with an anesthetic?"

"I'm sorry. This really isn't my field of expertise."

"But someone must have told you something. I need to know."

The physician bit his upper lip. "Your doctors have never seen levels like this."

Another person spoke. As far as I knew, he had not yet introduced himself, but he was wearing scrubs, so I assumed he was a doctor.

"Your liver metabolizes your medications. If we add more drugs, it's just going to make your liver work harder. We don't know yet what that would do to your anticonvulsant levels, and we don't want to risk triggering a seizure, which would require more medicine."

"So if you use an anesthetic, I might get more toxic?"

"We don't know," he repeated. "We're going to use local anesthetic but not a lot. So you need to be prepared. This is going to be painful."

The other doctor spoke. "Now, you must stay perfectly still. I'm going to inject a needle through the bone to get a marrow sample. Then we have to use another type of needle for the bone biopsy."

I wonder why he's switching his pronouns, I thought absentmindedly.

For the first time, I noticed the work being performed by the rest of the team. No conversation, every face serious. A woman removed wrapping from a tray. At some point, I noticed a sealed bag with a needle in it. By my guess, it was six inches long. Then I saw another device that looked like a giant corkscrew, only straight.

"Mom?" I said. She was nearby, behind all the staff dashing about.

I assumed she had been asking plenty of questions herself that I hadn't heard.

"Yes, Kurt."

"I want you to leave before they do this."

"I am. They told me I can't stay."

"Good." I looked around until I could see her face. "I'm going to be fine," I said.

"I know. Just know, I'm right outside. I love you."

"Love you too. I'll be fine."

I closed my eyes. I needed to prepare myself. I thought of Daniel Nevot, a war hero who fought in the Free French Forces during World War II and who later coached at St. Mark's, the school I attended as a kid. We called him Monsieur Nevot, and I considered him the toughest man I ever met. I'd heard his stories from others because he never discussed his exploits. One anecdote stuck with me: He and two others disguised as Arabs infiltrated an Italian garrison. He was captured but somehow convinced the enemy troops that they were surrounded by French fighters. Then he and his friends grabbed machine guns and held the soldiers prisoner until French reinforcements arrived.

When I was in first grade, Nevot ran a physical education class for a rambunctious group of six-year-old boys and frequently required us to run half a mile on the track. I despised the workout—I wasn't a runner. After the first lap, I always wanted to quit but knew that was not an option. Instead, every time I thought, *This is now. You hate it now. Soon it will be a memory. Keep running; soon it will be a memory.*

The doctor told me to roll onto my stomach. *Soon it will be a memory.* I gave silent thanks to Monsieur Nevot.

"Okay, Kurt," someone said. "Grab the headboard. Don't let go no matter what. Remember, hold perfectly still."

"Okay." I gripped the board tight.

A woman told me they were going to inject anesthetic. Given that they had warned the amount was going to be limited, I wasn't sure why they bothered. Afterward, time passed and someone pinched the spot.

"Did you feel that?" someone said.

"I know you did it. But it didn't hurt."

Someone wiped something onto my back.

"All right." I recognized the voice—it was the first doctor on the team who had spoken to me. "I'm going to insert the needle. Remember, you can't move."

"I know."

Soon a memory.

Sudden pain. I scrunched my face and dug my fingers into the headboard. It hurt, but I could bear it. I breathed hard.

"Don't move."

Monsieur Nevot. Monsieur Nevot. Monsieur Nevot.

And then, it was a memory. I relaxed my hands, listening as the doctors and nurses bustled about. I didn't ask or care to know what they were doing. I think I fell asleep.

"Kurt."

I opened my eyes. I was still facedown holding the headboard and believed a lot of time had passed. "Yeah?"

"Now we're going to do the bone biopsy. I don't want you to be surprised. This will hurt. But you cannot move."

"Got it. Give me a second."

Soon it will be a memory. Be calm. Soon a memory.

"Okay. I'm ready."

Something penetrated the skin over my hip. I could handle this.

Sudden, excruciating pain shot through my body, the worst I'd ever felt. I gritted my teeth and pushed my fingers so hard into the headboard I'm surprised it didn't break. I gasped.

"I know," the doctor said coolly. "Don't move."

Monsieur Nevot. Monsieur Nevot. Monsieur Nevot!

I couldn't take it. I never knew there could be such agony. In my mind, I saw the giant corkscrew in my back, twisting into my hip.

Monsieur Nevot.

I started crying.

"Don't move," the doctor said. "Almost done."

And then it was over. I took several deep breaths. *It's a memory.* I couldn't believe how painful that had been. *It's a memory.* I didn't move but hadn't let go of the headboard yet. No one spoke.

Then I heard it. A single soft word in a lilting, apologetic voice. "Kurt..."

No no no no no!

"... we didn't get the sample we need."

Wait, no. What? Wait—

"We need to do it again."

"No, wait! Give me a second! Stop, stop, stop! I need to ... just get ready!"

"It's better if we just do it now."

"No, just give me a second!"

Monsieur...

"Hold still."

Nevot...

Agonizing, nearly unbearable pain assaulted me.

Monsieur ... No, stop! Stop!

The tool penetrated the bone. I pictured it again in my mind's eye, digging into my hip. I made a noise, a combination of a soft scream and a sob.

"Don't move."

In my imagination, I saw the metal burrowing into bone, the straight corkscrew now curved, with the doctor bearing down as he rotated it into my back as if it were a bottle of wine.

Oh, God, if I have a seizure. The thing would break off. It would shatter my hip. Maybe they would never be able to remove it.

Did they think about that? What if I have a seizure? Wait. One's coming. It's coming! It's coming! It's going to kill me!

"I'm going to have a seizure!" I screamed.

"Hold still."

"No, get it out! Get it out! It's going to break! I'm going to have a seizure!"

"Just hold on."

My arms shook as I gripped the headboard tighter. I was crying and hyperventilating. This wasn't a seizure.

It's coming!

They finished and removed the instrument from my back. Then I lost consciousness, from the pain, from the cessation of pain, from the hyperventilation, from the overdoses—the possible causes were al-

most endless. The seizure I'd feared hadn't been real. Consumed by
alarm and agony while psychologically unprepared for the second biopsy, I had experienced a major panic attack.

I woke in my bed as someone bandaged my back. Some members of
the group who had performed the biopsy were still in the room. My
hip throbbed with pain, and I could barely open my mouth to speak.
My thoughts were clear, though all my energy had drained away.

Everything after that moment is a blur. I ended up in a clean bed on
the opposite side of the room; my mother told me later I had soaked
the sheets so badly with sweat that they moved me to Stale Cigarette's
old, now-clean bed rather than have me stand while they changed my
linens. I don't remember moving. A lower back muscle spasmed, and
trying to stretch it, I raised the head and foot of the bed as far as they
would go. I fell asleep in the mattress version of a taco shell.

A new roommate arrived and took my former spot while I dozed.
When I woke, he greeted me with a fulsome grin and a big "hello." He
appeared to be in his early eighties, and he introduced himself as Irwin
Henoch. His wife, Florence, waved at me and asked how I was feeling.
I replied that I was okay and introduced my mother, who told me they
had been speaking for a while.

Irwin and Florence treated me more like family than a hospital
roommate—in fact, within a day, he was calling me his ersatz grandson. He recounted their lives, ordinary talk that came alive with the
twinkle in his eye, the lilt of his voice, and the animation of his ges-
tures as he spun his tales; I was captivated. We discussed what had
brought him to the hospital, and Irwin explained that a part of his
spine near his brain had become clogged and needed to be cleared.*
The couple was open about his prognosis—Irwin required surgery,
and because of his age and poor health, he might die. He seemed resigned to whatever might happen, but I could see Florence was frightened, putting on a brave front for her husband.

The three of us talked and talked, and the conversation reminded

---

*In the course of my writing this book, doctors have told me that this is a rudimentary
and partly inaccurate description of a condition called spinal stenosis.

me that my life was filled with promise and opportunities. The anger, confusion, and fear that had eaten at me gave way to something: Determination? Empathy? I was content and resigned to my fate. For the first time in days, I cared about the outcome but also accepted it was beyond my control.

My mother listened to these conversations with a watchful eye and, at one point, seeing how relaxed I was, told me she was going to leave for a bit. She needed a break. She returned from the gift shop with a high-quality pen she had purchased for Irwin as a "thank you" for being so kind to her son.

That day, she explained to Carl that I was extremely ill, telling him about red blood cells and bone marrow and using terms he didn't recognize. It was only later when he spoke to his own mother, Lynne, that he came away believing I might have leukemia or some other cancer.

Not long after, Carl and Lynne showed up in my room; he carried a copy of a record by my new favorite band, the Roches. Had Carl bought me a present? That was odd, I thought. I studied their faces and detected a mixture of uncertainty and dread. Carl said something, but his tone was different than ever before. There was hesitation, no humor, no goofy put-downs.

Wait a minute. They all think I'm going to die.

Ridiculous. In my convoluted reasoning, I couldn't get sicker. I had told Craddock for months there was something wrong with the drugs, only to be dismissed with his "I've never heard of that as a side effect" mantra. Now everyone knew I had been correct. The *doctor* had been wrong. I couldn't *die* when I had been right all along.

The visit ended on an uncomfortable note. Carl clearly had no idea what to say. My mother was on the verge of breaking down. Lynne tried to be her usual upbeat self, but I saw through her forced cheerfulness. I was glad when everyone left.

I resumed my chats with Irwin and Florence. She started unpacking a suitcase, and I saw she couldn't find a place for her clothes. I understood—with Irwin's life at risk, Florence wanted to spend every moment with him until he was wheeled into the operating room.

I climbed out of bed, grabbed my IV pole, and wheeled forward. "Use my closet," I told her.

"Oh no, I can't," she said.

"Of course you can. You have nice clothing. I have a bunch of T-shirts and jeans. I'll put my stuff somewhere else."

She thanked me as I emptied my closet, then I stacked armfuls of clothes on the table used for meal trays. Florence finished unpacking and sat in a chair. Both she and Irwin sounded exhausted.

"I think everybody needs to go to sleep," I said.

They agreed. We turned out the lights.

I sat in the dark, the head of my bed still raised as high as possible to stretch my back. I could have slept but didn't want to. My mind flooded with thoughts, many inspired by the love and happiness I saw in Irwin and Florence as they accepted his own uncertain fate.

Why was I trying so hard? I was always in pain, fears were endless, and doctors made everything worse. Graduating with my class would give me the reassurance to know I wasn't letting epilepsy beat me, but that goal was not about life. There had to be a more important reason than that to keep pushing.

What's the purpose? What do I want?

For hours, I lay there, mulling my future. Obviously, I thought, I wanted to be happy, but what did that mean? For years, everyone I knew—including me—assumed I would be a lawyer. After all, I debated in high school, and litigation was sort of like that. It upset me terribly when Nicholson shot down that aspiration, saying someone with epilepsy couldn't practice law because of stress. But why did I want to be an attorney anyway? It took a second for the answer to hit me: I didn't. I'd drifted toward law because I hadn't given it much thought. I'd graduate from college, go to law school, become a lawyer, the end. But after facing my own mortality every day, fighting to overcome these challenges, it seemed like self-betrayal to travel the unthinking path. If my health improved, my future self owed me, the me in this hospital bed, not to blithely take the easy route. I remembered a phrase from a poem by William Blake: "mind-forg'd manacles." Before my seizures, I had chained myself, out of laziness or a lack of imagination, to a future I didn't want.

Suddenly, an epiphany. *Life is divided into two things—those that can be controlled and those that can't.* I couldn't control my seizures. What else? I couldn't control medication side effects. I couldn't control what others thought of me. I couldn't control whether a particular person loved me. I couldn't control whether someone chose to give me something I wanted, like a job. What did I control?

Everything else.

If I faced people who feared me or denied me work, I could control whether I gave up or tried to change their minds. I couldn't *force* someone to hire me, but I could work hard, assembling a strong enough résumé to prove that I was a candidate worth considering. I couldn't *make* someone love me, but I could be a person worthy of love. I could control the petty feelings that well up in everybody—jealousy, hatred, bitterness—by remembering that, in the scope of life, they were inconsequential. I controlled whether I pushed an elevator button, but I had no control over when—or if—it arrived.

So what did I want? The answer popped into my head: to be a newspaper reporter. In that job, I would always be learning, interacting with others, and seeing the world. That was almost what I was doing for the BGA, and I loved it.

I remembered my professor's comment on my first college essay. *Your writing is grotesque.* He had been right; when Michael wasn't around, it still was. But I could control how I handled that. I could give up, or I could learn the craft.

If I committed to working for a newspaper, I knew I would face challenges beyond my lack of talent. Unable to drive, I could live only in cities with mass transit, which meant I had to *start* at a major newspaper such as *The New York Times*, *The Wall Street Journal*, or *The Washington Post*. As my mind ranged over the obstacles I faced, it hit me again: I controlled whether I would accept the challenge. Slinking away to pity myself would mean Michael won. I was taking my life back. Despite the difficulties I recognized, I promised myself I would not let him defeat me. I would be a newspaper reporter.

What else? I wanted to be married to a fun, lively woman—I pictured Laura Petrie, the wife of the main character from the old television program *The Dick Van Dyke Show*. I wanted my marriage to mean something. I wanted to be an attentive father to several children. I wanted a life that mattered, at work, at home, to my descendants.

I finally understood—I possessed more control than I had believed. Healthy people didn't always understand the scope of how much could be overcome. I certainly never had before I got sick. As for what I didn't control—the seizures, how others reacted to me—to hell with it. I could control how I reacted to the uncontrollable.

Sometime after midnight, I closed my eyes, feeling far more powerful, far more in charge of my life, than ever before.

The next day, my doctors informed me there was no doubt—my anticonvulsants were killing me. They wanted my authorization to stop the drugs as fast as possible. My neurologist and a pharmacologist concluded that phenobarbital was the only safe anticonvulsant for me to take until my bone marrow recovered. A drip of that drug was attached to my IV, a necessary precaution since the withdrawal of Tegretol and Depakene could trigger seizures. Sometime later, the drip was removed, and I received the medication in pill form.

I slept a lot. Once I woke up deeply confused and realized Florence was asking if she should call the nurse. I rasped, "Why?" She told me she had just returned to the room, and Irwin had told her that while she was gone he heard me making odd sounds—my teeth crunching and strange breathing; he hadn't been able to see what was happening because the curtain between us was drawn. It was okay, I told her. I did a quick mental assessment of my body—yes, I'd had a seizure; all the post-episode feelings were there. I fell asleep.

Then there was a man beside my bed. He introduced himself as a psychologist and told me that my neurologist wanted him to examine me. He asked questions for about twenty minutes, administered a written test, and then was gone.

Technicians checked my blood every few hours, but I never asked about the results. The jitteriness of the medical staff had eased, so I assumed I was better. The first hematologist I'd met—the doctor who had been honest with me about the dangers I faced—was more upbeat. They pulled me off the drugs quickly after he estimated that my bone marrow had been five to seven days from shutting down. I asked whether I would have died if I had delayed my hospital stay by a few weeks.

"In the condition you were in, there was a good chance," he replied.

Maybe it was the passing of the danger, or Irwin and Florence, or the sense of control I developed in my night of contemplation that they inspired, but I felt calm. My fears, my desperation, had slipped away.

At one point, I woke in the middle of the night with my head on the floor and my foot stuck under one of the bed guardrails. I knew I had experienced a grand mal seizure, but it took me time to understand I had fallen out of bed. Extracting myself from this position proved impossible. I heard Irwin and Florence snoring and called to them, but they didn't awaken. A nurse or someone else—I couldn't tell who—turned up. She eased my foot out of the guardrail and helped me back to bed. When I awoke the next afternoon, my mother was there. She told me she had arrived in the morning and, based on how deeply I was sleeping, concluded I had convulsed during the night.

By the last day of my hospitalization, the Tegretol and Depakene had cleared my system, and I was instructed to never use either anticonvulsant again. Given how long I had been toxic on both drugs, a doctor said, no one knew what might happen if I resumed taking them.

My neurologist, Strauss, showed up that morning before my mother arrived. I realized I had barely seen him throughout my stay, but other people had come into my room and identified themselves as neurologists. I remembered—Northwestern was a teaching hospital. The other doctors had probably been medical residents.

I stood beside my bed in a robe. Strauss reviewed what had happened during my stay and confirmed that, yes, my levels of Tegretol and Depakene had been more toxic than he'd ever seen. He mentioned that one colleague had encountered someone with higher Tegretol blood levels in an emergency room, but that was a patient who intentionally overdosed in a suicide attempt.

He rambled on, but I paid little attention. The world struck me as blurry, but not in how it looked. I thought if I commented on that, no one would understand what I meant.

Wait. What?

"Did you hear me, Kurt?" Strauss asked.

"No, I'm sorry. I wasn't listening. What did you say?"

His face was firm.

"You don't have epilepsy," he said. "Your seizures are psychological."

In a conversation with

DR. ALLAN NAARDEN, 2017

Just think about the main problem with seizures. It's the chaos that it causes in your brain. It's very difficult to focus and to think coherently. You can imagine how people would believe when somebody else is telling them that they're mentally ill. How many patients wound up in mental hospitals with the diagnosis of suffering with psychological illness when that isn't what they had?

CHAPTER ELEVEN

My first reaction to Strauss's statement was gut-wrenching exasperation—another neurologist saying the others had been wrong. I had petit mal, I didn't have petit mal. My medications were fine, my medications were low, my medications were high. I had epilepsy, no I didn't. Then, disbelief: I had been throwing myself down stairs, biting my lip until it bled, breaking ribs, losing friends, living in fear, and it was all psychological? If those hadn't been seizures, I had to be insane.

"They're not epilepsy?" I snapped.

In a sharp tone, he told me to stay calm. I sat down on the bed, trying to absorb his words. A fear struck me. A doctor had just suggested I was mentally ill; perhaps his curtness toward me had been a warning. Maybe orderlies were in the hallway, ready to whisk me off to a psychiatric ward if I became argumentative. I felt a chill. I recognized I was being paranoid; there was no one ready to pounce. Probably. For a moment, I wished I could shut down my emotions whenever I wanted. I needed that now.

Watch your tone.

"Okay," I said. "If the problem is psychological, then we need to deal with that. But explain why you think it is."

He started with the bone biopsy. "Medical staff was here. You yelled you were going to have a seizure, and then you shook."

"My arms shook."

"Exactly. You know what happened. If that had been a real seizure, you wouldn't know. And the doctors who were there reported that you were speaking much of the time."

"But I never said it was a seizure."

"You did. And then you pretended to lose consciousness."

"I know it wasn't a seizure. When that thing was in my back, I got scared and thought one was coming. I never said it *was* a seizure. And I *did* pass out after it was over. At least, I think I did. I don't know why it happened. You're the one telling me you've never seen drug levels this toxic. Do you know how someone would react to that much pain with such high levels of those drugs in his system?"

"Kurt, it wasn't a real seizure."

"I *know!*" I shouted.

"Don't shout at me," Strauss said gruffly.

He was making short, staccato statements, and I was rambling. *Calm down.*

"Look, we agree," I said in a softer voice. "Why didn't someone just ask me if that was a seizure? If I said yes, you'd have a point. But you're assuming I thought it was. I was *scared* one was coming, but whatever happened, that wasn't one of them."

"The doctors who saw it say it was hysteria."

"Then it was hysteria. I don't know what it was. It wasn't a seizure. I had that thing in my back, they didn't give me a second to get ready before they did it the second time, and I got scared. It wasn't a seizure."

Strauss looked annoyed. "That's not the only problem. You've been here for days. You haven't had a seizure the entire time."

Wait a minute. "Yes, I did."

"No one saw you have a seizure."

Was I crazy? I woke up on the ground, having banged my head on the floor. A nurse—*was it a nurse?*—helped me to bed. I had been postictal; my mother told me. *That didn't happen?* I touched my head. A bump was there. It still hurt.

"Feel my head," I said. "You can feel where I hit it on the floor when I had a seizure."

"No one saw you on the floor."

That's not true!

Calm. Stay calm.

"A nurse saw it," I said. "Or somebody. I couldn't get my foot out of the railing. The nurse or whoever helped me."

"No one reported that. If you fell out of bed, they would file a report."

"But I have the bump on my head!"

"Kurt, no one reported finding you on the floor."

It happened. I know it did. But cracks in my certainty were widening. In mere minutes, Strauss had raised doubts I couldn't explain away. Why hadn't I had more seizures? Why had there been only one? I had already forgotten the others, the one Irwin had heard and the other times I woke up postictal. I wrote about those instances of confusion in my diaries on the days they happened but didn't think to check my records as I struggled with this new diagnosis. In fact, I wouldn't look at any of them for four years.

Strauss continued. "The most important part is your EEG. It showed no seizure activity."

I stayed silent. *The test showed no seizures.* No seizures. All of my injuries, all of the emotional trauma suffered by family and friends, and nothing had been detected in my brain, not even when they shoved coat hangers up my nose. *Could Strauss be right?*

"What's wrong with me, then?" I asked.

"It's called a conversion disorder, a form of hysteria. I ordered a psychological exam of you while you were here, and the conclusions are that you suffer from emotional disorganization and other symptoms consistent with hysteria."

Wait a minute. "You gave me the psychological exam at the same time I was coming off two anticonvulsants and adding another. How could anyone know if they were testing me or testing whatever the medications were doing to me?"

"Kurt, the diagnosis isn't from a single piece of information. It's everything together."

Crazy people never think they're crazy. I knew that. The EEGs showed nothing. I had to be mentally ill. This conversion thing had to be treatable. What difference did it make if I had epilepsy or a mental disorder? Either way, the episodes had to stop. I couldn't handle injuries anymore. *Oh my God. Everyone I hurt.* A wave of guilt struck, the worst I'd ever experienced. The anguish I caused so many people I cared about, people I loved—how could I have done that to them?

I folded my arms across my chest. "Okay, if it's psychological, what's the next step?"

"I'm going to refer you to a psychiatrist I've worked with. He's excellent, and I believe he'll be able to help you."

"Can I make an appointment to see him now?"

"I doubt he has an appointment now."

Why are neurologists so thickheaded?

"No, I meant, can you give me his number now so I can make an appointment?" I said. "I want to take care of this."

Strauss gave me the doctor's name and told me he was releasing me from the hospital. I would need my blood checked several times a week at the hematology lab, but otherwise there was nothing more for him to do. The discharge nurse would provide me with documents to sign and my prescriptions.

"Prescriptions for what?" I asked.

"For your phenobarbital."

I stared at Strauss, incredulous. "Why do I need an anticonvulsant? If this is psychological, can't I just stop the medicine? I'd rather not take anything."

He shook his head. "No, I want to leave you on it for now," he said. "Just in case."

I had arrived at Northwestern combative and afraid. I departed confused and consumed by guilt. My nausea, trembling, and headaches gradually disappeared, probably a result of coming off the Tegretol and Depakene. My white count remained low, but my red cells and platelet levels increased. I didn't know how my blood improved so quickly. I may have received a transfusion; doctors have since told me this would be standard for my low hemoglobin count. If so, I either forgot or was unaware it was happening.

After my discharge from the hospital, my mother and I went for lunch at a sandwich shop in Water Tower Place, the posh shopping

mall on Michigan Avenue. The strain on us was palpable, tacitly acknowledged by our silence after we found our table. She looked pale
but, unknown to me, had reached a turning point. She didn't believe
Strauss's diagnosis and was furious that he would proclaim, after one
appointment and a couple of drop-ins, that my seizures over the years
had been, essentially, fake. She had witnessed my episodes—the
crunching of my teeth, the biting of my lip, the saliva, the sounds as I
croaked out breaths through muscles contracting in my neck, the stiff-
ening of my body; Strauss had never asked what she thought, what
she had seen in the hundreds of days leading up to this moment. She
knew I had been postictal at least twice at Northwestern, although she
didn't mention that to me at the time.

As I sat in the deli, I had no idea I was watching my mother transform; she was resolving to no longer stand helplessly on the sidelines
and instead to fight to end the chaos. She had allowed my father to
seize the role of overseer of my medical care, then hadn't fought back
when I insisted on finding my own doctor in Pennsylvania—all with
disastrous results. If she hadn't forced me into Northwestern, I would
have been dead. Only her decisions had been correct; my father's and
mine had consistently been terrible. She knew taking control would
mean fighting us both. She had never been an aggressive person and
often allowed my father to dictate her life choices. No more. While she
didn't know her next step, she later told me that the day I left Northwestern, she began plotting how to get me to another doctor, someone
she would find by consulting experts.

First, though, came our usual dance. As I picked at my sandwich,
she pleaded with me to return home; again I refused. Now that we
knew what was happening, I told her, I should get better. If psychological distress triggered these whatever-they-were episodes, maybe I
could *will* them to stop. My first psychiatric appointment was in a few
days. Who knew what might happen after that? I wanted to finish my
internship. I would be home in August, just weeks away. I should be
better by then.

I parried every argument until she finally accepted that I would not
leave Chicago while I still had a job. Until another doctor confirmed
her suspicions, she had no grounds for declaring Strauss wrong. For
the next few weeks, she would have to endure her fear that the pheno-

barbital wouldn't work and I would be in more danger than before. She thought that trying to force me back to Dallas might backfire, and I might refuse care. She had no options available yet, no answers to give, no doctor waiting, no idea how to find a good one. She decided her only choice was to return home and prepare her next move.

I had almost reached the third floor of Carl's house, walking a couple of steps behind him, when I collapsed. I flipped twice as I plunged down the stairs, then crashed full force into a wall. I recall none of it.

Much of the rest of that summer has disappeared from my memory. I stopped recording and writing my diaries. I never told Carl of Strauss's diagnosis; I was embarrassed and remorseful about inflicting so much on my friend because of some psychological problem. Yet in my rattled state, it never occurred to me that by staying, I was wreaking more damage on him. The intensity of the seizures, their frequency, the injuries—all of them increased. Seeing the psychiatrist and swallowing phenobarbital accomplished nothing.

"It was just constant. You were so sick," Carl told me years later. "It's amazing you weren't hit by a car or didn't break your neck falling down the stairs or just wear yourself into the ground. It was awful. It was really awful."

By then, Carl and I were alone in the house; his parents had traveled to their home in New Mexico, and my mother, at my insistence, had returned to Dallas. That meant, as I got sicker, Carl—a twenty-year-old kid—faced every challenge by himself.

I knew my episodes had taken a sharp turn for the worse, but my thoughts were too unfocused for me to comprehend the magnitude of what was happening. According to Carl, I experienced grand mal seizures up to four times a week and frequently collapsed in drop attacks. I would awaken trying to make the postictal state disappear by force of will. If the seizures were psychological, then the post-seizure confusion was too. But no matter how hard I tried, I couldn't make anything stop. The disorientation became dramatically worse. I injured myself so badly during this time that I concluded that the psychological problem causing these episodes had to be severe.

I returned to the hospital, but not by choice. On July 3, 1981, Carl, his friend Tamar, and I boarded the "L" for the downtown business district, then walked to Grant Park for the second annual food festival Taste of Chicago. Crowds numbering in the thousands milled from tent to tent, where scores of the city's restaurants sold meals and snacks. As we ambled through the masses of people, I fell to the ground in convulsions. Carl did not know what to do—we were deep inside the park and surrounded by too many crowds for him and Tamar to bring me out. A passerby called an ambulance, which took me to the Northwestern emergency room.

On another day, I was in the kitchen near spaghetti that was cooking on a stove when I suffered a drop attack; I knocked over the pot of boiling water, and, while I was fully conscious, the liquid scalded my right arm. I banged my head on the street in several episodes. The left side of my chest hurt badly after one occurrence; I figured that I had broken another rib and ignored it.

The worst moment for Carl came when we were downstairs in the finished basement at his house. He was ironing a shirt, and foolishly, I was sitting on the washing machine nearby. A seizure struck, and I fell into the ironing board, knocking off the iron. Carl reached over the board and caught it by the handle before it crushed my skull. He screamed—not in pain, but in terror.

Afterward, as I convulsed on the floor, Carl couldn't stop shaking. Without his catching skills, he knew, I would have been killed. Terror welled up inside him. Suddenly, in what I have always believed was a moment he cracked under the emotional trauma, Carl imagined he heard someone upstairs. He scrambled around the basement, searching for a bat he could use in self-defense. Then he grabbed the phone and called a friend who lived nearby, begging him to come over because some stranger had broken in. When the friend arrived, Carl ran to the door, and the two searched the house. They found no one except for me, lying unconscious beside the washing machine.

Whenever I arrived at my psychiatrist's office, I reminded myself why I was there. This wasn't for me to blubber about my injuries; it was about treating my mental illness. I saw Dr. Robert Wolfe at least once a week, and he often changed my appointment if an episode left me incapable of attending. That was the word I used whenever I spoke to him—"episodes." If they were imaginary, I couldn't call them "seizures."

Wolfe looked like a psychiatrist from the popular imagination: glasses, brown hair, the furrows of time and experience etched in his lean face. I always sat in a chair instead of on the couch, occasionally glancing around the room before our session began. Dark wood panels, desk, bookcases. The sitting area was on a large rug that made me uncomfortable. What if one of my episodes happened there? If I bled on that rug, Wolfe would have to pay a fortune to clean it.

I never felt embarrassed when I discussed with Wolfe how my obvious madness hurt people; instead, he helped me manage my guilt. He listened more than any neurologist ever had. He never rushed me to make my point, and I'm sure I rambled.

Early on, he asked a question that struck me as absurd: "Where did you keep your clothes when you were in the hospital?"

"I'm sorry?"

"Where did you keep your clothes?"

"Um, in the closet."

He leveled his gaze over his glasses. "The whole time?"

"Yes."

Then I remembered. "No, wait, I didn't. When my second roommate arrived, his wife was staying with him, and she didn't have room to store her stuff. I let her have my closet."

"Where did you put your clothes?"

"On that table beside the bed. The one on wheels they use for meals."

"So you kept clothes on the table because you were helping your roommate's wife?"

"Yes."

This was bizarre. "Why are you asking me this?" I asked. "What does this have to do with anything?"

Wolfe brought out two pages stapled together. "It's in your psychological report from the hospital."

My psychological report? "Why would my psychological report talk about where I put my clothes?"

"The psychologist concluded that you stacked your clothes on the table so they would be near you, and that was a behavior consistent with you having disordered emotions."

"What does that mean?"

"Not much," he muttered.

I realized my mouth was hanging open. "So because I gave up my closet to my roommate, I'm crazy? Are you saying there is something wrong with what I did?"

"No. I assume the psychologist never asked you why the clothes were on the table?"

"No, he didn't. That's so stupid! How can he reach a conclusion based on where I keep my clothes without asking me why I did it?"

Wolfe put the report away. "We don't need to talk about this report. I'm not using it for anything."

"What else did he say?"

He brushed away my question. "It doesn't matter. I'm not going to rely on this report. Pretend it doesn't exist."

Panic. *Another doctor did something ridiculous?* What else had gone into that report? Analysis of my robe color? Whether I needed a haircut? Wolfe might ignore it, but would others? Strauss said his conclusions had been based on "everything together." Among the data he cited was this report, one that Wolfe clearly considered nonsense.

For all of Wolfe's graciousness, after several appointments, I grew antsy. We were getting nowhere. I had assumed we would be digging into my psyche, trying to unearth repressed emotions that led me to fake these episodes. But our sessions lapsed into recitations of the previous week's horrors—the ones I remembered and the ones Carl described. Occasionally, Wolfe asked to see my injuries; I showed him cuts on my arms, bumps on my head. He asked me to describe where my shoulder hurt. I told him about chest pain, dismissing it as another fractured rib; he suggested I see an internist, and I responded that it was no big deal. I'd broken ribs before and knew there was nothing to be done but wait for them to heal.

"If you keep falling, how is it going to heal?" he asked.

"Isn't that part of the reason I'm here? To find out why I'm hurting myself so much?"

Two days after scalding my forearm with the pot of boiling water, I arrived for a session in a state of exhaustion. Ugly shades of red and purple streaked across the skin. Wolfe asked to see, and I held my arm perpendicular to my shoulder. I commented on how the burn was beginning to look like a bruise, which I didn't know could happen.

As I spoke, Wolfe flopped back in his chair.

"I can't take this anymore," he exclaimed.

His statement shocked me. I had no experience with psychiatry but knew that reaction couldn't have been appropriate. What had I done? Had I insulted him?

He sat back up.

"Kurt," he said, "you have epilepsy."

I wanted to scream. *Don't do it*. If sharing my closet with my hospital roommate's wife had become part of my diagnosis, what would happen if I shrieked at my psychiatrist? I had accepted the diagnosis of mental illness, once again tricking myself into having hope, into believing someone would finally discover how to help me. Now back to epilepsy?

"That's not what Strauss said."

"Strauss is wrong."

"He's the neurologist."

"I'm the psychiatrist. And I'm board-certified in neurology."

I started crying. "How can you say I have epilepsy now? I had normal EEGs!"

Wolfe spoke softly in what I now recognize was an attempt to help me regain my composure. "People with epilepsy can have normal EEGs. It's quite common. What is *not* common is people with conversion hysteria injuring themselves. That doesn't happen. And every time we meet, you look like you just stepped off a battlefield."

People with epilepsy can have normal EEGs? "Why didn't Strauss tell me the test could be normal?" I snapped.

"I don't know."

I wiped away my tears. *So I'm back where I started?*

"Why didn't you tell me when I came in that people with fake seizures don't injure themselves?"

"It was farfetched, but you might injure yourself if you had a multiple personality disorder. But you don't have multiple personalities. You have epilepsy."

I closed my eyes and leaned my head back. *I want to feel the sun on my face. Why does this office have so little sun?* I brought my palms up to my eyes. *I want to feel the sun on my face.*

Time passed. Seconds, minutes—I don't know how much.

"Kurt."

I looked back down and reached for a tissue on a table next to my chair so I could blow my nose. "Yeah."

"You understand?"

I rubbed my hand across the back of my neck. "Yes, I understand. So what do I do?"

"You need to go back and see Dr. Strauss."

"I'm sorry. I don't accept his diagnosis," Strauss said.

He'd telephoned minutes earlier. I called him as soon as I returned to Carl's house and left a message with an assistant spelling out Wolfe's findings. Since then, Strauss had contacted Wolfe, and the two argued about their conflicting conclusions.

"But you said these seizures or whatever the hell they are were psychiatric, and the psychiatrist says you're wrong!" I snapped.

"I disagree with him. I'm convinced you have conversion hysteria."

"So why do you still have me on an anticonvulsant?"

His answer was a jumble of words, then a return to the psychological exam I took at the hospital, the non-seizure during the bone biopsy, the normal EEG. He finished by telling me that if I wanted the episodes to stop, I needed to return to my psychiatrist. I telephoned Wolfe and recounted my conversation with Strauss.

"I know what he thinks," he said. "I don't understand it."

"He says I can only get better if I keep seeing you."

Wolfe stayed silent for a moment. "Kurt, I can help you deal with your emotional reaction to the seizures. But I can't stop them. You have epilepsy."

My mother visited the Dallas Epilepsy Association for the second time since my diagnosis. My medical care had been terrible, she said, and the seizures wouldn't stop; she feared I would not bear up under the pressure much longer.

The counselor gave her a name: Dr. Allan Naarden, whom he described as the neurologist for hopeless cases. He worked at Medical City in Dallas. While he couldn't help everyone, Naarden would be the neurologist he would choose in my situation, the counselor said.

My father reacted with fury when he heard that my mother wanted me to see Naarden. That neurologist worked at a *for-profit* hospital! Those places hired only quacks! He raged at my mother for interfering in my healthcare, for trying to dump me with some sleazy doctor who would make things worse. But he offered no alternatives on how to help me.

Throughout the rant, my mother glared at him. Then her decades-long deference, her willingness to accept his instructions, simply collapsed.

"Stay out of it!" she snapped.

I stood beside the hot, open oven door. Then I fell, landing on the left side of my face. I heard my skin sizzle. Screaming, I reached with my right hand to push myself off the scorching metal. As I pressed on the door, I saw flesh on my palm smoke and bubble.

I bolted up in bed, shrieking. Was it a dream or real? I no longer always knew. Now, when something bad happened during a seizure, I sometimes dreamt during the postictal phase that the ugly event had been a dream. Then when I woke, I was plunged back into whatever reality my subconscious had tried to escape. The lines between imagination and reality blurred—nightmares plagued my sleep, and postictal dreams tricked me into believing real horrors had not occurred.

This time, I pulled at my sheets and pinched my skin as I hyperventilated, hoping I wasn't about to wake again to discover my face and hand had cooked. After about twenty seconds, I took a deep breath of relief—the oven episode had been a nightmare.

No one was treating me. I took my phenobarbital every day, but it may as well have been Tic Tacs. Strauss increased my dosage but still continued insisting I suffered no physical problems and only Wolfe could help me. Meanwhile, Wolfe kept repeating he could not stop the seizures, and finding a solution was in Strauss's hands.

I talked to Carl endlessly in our shared bedroom at night, trying to keep him awake in a pointless effort to fend off nightmares. When I gave in to his pleas to let him sleep, I sometimes retreated to the Moors' rooftop deck in the middle of the night. I knew exhaustion could trigger more seizures or hysteria or whatever was going on. But my nightmares had become so gruesome—falling off cliffs, plunging chest first into poles, being crushed by a truck, burning—that I took the risk. Sometimes, I was so frightened and lost, I just sat with Carl and sobbed. Everything was chaos. He didn't know what to do.

My job at the BGA was supposed to last until August 14, but eventually—as a result of my mother's pleas, in recognition of the harm I was inflicting on Carl, or simply out of feeling too sick—I agreed to abandon my work and fly home on August 6. In my mind, by quitting my job early, I had failed. And now I had this trail of medical records—*I'm crazy because I piled up my clothes; my EEGs are normal; oh no, I'm sane: I just have epilepsy; wait, no, something else*—that left me convinced this ordeal might never end. My mother told me about another neurologist—*another neurologist, another neurologist.* What difference did it make? They knew nothing. They hurt me. They berated me. They almost killed me.

Some nights as I sat on the rooftop, awaiting the sunrise, I struggled with my deepest fears. As it was, life was not worth living. I came up with two plans. The first: I would run away to Arizona, walk into a neurologist's office, announce I had just experienced a seizure, and start again. I don't know why I chose Arizona; I had never been there. But if I pretended my condition was new, I thought, I wouldn't be stalked by my medical records. Piling up my clothes, the bone-biopsy non-seizure, the fall from bed that apparently never happened—all would be gone. It was an irrational plan, but it was the only thing between me and my second idea:

I would kill myself. Strauss had mentioned hearing of someone becoming toxic on Tegretol after she swallowed a bunch of pills in a suicide attempt. A bottle of my phenobarbital, I figured, could do the job too. Once I obtained my next full refill, I could down them all.

On the night of August 5, I cried and hugged Carl. Going back to Dallas terrified me. I wouldn't kill myself in Chicago; I couldn't do that to a friend, since he would be the one to find me. I would swallow the pills in Dallas ... but I didn't want to die ... but I didn't want to suffer. I knew Arizona was unworkable, leaving only my second plan. And so I sobbed, knowing Dallas meant death, wanting to beg Carl for forgiveness without revealing he would never see me again.

The next day, two of Carl's friends drove me to the airport. I didn't pack some of the new clothes we had purchased that summer, instead leaving them at the Moors' house. I figured the shirts might fit somebody they knew. I wasn't going to need them anymore.

CARL: *After the hospital you were emotionally, physically much worse off. But you became so obsessed with living a normal life that you made a normal life impossible. You were so obsessed with not losing your job at the BGA and proving that you could work. Every day, you had to go to the office. You would absolutely not stay home. And it would take us sometimes forever to walk to the "L" station, which is five minutes from my house, because you were so beat up and walking so slowly. But you just wouldn't skip work. And I thought, This is crazy. That you should go home and you should do what you can to get better.*

KURT: *Why didn't you tell me you needed me to leave?*

CARL: *Because that would have been the worst slap in the face of all. Kurt, I can't stand it anymore. Go home. That was what you feared worst. That was readily apparent—that you were terrified everyone would abandon you. I couldn't do that to you.*

An audio diary from

ELVA EICHENWALD, 1982

I got strength somewhere to decide that I was going to fight for my son and get him the care that he needed, and I was prepared to go to any length to do that. Toward the end of July, Kurt was obviously doing very, very badly. I begged him to come home. He wouldn't come home. He said that he had to finish this investigation he was doing, and I begged him, and I begged him. His father ordered him, and nothing happened. He scared me, because he was accepting his seizures as a way of life, and I kept saying, "That's not a way of life." Seizures every day is not a way of life, it's an existence, and I was afraid that at some point it all would be too much and that he would decide to end his life. I know that I would.

I chose to find out more about epilepsy, everything I could. Went to the Epilepsy [Association] again, talked with the counselor there, who was absolutely fantastic. I visited with him and expressed my fears and concerns, and he gave me the support I needed to continue to let Kurt do what he had to do. Kurt had told me that if I did come to Chicago again, he would not come home, and the counselor told me that he felt Kurt very well might run away. He believed Kurt was very frightened and very confused and that he must be allowed to come to terms with this in his best way.

We finally did get Kurt to come home; he looked awful when he got off the plane. He looked like a scarecrow. He looked very sick and very tired, and he was the son that I didn't know. Dark circles under his eyes, and his normally sparkling eyes and bright, cheerful outlook were gone.

CHAPTER TWELVE

I lay on my bed in Dallas, propped on pillows and wearing a now-loose-fitting Mickey Mouse T-shirt that I'd outgrown years before. The bottle of phenobarbital in my hand rattled when I shook it. One-quarter full. I wondered if that would be enough to end my life. I thought through my Arizona plan again. I couldn't afford plane tickets, I couldn't drive, I couldn't pay the medical bills. But a suicide attempt, I knew, had to succeed on the first try. I decided to wait until I had a full, fresh bottle of the anticonvulsant before reaching a verdict about whether to kill myself.

It was August 8, a Saturday. I'd arrived home two days earlier and experienced a grand mal seizure the previous evening. My father had fully subscribed to Strauss's diagnosis that this problem was psychological, so my mother forced him to stand over me as I clenched, bit, and convulsed. "Look at him!" she shouted.

I didn't care what the truth was. Fear, embarrassment, anger, guilt, and a desire to make it all go away overwhelmed me. I glanced around my room at the ceremonial masks hanging on the walls, decorations my father brought back from overseas trips. I wondered if any of them represented death. Or health. I realized I'd never asked how the various tribes, religions, and indigenous people used the masks or why. I just thought they looked cool.

I heard footsteps and tossed the pill bottle into a bedside table so no one would ask why I was holding it. My mother appeared. I never closed my bedroom door anymore to make sure I could be heard if I had an episode.

"How are you feeling?" she asked.

"Same as always," I replied, emotionless.

"Your speech sounds good."

"Yeah, well. Give it time."

She sat at the end of my twin bed, the only spot with enough room. "We need to talk about—"

"No." *Again with this Naarden guy.*

"Kurt . . ."

"What's the point?" I argued. "He'll tell me I have rabies or aliens are shooting beams into my head or say I'm not taking my meds. I hate neurologists. They're all the same."

She took my hand. "Kurt, I can't make what's happened go away. And I'm sorry you have been so alone in fighting this. We made a lot of mistakes. But this is not the time to give up."

I was about to speak but she interrupted. "You need to go. And if he is not the right neurologist, we will find another one. Things can't go on like this. But you won't be alone anymore. You're a fighter, and I'm going to fight with you."

I looked in her pleading eyes. A stab of guilt cut through me. If I didn't go, I knew I would just hurt her more and we would spend my final days—well, maybe my final days—arguing about Naarden. I had caused enough pain. I could waste time with another quack if it would make her happy.

"Fine," I said.

Days later, I sat in sullen silence in the passenger seat as my mother drove the fifteen minutes from our house to Medical City. I knew my surliness only added to the pressure on my mother—the night before, my father had again complained bitterly about her taking me to a doctor at a for-profit hospital. I silently rooted for him to win the argument but couldn't help applauding her newfound assertiveness.

We headed to the crowded parking lot and maneuvered into a space. My mother uttered a few words of encouragement, then stepped out of the car. I didn't budge, not even to unfasten my seat belt, as I imagined the coming medical interrogation: *Why don't you know the answer to this question? Why didn't you ask other people what happened? Why didn't you have a seizure on Tuesday? Why are your EEGs normal?*

The driver's-side door was still open, and my mother leaned down to talk to me. "Kurt," she said, "I know you don't want to go. Please do this for me."

I unfastened my seat belt and climbed out of the car, shuffling behind my mother. She walked with such self-assurance that I realized she must have been to this place before. After riding the elevator upstairs, we stepped into a long hallway. No pictures hung on the wall, creating an illusion that the corridor became narrower and narrower.

Great. This neurologist works in a funhouse.

When we reached the end of the hall, I noticed a sign that read, "Texas Neurological Institute" with names listed beneath it. For the first time, I saw how "Naarden" was spelled. The two *a*'s together left me wondering about the name's country of origin.

Inside, I flopped into a chair in the waiting room while my mother went to the reception desk. I knew I was being petulant by refusing to do more than just show up. I wouldn't even greet members of the staff.

The room was packed with patients, some in wheelchairs, others with noticeable neurological impairments. I realized I had never seen a person with an obvious, significant health problem in any other neurologist's office.

After about twenty minutes, I was called to the back by Naarden himself. My mother went with me, a good idea given the likelihood that without her, I would bolt if this doctor started spewing nonsense.

Naarden ushered us into his office. He was a heavyset man with a mass of black hair and a bushy mustache. He flashed a broad smile, his demeanor conveying an animated charm, but I vowed not to be fooled by his façade of affability. I took my seat in silence as Naarden sized me up. He knew I was irritable, likely belligerent, but he was unfazed. He witnessed those emotions and behaviors frequently in seizure patients. I never imagined as I glowered at him that this doctor already understood the psychological struggles I faced because of my seizures. Despite my father's protestations about Naarden working with a for-profit hospital, I would soon learn that he was the best-trained neurologist I had ever consulted, one who bristled with credentials.

Borough Park in Brooklyn teemed with energy in the 1950s, its streets packed with Orthodox Jews clad in black coats, prayer shawls, or long-sleeved dresses. A kaleidoscope of residents headed down Thirteenth Avenue toward an open market where pushcart vendors once lined the road. Young and old obsessed over the Brooklyn Dodgers, and the boys emulated their heroes with games of stickball in the streets, swinging broomstick bats as their shoes grew tacky on the hot asphalt.

That was the world Allan Naarden experienced growing up on a treelined street in the Kensington neighborhood, but he was not the kind of boy to be found in a pickup game. Never an athlete, he spent hours reading in his beloved Brooklyn libraries, captivated by worlds he could explore only in books. Like many Jewish families of the day, the Naardens considered education a great leveler, a gift that opened opportunities to anyone with determination, and they urged young Allan to pursue learning without compromise. While Naarden's father was a diamond merchant, his mother and grandmother pushed relentlessly for Allan to achieve more—he should be a doctor, they said, the pinnacle for an educated man.

By junior high, Naarden realized he had a knack for academics and decided he wanted a life dedicated to expanding his mind. The public-school system allowed for the brightest sixth graders to graduate into a special rapid advanced class, and Naarden's mother made sure he was ready for that program. From there, he skipped eighth grade and headed straight to Erasmus Hall, one of the oldest public high schools in Brooklyn. Coming from a family with little money, Naarden relied on the taxpayers for the rest of his education. He earned his undergraduate degree with honors at Brooklyn College and went to medical school training just over two miles from his boyhood home, at the

State University of New York Downstate College of Medicine, graduating magna cum laude. Then it was off to an internship and medical residency at Maimonides Medical Center, also in Brooklyn.

It was there that Naarden began to wonder. He'd spent his entire life in this one borough, and that was all he knew. If he didn't leave, he realized, that parochial mindset that affected so many New Yorkers could infect him. He wanted to meet different people, see other places. By then, he had married, and his wife, Audrey, entered a master's program in music at Yale University. A neurologist at Maimonides piqued Naarden's interest in the brain, so he decided to attend Yale for a fellowship in that field of medicine.

He arrived feeling out of place, a kid from Brooklyn about to walk the halls of the school that taught some of the world's greatest medical minds. *Now I'm going to be let in on the secrets of medicine*, he thought. Instead, he discovered that his training had been top-notch—he had more experience with the most frequent neurological conditions and with hands-on patient care than many of his Yale colleagues. He worked under Drs. Gilbert Glaser and Richard Mattson, giants in the field whose interest in epilepsy played a major role in Naarden's professional journey.

He never lost the humor and sparkle that infused life in Brooklyn. As the senior fellow under Glaser, Naarden had the job of driving the world-renowned doctor to the nearby Veterans Administration hospital, and if his boss was in a bad mood, the young neurologist would catch the brunt of it. After realizing that Glaser had an obsessive fondness for Britain, whenever he climbed into the car seeming grouchy, Naarden would mention fog, umbrellas, tea, or whatever; the conversation between boss and driver invariably transformed.

Naarden also was willing to play jokes on his colleagues. Once he learned that a nurse owned a poodle with seizures. He made a plan—translate the dog's age into human years, and present him as a case to other doctors at the weekly neurology grand rounds. Then he would ask Glaser if he would like the patient brought in. Naarden felt sure when the poodle arrived, everyone would crack up. He discussed the idea with his other boss, Mattson. He didn't laugh.

"Do you like being a neurologist?" Mattson asked.

"Yeah."

"Then I wouldn't do that."

The poodle lecture never occurred.

Research was central to Naarden's work. The Yale neurology department was among the first to conduct long-term monitoring of seizure patients using video cameras, now relatively common. They performed clinical trials seeking to expand the number of available anticonvulsants; their work contributed to an explosion of drug options for seizure patients over the decades that followed.

Despite the opportunities at Yale and his prestigious title of assistant professor, Naarden grew restless. Staying in academia meant publishing research as he climbed the medical school career ladder. Caring for patients interested him far more. He decided to leave Yale and instead go into a clinical practice that also offered opportunities for research. That way, he could treat patients as well as spend time conducting studies without facing relentless pressure to publish.

He learned from a surgeon friend that a prestigious hospital in Dallas desperately needed neurologists. He landed a job there, and in 1973, he and his wife loaded their belongings into their car and drove from Connecticut to Texas.

Things didn't work out as planned. In a matter of months, Naarden grew disenchanted by the quality of work at his new employer. The EEG lab particularly disappointed him; the technicians were poorly trained, and it overall did not live up to the standards of quality he had come to expect from his previous training and work. He reviewed EEGs, both old and new, and concluded they would be unlikely to pass independent scrutiny from national certifying organizations.

Naarden decided to move on again. In 1974, two neurosurgeons from Dallas academic hospitals invited Naarden to join them in a group dedicated to both research and patient treatment that would practice at a new for-profit hospital, Medical City. It was the perfect scenario, putting him together with top doctors and allowing him to treat patients while still keeping a hand in research.

By then, Naarden had cared for large numbers of epilepsy patients. He knew not only the latest treatments and diagnostic tools but also the emotional impact of the condition. He understood seizure disorders entailed a loss of control that could be more terrifying to patients than even death. That explained their willingness to surrender authority over their lives to a stranger certified in neurology and their reluctance to change doctors even if mistreated.

Naarden would never claim to fully comprehend those emotions, but he would also never argue with patients about how they should feel. He wanted to be a doctor who offered these people a chance at a life. He might have been able to save me, but I was no longer ready to trust anyone. Fortunately, he knew how to break through the defenses of patients who had given up.

After walking into Naarden's office, I slumped into a chair ready for the usual questions and tests, then the tired promises: He knew the problem, other neurologists had been wrong, he could stop the episodes. I wondered if he would prescribe a phenobarbital refill; at least then I would have a full bottle available to end my ordeal.

He sat and we started by discussing my staring spells, then moved on to the grand mal seizures and drop attacks. The rest was a rote recitation of history—low medication, high medication, toxic medication, bone marrow problems, and oh, by the way, I'm crazy.

To my surprise, the questions kept coming. He asked whether I was left or right handed. "Left," I replied, wondering why he cared. Then he pursued details no previous doctor had ever wanted to know. When I didn't have the answer, he didn't chastise me or demand I explain my lack of information. After twenty minutes, Naarden had already spent more time speaking with me than any other neurologist ever had, so I figured we were almost done. Then the conversation took an unexpected turn.

"Have you ever read *The Brothers Karamazov?*" he asked.

A beat passed. *Who cares?*

"No," I said.

"You should. Dostoyevsky is thought to have had epilepsy, and it gave him profound insight. He wrote about his own symptoms. The central character in *The Brothers Karamazov* has epilepsy and experiences seizures of different severity . . ."

What the hell is he talking about?

"...and in his other writings, Dostoyevsky gave very vivid descriptions of auras and seizures. But he also wrote about the struggles that can present and how epilepsy was perceived by society at the time."

Jesus Christ. I'm getting a book report from this guy.

"Now, the word 'epilepsy' is derived from the Greek, and it means 'to be shaken from without.' You might have felt like the seizure isn't coming from you. It's almost like it's emanating from outside of you ..."

Ha. You listening, Michael?

"... but different societies have had different ideas about what this thing emanating from outside really is."

He stood and paced toward my right. I turned my head as I watched him. My anger was giving way to fascination.

"There was an interesting safari that took place in central Africa back in the thirties where researchers went to gain an understanding of how Pygmies viewed disease. They found the Pygmies had a concept of seizures but thought you were being visited by your ancestors. That kind of idea isn't confined to Africa. In many cultures, there's been a belief that ancestors visit you and cause mischief if you don't honor them."

I wonder if I have an ancestor named Michael. That would be funny.

Naarden was taking me on a literary and anthropological journey through the history of epilepsy and wasn't stopping soon. He mentioned that some ancient civilizations had discovered imperfect ways to detect epilepsy. "In Greco-Roman times, they suggested that before you buy a slave, you have them look at a spinning potter's wheel. Now, why do that? It's because you're being strobed. And a strobing light can trigger a seizure ..."

Wait, what? Somebody told me I had a seizure after a strobe light went on at a dance. Strobes set off seizures?

I interrupted. "I think I've had that happen," I said softly. "I had a seizure after a strobe went on."

Naarden seemed delighted that I'd joined the conversation and grew more animated. "That happens to some people with epilepsy. Now, the mistake they made with having slaves look at the potter's wheel is that not everyone with seizures has that problem, and it had to be spinning at a particular speed."

How did they get the wheel to flash? Before I could ask the question, Naarden moved on.

"In fact, in southern France, there was a road where a pattern emerged of some people with seizure disorders having seizures as they rode through on horseback. There had been some trees planted along the side of the road about equidistant from each other, and they thought that might be the problem. They decided to test it and tried to induce a seizure by having those people ride down the road in a carriage with a fast horse, but nothing happened. Then some smart fellow suggested maybe the sun had to be low on the horizon. At that point, the sun would be behind the trees, and when you rode past them quickly, the light from the sun strobed. That's what caused the seizures."

I wasn't slouching anymore. I had arrived in Naarden's office committed to showing contempt through my tone of voice and body language, but now I sat up straight, captivated. Epilepsy was fascinating.

I recognized my guard was down. "None of that has anything to do with me," I fumed. "One of my neurologists told me I'm not a textbook case. I'm crazy."

Naarden smiled. "There are no textbook cases with epilepsy. Anyone who said that didn't know what they were talking about. One of my patients' recurrent seizures presented as seeing Abraham Lincoln in a closed convertible with his head sticking through the roof. That sounds ridiculous, and it certainly could lead to misinterpretation by a doctor. But when she saw that image during an EEG, it revealed the seizure."

"Yeah, but an EEG never detected my seizures."

"An EEG only measures a small amount of brain activity. It's a diagnostic tool. Plenty of people with epilepsy have either nonspecific or normal EEGs."

I swallowed. I wanted to cry. I wanted him to tell me I was mentally ill. That would be easier. Then I remembered.

"At Northwestern they gave me an EEG with nasopharyngeals. They slid those electrodes up my nose and still didn't find anything."

He sat back down. "Let me ask you some questions. Were you on your medication when they performed that EEG?"

"Yes."

"And what is the medication supposed to do?"

He's enjoying this, I thought.

"Stop the seizures," I said.

"So why would anybody check for seizure activity while using medication to stop seizure activity? Also, were you well rested? Did they keep you from sleeping before the test?"

"No, I slept a lot beforehand. But they wanted me to sleep during the test."

"So, how did you manage to sleep during the test when you were already well rested?"

"They gave me a sedative."

"You mean the type of drug that is used to stop seizures?"

It seemed as if the floor had dropped out from under me. "Wait, what?"

Naarden leaned forward. "Sedatives are often used to stop seizures. Your phenobarbital is a sedative. IV Valium can be used to stop a seizure as it's happening. It has sedative effects. If they used a sedative on you before the EEG, they were making it less likely that seizure activity would be detected."

I couldn't speak. I was told I was crazy because I let my hospital roommate's wife use my closet, because some nurse didn't report that she found me on the floor, because the neurologist didn't speak to my mother, and now also because an EEG didn't detect seizure activity when I was on drugs to stop seizure activity. Had *no one* given thought to what they were doing?

For a second, I considered asking why Strauss kept me on anticonvulsants while also insisting I didn't have convulsions, but I decided not to interrupt. Everything Naarden was telling me was amazing.

In a moment, we were off to the exam room, where Naarden conducted another neurological test—"push my hands; squeeze my fingers". He asked me to touch each finger on my left hand to my thumb rapidly. He pointed out that my right hand was mimicking my left, making the same movements. He told me to keep my right fingers still, and I repeated the movement on my left hand with much more difficulty. Minutes later, we were back in his office.

"Based on your history, I believe you're experiencing partial complex and generalized seizures with the focus seemingly in the temporal lobe," he said.

"The focus?" Another word I had never heard from a neurologist.

"The part of your brain where the seizure originates. Or there could be projections from other parts of the brain to that area."

Sensing my bewilderment, Naarden launched into a lecture about how even a small number of "bad" neurons could fire, triggering an electrical storm across the brain. I had heard so much at that point I could scarcely take it all in.

"I want to put you in the hospital for a full workup," he said. "Then after I've finished, I'll get you on a proper regimen of anticonvulsants."

I smirked. I knew what he was about to say. Every neurologist used the same words. I decided to beat him to the punch. "And then the seizures will stop, right?"

Naarden's smile faded. "Kurt," he replied, "I don't know. I can't know. A great doctor once said, 'When we understand seizures, we will understand the human brain.' We do not as yet understand the human brain."

His voice softened. "If the anticonvulsants don't work for you, I'll try again. I will keep trying to get the best seizure control for you possible, with the lowest level of side effects. I can't tell you now what that means or how long it will take. But I won't quit on you."

As Naarden spoke, I blinked away tears. For the first time, a doctor was admitting the truth about the elegant complexities of the brain, showing humility before this beautiful and incomprehensible collection of cells that determines personality, intelligence, emotions, and abilities. He was admitting, finally, that there weren't always simple answers, that choosing medication was trial and error and that this amazing organ guiding our central nervous system required respect and awe before treating problems with its functioning.

"If I'm going to help you," he concluded, "you have to let me put you in the hospital. That will be our next step."

I pursed my lips, then wiped my eyes. "Okay," I said. "I'll go."

ELVA EICHENWALD, 1982

Dr. Naarden said he wanted to get a sleep-deprived EEG and wanted to cut back on Kurt's phenobarbital in the days before that to increase the chance of finding something. Heinz was very angry that he was cutting back on the medication, which wasn't doing anything anyway. Kurt had a seizure on a night his brother, Eric, was home, and it was the first seizure he had seen, and, bless his heart, he cried. Heinz again blasted the neurologist for taking Kurt off the medication and blasted me for something, I don't remember what.

CHAPTER THIRTEEN

In the third week of August 1981, Naarden admitted me to Medical City, and I sneered as soon as I walked into my room. Despite years of disastrous experiences at academic hospitals, I reacted with long-ingrained disdain toward the trappings of for-profit hospitals. Lots of closet space, bright lights, window with a view, no roommate—this was more like a hotel than the cramped, hastily cleaned hospitals I had seen. They even spent money on wallpaper. Wallpaper! What kind of hospital needed wallpaper?

Glancing outside, I saw a strip mall nearby with a hole-in-the-wall eatery called The Feed Bag, which served up big, greasy hamburgers. A month earlier, just thinking about that kind of food would have nauseated me. Now I craved one of those juicy delights and a pile of french fries.

I heard my mother arrive. "Hey, Mom, can you go to The Feed Bag and get me a burger and fries?" I asked.

She laughed. "It's nine in the morning. I doubt they're open."

Hopes crushed. "Oh yeah."

"I'll get you some later today."

The moment meant nothing to me, but it gave her an enormous lift. Since returning from Chicago, I had pushed food around on my plate at every meal, barely taking a bite. This was the first time she had heard me express an appetite in a long while.

A nurse appeared with a hospital gown, and I took it into the bathroom to change. I had brought a blue robe with me and slipped it on. Afterward, I folded my shirt and pants, then rolled my white socks together. I piled my clothes with my shoes on top, left the bathroom, and put them in the closet. My mother had unpacked the rest of my items, and I inspected them. Everything looked orderly and in place. Any psychologist who again wondered where I put my clothes might conclude I was a neat freak instead of someone suffering from "emotional disorganization." And I would not share this closet with anyone, even family. No way I'd allow courtesy to be used as proof of mental illness again.

I was lying on my bed when Naarden dropped by. I sat up, legs dangling over the side, as we chatted. He told me to uncross my feet, and I did. Our conversation continued, and he told me to uncross my feet again. A minute later, again. Why did I keep doing that? Was it seizure related? I didn't ask.

He performed a neurological test. He scraped a blunt metal instrument along the bottom of each foot; my toes bent downward. This was a normal reflex, he told me, like when a leg kicks out after a doctor hits a knee-joint ligament with a rubber hammer.

Then he told me the plan. My hematologist was Dr. Charles White, and he would monitor my bone marrow recovery with frequent blood tests. They would conduct an EEG, as well as a CAT scan. Afterward, a Holter monitor would be attached to me.

"It's an ambulatory EKG," he explained. "It's about the size of a portable cassette player, and it will stay on for at least twenty-four hours so we can measure heart rhythms."

Fear struck. "Did you find something wrong with my heart?"

"No, no," Naarden replied. "Everyone has assumed the drop attacks are seizures. The monitor may help us eliminate the possibility of irregular heart rhythms causing them. If there is a problem, it's certainly something we want to know right away."

Right away. My drop attacks had started, what, half a year ago? No doctor had ever thought to check my heart. Now that Naarden mentioned the possible relationship between sudden falls and heart issues,

I marveled that everyone else had failed to conduct an EKG. How could they have overlooked something so obvious?

"Also," Naarden continued. "You're going to be kept awake all night."

For days, Naarden had been slowly cutting back my phenobarbital. Now he wanted me to have no sleep? "Why?"

"You're going to have another EEG tomorrow. Remember, we want to increase the chance of recording seizure activity, so you shouldn't be medicated or rested. Also, we'll be using sphenoidal leads. Those are electrodes injected through the opening in the temporomandibular joints, which connect your jawbone to the skull. Instead of just getting an EEG reading from the top of the skull, we're recording from a different place and getting a better reading from the temporal lobe."

For a moment, I thought about how the coat hangers—the nasopharyngeals—slid up my nose and where those electrodes must have ended up. It seemed like the same place.

"Didn't they already do that with the nasopharyngeals?" I asked.

"No, with those you're looking at the medial side. With the sphenoidal leads, you're checking the lateral side."

My brow furrowed in puzzlement.

Naarden noticed. "It's like you're listening to someone from across a lake, trying to tell what they're saying. If you move to a different spot, you might be able to hear them."

I knew this was a gross oversimplification, but it satisfied me.

After a few more comments and questions, Naarden left the room. Minutes later, a technician arrived to draw blood, and then White, the hematologist, stopped by. He asked about my experiences at Northwestern and what I understood of their findings, then cleared up a few misconceptions. He explained the details of how he would be monitoring my blood while I was in Dallas and why. He also wanted me to arrange for a doctor to continue a testing schedule when I returned to Swarthmore and have the results sent to him in Dallas.

"What are you checking for?" I asked.

"Changes in your platelets, red cells, white cells."

"Got it," I said. "White's watching my whites."

He gave me the pained smile of a man who heard the same joke every day.

Nurses and technicians came and went. I noticed that all of them introduced themselves and described not only what they were doing but also what they planned to do. At Northwestern, most doctors, nurses, and technicians had fluttered through my room like busboys at a busy restaurant. The few doctors who introduced themselves rarely told me why they were there. I realized: Northwestern was a medical school. Those people had all been residents and medical students. Was that psychologist—*you're crazy because you have clothes on your tray*—in training? Was he a doctor or a medical student? Was that doctor who tortured me with two bone biopsies a resident? Had they allowed someone just learning the job to perform such a painful test? Had he rushed the second one, not allowing me to prepare myself, because he was embarrassed for screwing up the first time?

I tried to remember their faces. Most were young. *Omigod.* Had it been residents, interns, and medical students with no experience in neurology who relayed their belief that I had faked a seizure? None of them asked me about what had happened. Did they not understand that human beings have emotional reactions to pain and fear?

I didn't mind being treated by doctors in training. But how could they not regard patients as living, breathing human beings with real dreads and anxieties? It amazed me that, despite their wealth of knowledge, their basic lack of understanding about the importance of doctor-patient interactions may have led to misdiagnosis. These whoever-they-weres had told me nothing, made assumptions, blithely passed nonsense to attending physicians, and unknowingly pushed me toward suicide.

Or wait. Maybe I was crazy. Chicago was a split decision, psychiatrist versus neurologist. I decided to wait until Naarden ruled out insanity before condemning the Northwestern doctors. If the physicians in training ended up being right, well, kudos to them.

As promised, my mother picked up my lunch from The Feed Bag, and I thought it was the best, fattiest food I'd ever eaten. Soon after I finished wiping the drippings off my hands, a man arrived with a wheelchair to take me for some tests. First, off to the lab for one of two EEGs I would have during my stay. The technicians there already knew I would be having one the next morning with sphenoidal leads injected and asked if I had ever experienced that before.

"No," I replied. "But I had an EEG in Chicago where they used nasopharyngeals."

I remember a gasp.

"How could you let them do that to you?" one of the technicians thundered, her voice raised in disbelief. "Those are *barbaric! No one* uses them anymore."

I stared at her, trying to hide my emotions. "I don't know. That's what they did."

For the first time since I'd arrived at Medical City, anger flashed through me, but not toward Northwestern. Instead, my silent ire was directed at the graceless lady who'd just implied I bore some responsibility for doctors' recommendations. "*How could you let them do that to you?*" she had cried out. Patients do what they're told. I'd expected doctors to exercise care. I couldn't have known I had to protect myself from hospitals inflicting unnecessary discomfort and pain.

They finished the EEG, and the man with the wheelchair rolled me to the CAT scan. Inside the machine, listening to whirring and thudding, I thought about how commonplace this had become for me. Put electrodes on my head; stick me into a giant donut hole—sure, why not?

With tests completed, I returned to my room. My mother was waiting there, and I noticed how relaxed she seemed. Then I realized—I felt calm too. I knew everything my doctors were doing, everything they were planning, and why.

For the first time in months, I wasn't scared. I knew, even if I had a seizure or whatever they were, I would be okay.

The last thing I remember is walking the hallways with my mother sometime past midnight, trying to stay awake. Earlier, a technician attached electrodes to my chest that connected to the Holter monitor, which looked like a camera hung around my neck. I wondered what would happen if I fell on it.

After that, everything is blank. I fell into convulsions at 4:30 A.M. near the nurses' station. A group of people helped me to my bed, then lifted the padded guardrails to protect me. An hour later, more convulsions. My mother hit the CALL button, and five nurses appeared. The night supervisor mentioned that a neurologist named Dr. Steve Lindner was in the emergency room and asked if my mother wanted him to come up. She was astonished—she knew Lindner, having met him at an event she attended with my father at the local medical school.

"Yes, please," she said.

Another severe episode struck, the most violent my mother ever saw, just before Lindner walked into the room. For the first time, a trained specialist witnessed one of my grand mal seizures. Lindner knew my story—I never found out how—and watched as I convulsed, shocked that anyone could have ever misdiagnosed me. He grew anxious that the episode was lasting too long and prepared to load an anticonvulsant intravenously. Before he did, the seizure stopped.

Lindner decided to conduct a neurological exam. He ran a blunt instrument up the bottom of my foot; rather than turning downward as before, my big toe pointed upward, and the others fanned out. He lifted my arm, held it for a second, then let go. My hand hit my face. He placed his knuckle on my sternum and rubbed hard. No response.

No doubt. All this talk about hysteria was nonsense. Lindner knew he had just seen an epileptic seizure.

Someone drew blood to check its chemistry. Then while I was still unconscious, I was wheeled away for my EEG. Needles were injected through my jaw joint in what is usually a painful procedure. I didn't flinch. Once they finished the test, I was brought back to my room. I never woke up for any of it.

Naarden reviewed the results. My blood showed changes that can emerge post-seizure. The EEG caught abnormal activity. The focus was in the right temporal lobe, exactly where Naarden had hypothesized based on nothing more than a comprehensive medical history.

I awoke to the sound of snoring. *Wait. I'm awake. I don't snore when I'm awake.* I touched a blanket. *Why am I snoring awake?*

Time passed. I opened my eyes. I turned my head and saw my mother in a chair. She was snoring. It wasn't me. She was snoring.

I glanced around the room. A hospital. My head hurt. *Okay. No one talking to me.* I was alone. Except for my mother. Body assessment—my cheekbone hurt. I must have hit it. Muscles weak. *Okay.* Licked my lips. No blood. I touched my head. Nothing sticky. No bleeding. *Wait.* My jaw hurt. No, it just ached.

I was in a bed. *Of course.* I was in a hospital. *What led up to this?* I needed someone to tell me what had happened, to place me in time. I think I fell asleep.

I was awake. I heard my mother say my name. I looked at her.

"Anything good on television?" I asked, my speech slurred.

She grinned. She had never found my choice to crack jokes as soon as I started recovering from a seizure to be funny, but she understood it was my signal that I was all right.

I drifted off again. Someone mentioned my name. I opened my eyes. A man I never met before, dressed in a lab coat, stood next to my bed.

"How are you feeling?"

"Rather be in Philadelphia," I slurred.

I remembered this was a stranger. He might take that line as a sign of a psychological problem. "Old joke. W. C. Fields," I murmured.

"I know," the stranger replied.

I closed my eyes.

"Kurt."

I opened my eyes and looked at the man.

"I'm Dr. Lindner," he said. "I'm a neurologist at Medical City. I was here last night when you had a seizure."

Okay, it happened at night.

"When is it now?"

He told me. "I know you've been told that your seizures might be hysteria. They aren't. What I witnessed was a grand mal seizure."

I closed my eyes. *Okay. Says you.*

"Kurt."

I opened my eyes. "Yeah."

"There is no doubt you have epilepsy."

He explained something about the neurological test. The only thing that sunk in was that something weird had happened when he scraped the bottom of my foot.

I thought I heard him say "Brzezinski reflex."

"Like the guy who worked for Carter?" At that moment, I could not have spoken the full name of Zbigniew Brzezinski, former president Jimmy Carter's national security advisor.

My mother laughed.

"No, not Brzezinski," Lindner said. "Babinski. The Babinski reflex."

"Okay." I wasn't understanding his point.

He saw my confusion. "An abnormal Babinski reflex is a sign of a neurological problem. It happened after the seizure I witnessed."

"Okay."

"Also, I lifted your arm above your face and let it go. People with hysterical seizures don't hit themselves when it falls."

"Did mine hit?"

"Yes."

"Is that why my jaw hurts?"

"Unlikely. It wasn't that hard."

My mother interrupted. "He had an EEG this morning with sphenoidal leads."

"That would leave your jaw aching for a few hours," Lindner explained. "Is it sharp or dull pain?"

"Just . . ." I stopped speaking.

I heard my mom's voice. "Kurt."

"Yeah?" I opened my eyes. I hadn't realized they were closed.

"Is it a sharp or dull pain in your jaw?"

"Just uncomfortable."

I looked to my right. Oh yeah. That doctor.

"You need to sleep," Lindner said. "I just wanted you to know, there is no reason for you to question what is going on. This is not psychological. These are epileptic seizures."

"Okay," I said.

My mother came around the bed and spoke to Lindner. I heard her thank him.

"Oh yeah," I said. "Thank you."

Sometime later, Naarden arrived. He explained that the EEG with the sphenoidal leads confirmed I had epilepsy with the focus in the right temporal lobe. "So you're crazy if you think you're crazy," he said.

Confirmed. Almost two years of nonsense, and it had taken Naarden a few days to diagnose epilepsy and find where the seizures started. All the wasted time, all the tests, all the pain, and Naarden had figured out what was happening just by asking questions.

"Okay," I declared excitedly. "Now what?"

"We proceed as planned."

An unspoken fury exploded inside me. While I understood the importance of confirming a diagnosis, at that moment, I was enraged that every diagnostic test—not just the ones at Medical City, but all of them from day one—had been useless. All the needles and electrodes and blood and pain, all the claustrophobia and fear as I stayed motionless inside of giant machines, all the accusations and false assumptions, all of it was less important than asking me questions. These doctors thought their electronic toys and numbers and charts were the key, so they shortchanged digging for every detail I could provide or teaching me what I needed to know so I could help fill in the blanks.

They gained no greater insight into my medical problems by subjecting me to so much discomfort and pain. Everything they had done to me, in the end, was for nothing.

THERESA EICHENWALD, 2017

My wife

As an internist, I learned that taking a good medical history is the most important part of diagnosing a patient. That's what Naarden did with you, which is why he could figure out what was happening. Medicine is a puzzle, and there are lots of pieces to it. You have to observe people and pick up clues from them, and their behavior, and how they sit, and what they say, and their history. You just have to listen for some of the pieces and know the right questions to ask.

There's no way a machine can do it. People will explain things differently that a machine would not be able to recognize. The machines provide just another piece and usually should just be confirming or disproving the doctor's preliminary diagnosis.

I know from my own patients what people go through when other doctors are careless or inattentive or sloppy. I see suffering, and I see fear. I see it in my patients the same way that I see it in you. And I hate it. I want to erase it from you, and I want to erase it from them. Physicians have no right to play with people's lives and pretend they know when they don't. Writing a prescription has a consequence; it's not just a scrawl on a piece of paper . . . It translates to a pill that can hurt somebody or help them. Physicians have to care enough to recognize that even what they say to patients matters, that it can make the difference between hope and hopelessness, between a patient living a good life or throwing it away.

The doctors who did not treat you correctly, who robbed you of your hope and your health for all those years, make me so angry. I would like to go back and protect that person who went through all of that abuse, because it was unnecessary. The answer was much simpler. I am embarrassed for medicine, because this is not who we should be. This is not what medicine should be. Those people had MDs, but they were not doctors.

CHAPTER FOURTEEN

The day after my release from the hospital, I returned to Naarden's office. While there was no longer a chance I would run out of the room, I still asked my mother to join us. I wanted her there to help me recall what Naarden said. While certain events, such as emotional or humorous experiences, lasted as memories, instructions did not.

Naarden began by repeating his findings from my hospital stay. A cardiologist had reviewed the results from the Holter monitor—no problem. White had confirmed my bone marrow was recovering from the previous onslaught of toxic drug levels, and my condition had improved since the last tests in Chicago.

"I'm going to be prescribing Dilantin," Naarden said. "It has been around for decades and is very effective."

"Does it do anything to bone marrow?" I asked.

"There have been some reports in the medical literature that there can be hematopoietic complications . . ."

I stopped listening for a moment and marveled at his words. "Reports." "Medical literature." I didn't know what "hematopoietic" meant, but I assumed it was a blood problem. I knew I could ask, and that

Naarden would delight in telling me—and perhaps be embarrassed that he had used a word beyond his patient's vocabulary—but I didn't need to know specifics. He was answering my question, based on research he could cite off the top of his head. All those academics never mentioned medical literature. They just threw drugs at me.

". . . so you need to see Dr. White frequently while you're home. He wants your blood checked three times a week."

"Will you be taking me off phenobarbital?"

I should have known the answer to that question. My anticonvulsant had already been boosted back to previous levels. But I could see in Naarden's expression that he was going to use my thoughtless query as an opportunity for a teaching moment.

"No one seems to have ever told you the words 'everything in moderation.' We're not going to rush you on or off a drug. We're going to build up the Dilantin slowly and see if it decreases the seizures with limited adverse effects. If we do more than one thing at a time, and there's a problem, we have no way of knowing the cause. That's why no one knows if it was Tegretol or Depakene or both that caused your bone marrow problems, because the dosages were increased simultaneously. And the result of that rushing in and adding medications is that, at least for now, we can't use either one anymore because of the potential danger to you."

Again, the proper approach seemed so obvious.

"Now, I do want to take you off phenobarbital once we get the Dilantin set," Naarden said. "Maybe you won't need anything else, but if you do, phenobarbital is not the best choice. Hopefully by November, if necessary, I want to start switching you from phenobarbital to another drug called Mysoline. It metabolizes into phenobarbital and other anticonvulsants. It's a better drug."

"What if the Mysoline doesn't work?" I asked. "Are we out of options after that?"

Naarden smiled. "No, not at all. If the Mysoline causes problems or the seizures aren't better, come spring we can try another drug called Tranxene," he said. "But this is all up to you. You know, anticonvulsants have side effects. The idea is to get the best balance between side effects and seizures. You're the one who decides the right balance."

I could scarcely believe it. Naarden wasn't just telling me what he was going to do now. He was laying out a plan of action in case his original treatment didn't work. He was empowering me, as the patient, to take control of the decisions. I would not have to fight to convince him to do something if the seizures continued. He wouldn't ignore me, as Nicholson had. And if I wanted to stop changing drugs, Naarden would listen.

"But 'everything in moderation' is not just about medication," Naarden continued. "It's about how you live. You need adequate sleep; you need to eat well. Don't drink alcohol; don't take other drugs. And decrease stress. Stress can trigger seizures."

I braced myself. I was about to hear the *avoid these kinds of jobs; shelve the plans for your life* speech.

"Now, your mother told me a lot about the things you've heard from doctors in the past. And I want to talk about that. Tell me: Do you have any plans for your future?"

I nodded apprehensively. "Yes," I replied softly. "I want to be a newspaper reporter."

"That's great. Now—"

"Wait a minute," I interrupted. "Can I be a newspaper reporter?"

"Of course!" Naarden beamed. "You can be pretty much anything you want to be. Not a school-bus driver or a boat captain if you're having seizures, but epilepsy doesn't decide your life."

I blinked. "Nicholson told me I couldn't take any job that had stress," I said.

"Well, he's wrong. You can be a newspaper reporter—"

"Could I be a lawyer?"

"Of course. Do you want to be a lawyer?"

"No," I replied.

Naarden shot me a puzzled look, apparently wondering why I would ask about a career that held no interest for me. I just wanted to hear his response to the example Nicholson had ruled out.

"Again, you can do almost anything. But everything in moderation. Learning to handle stress is an important part of that."

"Okay."

Silence.

"There is something else we have to talk about," he said. "Your mother told me what's been going on at school, how you've been hiding in your room, keeping secrets, letting your roommates handle this. That has to stop."

He waited to see my reaction. I didn't know what to say.

"Kurt, you have no reason to hide. Epilepsy is a medical condition. That's all. I know there are people who might react badly if they see a seizure, but ignore them. By hiding, you're letting epilepsy control you. It's not who you are."

He let that sink in. I thought about his words, then changed them into my own slogan. *Epilepsy is like brown hair. Some people have it.*

"You have to stop depending on your roommates. I want you to speak to the Swarthmore administration, the health center, and school security. If they know what's going on and how to deal with it, you can go anywhere by yourself. So promise me you'll speak to those people."

The thought terrified me, but I agreed.

"You also need a doctor at the health center, and I want you to see a school psychologist, to help you handle the emotional challenges that come along with epilepsy."

Naarden saved me. How could I refuse?

We weren't done. "Now, the medication transition might be difficult, and I want you to have the least amount of stress possible. What is your normal course load?"

"Four classes."

"I think you should cut it to three while we work on medication levels."

Wait—I need to graduate with my class. I started to speak, then stopped. I remembered that I had taken two Advanced Placement tests in high school and scored fives on both. Swarthmore gave me two college credits for those. If I cut my first semester course load to three classes, I wouldn't fall behind my peers—the AP tests would make up the difference, with one credit to spare. I could do as Naarden asked and still graduate with my class. Okay, I told him—three classes.

We then discussed a recommendation my mother received from the Epilepsy Association. They advised that, while I was in Dallas, I see a rehabilitative psychologist who focused his practice on people with chronic medical conditions. Naarden thought it an excellent idea;

I had been through a lot, he said, and the psychologist could help me adjust.

At this point, I would do anything Naarden told me.

My mother dropped me off at the medical building where I was scheduled to see the rehabilitative psychologist. She didn't want to leave me alone for fear I'd have a seizure, but we agreed that for me to have a normal life, I would have to take risks. I rode an elevator upstairs, found the office, and walked into an empty waiting room. There was another door opposite the entryway, but I took a seat rather than knocking.

Minutes passed. Then a man opened the door and introduced himself as Dr. David Talbot. At first, I had trouble taking him seriously. His voice was nasal, and he had wild, dark hair that made him resemble Gallagher, the comedian best known for slamming watermelons with sledgehammers.

I accompanied Talbot into his office and sat on a couch. He took a chair across from me, with a small table between us. He asked me to tell my story. As I recounted the events of the previous two years, he posed an occasional question. I found myself rambling until I was finally talked out.

"So," he asked, "how do you feel about what happened?"

"I bounce back and forth between fear and hate."

"Hate for who?"

"Nicholson. Craddock. Everyone who wouldn't take time to figure out what was happening."

"How do you feel about yourself?"

I considered the question. There were many possible answers. "Well, I don't *hate* myself if that's what you mean. I don't know. I guess I'm mad at myself."

"For what?"

"For being stupid. I listened to doctors even when I knew they were hurting me. And guilty. I kept so many secrets and hurt so many people."

I struggled to put my thoughts into words. "I hurt myself. I hurt others. I should've . . . I don't know."

I stopped, expecting Talbot to ask me something. He just watched me. The silence grew oppressive.

"I miss my old life," I finally said. "Everything I think and feel is different than it was. In some ways that's good, but I still wish I could go back to the life I had before all this."

Talbot picked up a yellow pad of paper from the table. "You can't," he said firmly. "The person you were is gone."

Experience shapes and transforms people, he explained, and that can be shocking. Everyone forms mental conceptions of themselves—their values and beliefs, their expectations of how the day will unfold, their challenges and goals. When they look in the mirror, they recognize and understand the person looking back at them, he said.

He drew a circle on the pad. "This was you," he said. "This was your self-conception. You never thought of seizures as part of you. The fear and the guilt you talk about now had nothing to do with your life then."

He drew another circle intersecting with the first.

"This is you now," he said. It's not a completely different person, he explained—that was why the circles overlapped. But things had shifted to a place I hadn't planned for them to go. The first circle existed until I was eighteen, when my seizures began. The second had been my reality ever since.

"When you accept that the person you were is gone, you can start to accept the person you are," he said.

I mulled that over. I mentioned that I'd planned for years to drive cross-country after college graduation but had already let that dream go. So at least I was beginning to recognize my life was not the same as it had been, I said.

He answered in a clear voice. Some plans would have to be dropped and new ones adopted. And no matter what happened, even if the seizures stopped, I would never return to who I had been; experience changed me. Once I abandoned my original conception of myself, I could love the person I had become.

Our session ended, and I headed to the elevator. I didn't know what to make of Talbot. I was tempted to dismiss his advice as platitudes, feel-good bromides from a fortune cookie.

Outside, as I waited for my mother, I sat on the sidewalk to protect myself from a fall. Talbot's words echoed in my mind. I thought about who I had been before my first grand mal seizure—largely carefree, immature, without much worry or planning for the future.

That person was gone. Now I was scared every day, checking where I stood for dangers, wondering when consciousness would disappear, but also deeply contemplative about my future and my values. I had recently said to my mother, "I'm too young to be this old." Circumstances forced me to face my present and future with a world-weariness I never would have expected at my age.

Talbot was right. I had to face the truth. My old self was gone. This other person, this different me, had taken his place. A sadness swept over me as if a loved one had passed. I hesitated. Then, acceptance.

"Goodbye," I whispered to the person I had been.

My days became a series of doctor visits to check my blood count, Dilantin and phenobarbital levels, seizures, emotions. My mother made an appointment for me with an internist to assess lingering damage from my injuries over the years. He confirmed that the white growth inside my lower lip was scar tissue from repeated biting during seizures and recommended I have it removed. *No way.* I would not allow a procedure requiring anesthesia while adding Dilantin to my medication regimen.

He found a few scars and other old wounds, then recommended I visit an orthopedist about my ribs. A few days later, I sat on an exam table as a sports medicine specialist examined an X ray of my chest. Some rib fractures had mended. One rib was still broken on two sides, creating unattached pieces of bone that would take time to heal.

"Be careful not to hit your chest," he warned. "A hard impact could shift one of those pieces and puncture a lung."

I snorted a laugh. "That's going to be difficult. My epilepsy still isn't controlled. I could fall at any point."

The doctor looked taken aback. "Do your best," he said.

I once again recounted my history later that week, this time in a law-yer's office. I was meeting with Marc Barta, a family friend and the husband of one of my favorite high school teachers, Stephanie Barta. I had decided I couldn't let Nicholson, Craddock, and Strauss off the hook; I wanted to reveal their incompetence and the harm they caused. To regain my strength and self-respect, I needed a jury to hear the story. I cared nothing about money. I just hoped to shine a light on their actions and force them to explain themselves.

I finished the tale, and Barta leaned forward. "That's horrifying," he said. "I am so sorry all of this happened to you."

He glanced at my mother before continuing.

"I have some questions," he said. "You said that Nicholson works at the medical school under your father. Do you think your dad will support you in a lawsuit?"

I paused for several seconds, staring at my lap. "I don't know," I replied softly.

"Do you think he'll testify on behalf of his colleague?"

A much longer pause. My mother could see my thoughts about the question were tearing me up. She considered calling for an end to the discussion.

Finally, I spoke, still averting my eyes from Barta. "I don't know," I said again.

My mother shifted her gaze from me to Barta. His expression was compassionate; she knew he recognized the anguish from my uncertainty about my father's allegiance.

Barta spoke briskly. "It doesn't matter what he does," he said. "I have no doubt that you'll win this case."

I felt a moment of elation, then realized a "but" was coming.

"But we need to discuss something, and I want you to think carefully about it," Barta said.

A lawsuit wasn't just filing a complaint followed by victory. I would have to go through my story again and again. These doctors weren't going to cave and recite mea culpas. They would fight fiercely. Their malpractice insurance companies would hire lawyers to wage war against me. I might have to watch my father testify against me.

"So the question is, do you want to live the past two years of your life for the next two years of your life?" Barta asked.

I knew the answer instantly; I needed to move on. "No," I said.

"Then don't sue. Take care of yourself, and don't let the past destroy your future."

The words hit hard, but I knew that Barta was right. I told him I would not be able to bear up under the fight. We thanked him for his time, and he showed us out.

That same evening, a hostess at Chili's whisked my mother and me to a two-person tile-covered table. We ordered our standard fare—Oldtimers with cheese, fries, and Cokes—then settled into a conversation about doctors' visits, the meeting with Barta, plans for school. And something more astonishing: Five days had passed without a seizure. My growing dosage of the Dilantin—a little white capsule with a gelatinous red band around it—seemed to help. For the first time in months, I went days with no new pains, my mind clear, my appetite ravenous. I accepted with greater clarity each day that sickness had changed me, that the Kurt I had been was gone, and that I could accept the person I had become.

The waitress placed baskets of food in front of us. As I ate a few bites of my cheeseburger, my mind drifted back to the meal my mother brought me from The Feed Bag when I was in the hospital. That had been two weeks ago. When I ate that lunch, I still believed I might be mentally ill and had not yet shaken thoughts of suicide. I had been despondent, but between the time I ate that cheeseburger and the one I was chewing now, doctors had rescued me, turning my life around.

I thought about my former neurologists—Nicholson, Craddock, Strauss—who, through arrogance or inattention or incompetence, had placed my life in jeopardy, leaving me beaten and scarred, hurting my friends, hurting my family. And those doctors would never pay a price for what they had done.

Nicholson. My father's colleague. A fury smoldered inside me. I was gripping my cheeseburger, crushing it. I placed it back in the basket.

"Kurt, what's wrong?" my mother asked.

I closed my eyes tight and pushed my fists against my forehead.

"*Nicholson!* That son of a bitch! He did this to me! All he had to do was listen! Just for twenty minutes! He treated me like shit on his shoe, answering nothing, telling me to be afraid of everything. That fucking *sadist*! He got off on this! He didn't call me back, he berated me, he ignored me because causing pain thrilled him. He's a psychopath! He's a fucking psychopath!"

I wiped my palms across my face. "And nothing's gonna happen to him! He put me through two years of hell, and *nothing*! *Nothing*! He'll just do it to someone else. Maybe next time he'll kill somebody. He'll enjoy it. *And I can't stop him!*"

My mother listened in silence, knowing she had to let me release my rage against the man who could have stopped the horrors of the past two years. She struggled not to cry as she watched the explosion of my temper. *The pain this poor boy is experiencing is unbelievable*, she thought. *If I could take just a little bit of the pain he's experiencing . . . But I can't do that. I can only reach out to him and hold him and hug him.*

"*Dad* could stop him!" I yelled. "Dad could get him fucking *fired*! But he won't do it! No, he won't do it."

I pounded the table twice as I curled my back, bringing my face to just above the tile as I started to sob. "'Would your dad testify for Nicholson?'" I said. "I couldn't answer Mr. Barta. I couldn't answer! I didn't know! How could I not know? My *friends* would know if their dads would side with them against a man who could have killed them. Everybody knows! I don't know. Why can't I know?"

I started shaking my head. "I can't deal with this," I moaned.

The explosion was getting out of control. My mother decided the time had come to intervene. "Kurt—"

"No!" I barked. "There's nothing to say."

My father had trusted Nicholson and the rest of those doctors. I had heard about how, even as he watched my convulsions, he believed—no, I was sure he *wanted* to believe—that I was mentally ill. Now there was no doubt that I had a neurological problem, something that could be controlled with medication. Was my father so repulsed by epilepsy that he *preferred* for me to have a possibly untreatable psychological problem? Nicholson worked for him—had my father played a role in that son of a bitch refusing to speak to me? Was this my father's fault?

My mother watched my face and grew concerned. She could tell something bad was happening. The growing fury she saw was greater than anything she had witnessed before.

I spoke through gritted teeth. "How could he have believed them?" I said in a soft, contained rage.

"What do you mean?"

"Dad. How could he believe them? He wanted me to be crazy! He thought that was better than me having epilepsy."

"That's not true."

"Then why did you have to work so hard to convince him?" I raised my voice. "He did *nothing* to help me! Not a *fucking* thing! He got me to see those bastards who tore me to shreds. Then just walked away! He *walked away*! He left me out there, going through all this, because he'd rather I die than have epilepsy. He's a *fucking doctor!*"

"Kurt . . ."

"He was always the one who demanded he manage our medical care. 'Oh, only I know good doctors. Only I know what to do.'" My breathing grew heavy. "*Fuck* him!" I shouted. "*Fuck* him!"

"You need to stop. You can't—"

"These people almost killed me! Naarden is saving my life. Has Dad ever *spoken* to Naarden?"

My mother squeezed my arm. She couldn't get a word in and hoped physical contact would bring me to my senses.

"Did he ever come to the hospital? Was it *so fucking important* to him that this wasn't a medical school, that it was a for-profit hospital? More important than me, than my life?"

"Kurt—"

"Goddamn him!" I screamed.

The entire room watched in silence. A waitress recoiled in apparent fear, then hurried away. My mother thought she was getting the manager, maybe calling the police.

"Kurt, stop!" she shouted.

"*Fuck* him! Fuck him and his medical schools! How could he do this? How could he put me into hell and abandon me! Why did he want me to be crazy? Was that *really better* than what I am?"

My mother had never seen me so out of control. My words tumbled out faster, a mishmash of shouts and curses. This eruption of rage seemed to have no limit.

Then she remembered. Naarden had told her that rage episodes could be a sign of an oncoming seizure. Many people had auras that were emanations of explosive anger. Or my new medication might have triggered my outburst. Or maybe, she thought, after so many years of trauma, the sudden relief of seeing my health improving had broken an emotional dam.

"Kurt, stop it!"

My words grew incoherent as I continued spewing venom against my father. Then my speech slowed, and my mother saw the redness in my face transform to a white pallor. My eyes changed in a way she could not explain.

She stood, certain I was about to have a grand mal seizure and hoping to clear the area so I wouldn't get hurt. She heard me gasp as if all the air in my lungs had been pushed out at once. I fell to the ground as intense convulsions began. People sitting near us jumped up and started to approach.

My mother slid her hands under my head to keep me from banging it on the floor. Someone shouted she needed to put a spoon in my mouth before I swallowed my tongue. She ignored the ill-informed advice until this customer repeated herself in angry tones. My mother looked at her.

"I'm sorry," she said firmly. "You don't know what you're talking about."

A manager appeared. "Should I call an ambulance?" he asked.

"No," my mother replied. "This will stop soon. I could just use some help getting him out to the car afterward."

The convulsions ended, and I lay on the floor unconscious. The manager asked two waiters to bring me out to our car.

"Don't worry about the bill," he said. "It's on the house."

I woke the next day in my bedroom with the familiar post-seizure confusion. I ran through the full body check in my mind; no unusual pains or injuries. I touched my hand to my head, inspecting for blood, and it felt strange, almost slippery. I looked at one hand, then the other, and rubbed my thumbs along the fingers. They were vaguely greasy.

Time passed, and then my mother appeared.

"Do you remember what happened?" she asked.

"I'm not sure," I replied. "Where was it?"

"At Chili's."

That's right. We had gone to Chili's.

I held up my hands. "This is amazing," I said. "My fingers are still greasy."

She laughed. "Do you remember how angry you got?"

A few scattered memories returned. I knew I had been screaming about my father. "I really lost it, didn't I?"

"The worst I've seen," my mother said. "You need to call Dr. Naarden and tell him about what happened when you're feeling better."

I promised I would, and after a short discussion, she left the room. I thought about everything I'd said at Chili's—at least, everything I remembered. I had no regrets about my fury toward my former neurologists. But what about my father?

For so much of my life, I had considered him a towering figure who stopped disease outbreaks worldwide. But with me, he failed. I knew he loved me, but he was human, with accompanying flaws he couldn't overcome.

He hadn't *wanted* to hurt me. He believed he was finding the best care. Now I knew, with his convictions about academic hospitals and medical care upended, he was unable to face reality: He botched everything because of his shortcomings. But all of us had those. I certainly did.

Those thoughts tumbled through my mind for about thirty minutes. Slowly, as time passed, my anger dissipated. Then in a single second, I let it go.

I forgave my father, forever.

KURT: *In the end, there's no reason to feel bad, because what happened, happened. Just like the bad decisions I made were not my fault, what happened with you wasn't intentional. I won't deny that you failed, but it wasn't on purpose, and I love you very much.*

DAD: *I love you too, dear. But you know, one can't help saying, "What if?" It's always "What if?" If this had happened, if I'd done this. It certainly might have made your life easier.*

KURT: *But no matter what, I'm living a happy life.*

DAD: *Yeah. You're doing okay.*

The one thing that surprises me with Kurt is his ability to forgive his father. I probably should thank his father because maybe if Kurt had not been so sick, I might not have met him, but once again, I cannot forgive his father. Part of it may have some element of my not forgiving my father, another trained physician always worried about his colleagues, for the poor medical care we got and the fact that arrogant doctors of that generation seem to have wreaked a lot of havoc on their families. I think that I just cannot forgive Heinz for ignoring the fact that his son was having a medical problem, for not standing up for him, and for allowing his pride and pleasure in being the boss—allowing that to interfere with Kurt getting good medical care.

CHAPTER FIFTEEN

From the top of a hill in front of Parrish Hall, I marveled at the foliage dotting the Swarthmore campus. I inhaled the sweet air, perfumed by trees nearing the explosion of reds and greens and purples that would define the final days of fall. In the past, I had smelled these invigorating aromas, seen these majestic giants, and walked by these sweeping green fields, but never appreciated their life-affirming beauty.

My mind reeled. With Talbot's help, I accepted the new me, and now I saw and heard and felt things as never before. I cherished the knowledge of my own mortality, the recognition that every moment I let slip past unappreciated—whether embracing in love or washing the dishes—was a moment wasted, a moment when I may as well have been dead.

This was my second try at starting my junior year. I had insisted I would arrive at school the day before classes began, and despite widespread warnings that I was too sedated from the anticonvulsants, I showed up on time. My mother stayed nearby as she waited for me to come to my senses. I slept constantly, my speech was always slurred, and my roommates insisted I was not in shape to attend school. When I realized I couldn't walk to class, I agreed to return to Dallas, where

Naarden cut my dosage. Once I was better, I returned, two weeks into the semester. The incidence of seizures had improved dramatically. The drop attacks had ended, and convulsions occurred as infrequently as every two weeks. A stranger might have reacted with dismay and pity over that frequency; for me, who just weeks before had been having seizures every other day, it was as if I had been released from a dank prison and chauffeured to a country estate.

My mother accompanied me on my second attempt to start school that semester, helping me settle in and making sure I arranged to meet with school officials. I moved in to the triple suite I was sharing with my longtime roommates. Franz and I would stay in the double; Carl had taken the single. After an emotional experience with his family in Santa Fe—Carl had jumped to the aid of his healthy younger brother, irrationally fearing that Peter was about to have a seizure—he decided that he needed to put some distance between us.

Then I made appointments to meet with the security department, as well as with an internist and a psychologist at the health center.

Afterward, I walked my mother to her rental car, and we hugged goodbye. She clasped my chin and looked me in the eyes.

"Remember," she said. "No hiding. No secrets. If there are problems, you call me or Dr. Naarden right away. Promise?"

I nodded. "I promise."

She held my gaze, reluctant to leave. She reminded me to watch for side effects from the Dilantin. Naarden had told me that, barring drug problems, if the seizures had not stopped by early November, he might increase the dosage. To me that meant, as good as things were already, they could be better when I returned from break. Everything was falling into place.

After another set of goodbyes, my mother drove away. A thrill ran through me. I was on my own, ready to be a regular college student with no more drama or pain.

The first step was to meet with Janet Dickerson, Swarthmore's new dean. I reviewed the basics with her: My epilepsy had been poorly controlled for years, but now my new neurologist was making great strides. She asked some questions, and I explained that medication changes require a lot of time and educated guesswork. It could take weeks to determine if a new dosage worked and whether side effects were bearable. Gaining control was not a process of throwing drugs at the problem and then trying more the next week. There would be ups and downs, but the worst was over.

We discussed my schedule. As Naarden recommended, I took a lighter load, signing up for only three courses. She advised that, with two Advanced Placement credits available, I could drop another class, since that would not affect my graduation timetable. Then, if the Dilantin caused unexpected problems, the academic pressure would not be so high. I agreed, leaving me with one class in statistics and another in public policy.

On to the health center. One member of the staff, Dr. Jeffrey Millington, maintained a medical practice and also saw students at the college; he had known about my seizures since May and had advised me to find better care, but back then I had no reason to question the skills of Craddock, my neurologist. Millington wasn't around when I dropped by, so I met with the health center director and nurses to discuss my condition. I assured them they did not need to panic if someone brought me there after a convulsion.

Next, I headed to the security department for a meeting I had scheduled to speak with the staff. Once again, I explained my seizures—they might frighten people, but I would be okay so long as the convulsions didn't last for many minutes on end. I dismissed myths believed by several of them—*no, don't put anything in my mouth; no, I won't swallow my tongue; no, don't hold me down.* "It's best not to touch me and just let the seizure run its course," I said. "Then you can take me back to my room or to the health center so I can sleep it off."

The session ended with my self-confidence soaring. I was discussing my epilepsy openly, and I wasn't frightened of how my audience might respond. One officer approached me. He was an emergency medical technician, he said, and wanted to tell me about a conversation he'd had with the health center director.

"She seems scared," he said. "I tried to tell her it's really not a problem unless the seizure won't stop, but she doesn't get it."

I thanked him and promised to speak with her again. We both joked about the absurdity of the person running a health center being frightened of epilepsy. Maybe, I suggested with a laugh, the school's medical team was trained to deal with only stubbed toes and colds.

Then the hard part: telling friends. I procrastinated, but Carl would have none of it. The secrecy had to end, he said. I was insulting my other friends through my lack of trust, and I was being unfair to him and Franz by burdening them with keeping this secret out of an irrational fear. In the end, both Carl and Franz accompanied me to tell two mutual friends. Both were surprised I had assumed I needed to hide my epilepsy from them and asked what to do in the case of a seizure. Relieved, I went to others. The reaction was always the same: understanding, support, and a trace of annoyance that I had doubted how they would respond.

It was over. Everyone I cared about knew. There was no reason to hide. I could walk the campus, even alone, confident I didn't have to dread what would happen if a classmate or school officials saw a seizure.

A week after returning to school, I headed to the health center for my first appointment with the school psychologist, Leighton Whitaker. My sessions with Talbot had continued until I left Dallas, and with his help, I was in a much healthier place emotionally than I'd been since the seizures began. I doubted a college shrink who spent his time dealing with the woes of breakups and depression would have anything to contribute. But I promised Naarden and my mother that I would seek counseling on campus, and I would not break that vow.

We took our seats. Whitaker already knew the basics; apparently, he had been briefed about me. I recounted the same gloomy history of recent years that I'd rehashed so many times. The events of even weeks earlier seemed like dreams of a distant past.

He asked if I had ever received a particular type of brain scan or taken the Halstead-Reitan Neuropsychological Battery. I replied that I didn't know but that many tests had been conducted—including a CAT scan—that helped my neurologist reach his diagnosis. I told him that Naarden had turned everything around and that the breakthrough had come when I was given an EEG with sphenoidal leads . . .

Whitaker interrupted me. "Oh, I was on the research team that developed sphenoidal leads!" he exclaimed.

For many minutes, he rambled on, bragging about his supposed accomplishments. I listened in silence, growing more uncomfortable with each word.

How stupid does this guy think I am? I thought. He was a psychologist. He had no medical degree, no specialty in neurology, and he certainly wasn't an engineer. How could someone with so little relevant expertise, working at a tiny college in a speck of a little-known village, have assisted top specialists in developing advanced equipment for electroencephalograms?[*]

As Whitaker droned on, I pegged him as another potential danger to me. *What psychologist spends so much time bragging to his patients about his résumé?* No worries; I had Naarden. Whitaker was a nobody. I didn't need him. And I didn't trust him.

Our session ended, and I left having made two firm decisions. I would continue meeting with Whitaker, but only to keep my promise. I would chat with him about classes, extracurricular activities, friends, the weather, but I would never tell this guy about my state of mind or my emotions. He would be just an occasional intrusion on my schedule. He would have no power to cause any trouble.

In my dorm suite, things were tense. Carl was antagonistic and distant, in what he described years later as his period of "backlash and resentment." I knew I had selfishly put him through hell. Whipsawed by conflicting diagnoses in Chicago and the years of medical incompetence that preceded them, I had saddled him with the bleakness of my life for too long.

With my physical and emotional health improved, I finally had the clarity of mind to take stock of the damage I had inflicted on Carl. He always swung between happy-go-lucky and doom and gloom; now, at least when I was around, the sour outlook and anger were constant. I tried to stay out of his way, which was largely impossible in a three-person suite. I didn't speak much with Franz either; he had a new

---

[*]I have since conducted a computer search of all published studies about sphenoidal leads conducted before 1982. Whitaker appears in none of them.

girlfriend, a heavy academic load, and endless extracurricular commitments.

The strains were apparent, and Carl had a low boiling point with me. After one explosion of screaming, he stormed out. I ached with guilt, believing that my failure to leave Chicago had injured him so badly that I had triggered uncharacteristic fury. Even so, I sometimes lashed back at him, leading to intense, childish arguments. Once we got into a shouting match about a red cloth I hung on my dresser; he called it an eyesore. Rather than removing it, I argued that I had the right to decorate my things the way I wanted. The confrontation escalated until we were screaming at each other. Afterward, I realized our nonsensical fight had nothing to do with the red cloth. It was about his rightful anger at me, conscious or not, for what I had put him through.

Still, we spent some time together outside the room. Over the summer, we'd decided to form an a cappella octet, and we stuck with the plan, recruiting singers from the previous year's musical and holding auditions for other spots. One member, John Fischer, suggested that, since we had eight members, we call the group Sixteen Feet. Carl hated the name—he preferred the Swarthtones—but he was outvoted.

The a cappella group proved to be a boon for all of us. Carl seemed happy at rehearsals. He and Franz gathered a new set of friends, and through Sixteen Feet, I did the same: Harry Schulz, Neil Fisher, and John Fischer were among my new buddies. Then Harry introduced me to his own circle of friends, and we all clicked.

I also started connecting with residents of the village of Swarthmore. Given my frequent visits to pick up my anticonvulsants, the town pharmacist, Jack McDonnell, and I often engaged in friendly, meandering conversations. I learned he was part of a theater group called the Swarthmore Players Club and that they owned plenty of high-end stage gear. Since I would be directing the spring musical, I realized this could be a huge opportunity to get my hands on expensive lights, curtains, and props. At that time, the club was preparing to perform *The Diary of Anne Frank*. I offered to help in exchange for permission to borrow some quality equipment in the spring. Jack agreed.

Life was wonderful. I was busy, making friends, taking on new challenges, out and about on campus. My fears and hopelessness were gone.

Befuddled as usual, I watched as my statistics professor, Rob Hollister, scribbled symbols on the blackboard. I knew I must be looking at numbers and letters, but they may as well have been Chinese characters. I had never experienced anything like this.

I was doing well in my public policy course; my professor, Richard Rubin, often thanked me for my contributions to class discussion. But statistics was a disaster. Equations in the textbook were a muddle, and so were the hieroglyphics on the blackboard. I was glad there had been no homework, quizzes, or exams yet. I kept hoping I would find some secret to crack the riddle of these symbols.

Hollister printed something on the board that he had written many times before:

$E = 0.$

For me, it may as well have been $\nearrow \rightleftharpoons \nVdash$.

He turned to the class and, for the first time, spoke the equation out loud: "So the error is equal to zero."

Just like that, it seemed as if the computing part of my mind entered hyperspace. His utterance made perfect sense, I comprehended why the formula was important, and a bit of the nonsense on the blackboard transformed into knowledge.

What the hell was that?

I walked back to my dorm, my mind spinning in wonderment as the answer came to me: My brain couldn't translate written symbols but understood them if said out loud. What else could explain my sudden grasp of a range of statistical concepts after hearing the spoken definition of a single equation?

Naarden had told me to call whenever something odd turned up. *But this.* This was too weird. I knew what was coming if I phoned him—a dismissive chuckle, an assurance that I was imagining things, or maybe the old refrain "I've never heard of that as a side effect of the medication."

I fretted for an hour over whether to contact him. What if he decided I was mentally ill and took me off the Dilantin? But I had promised not to keep secrets. Finally, I walked down the hallway to the pay phone and dialed his office. Someone placed me on hold, and he quickly picked up.

"Kurt, how are you doing?" he asked.

"Fine," I said hesitantly. "The seizures are still a lot less. But there's something else really weird going on—"

Naarden interrupted. "Is it math?"

A few days later, I visited Hollister's office. I never discovered how Naarden guessed my problem, but he told me that either seizures or the anticonvulsants might be interfering with my brain's ability to translate symbols and perform mathematical tasks. When I explained that I *could* understand if someone spoke the words each symbol represented, he suggested I contact my professor to discuss options to address the problem.

I worried about what Hollister might think. He had probably heard every excuse from students struggling with their work. This one was a doozy: *I can't recognize symbols that any first grader could understand.* I was sure the meeting would be a disaster.

Instead, about a minute into my explanation, Hollister's eyes lit up. "I know about this!" he said excitedly. "My wife is conducting research on it. It's really fascinating."

I blinked. Every day was new proof that telling the truth was the best approach.

"You know," Hollister said, "she's looking for subjects for her research. Would you be willing to participate?"

"I don't think so. I've been through so many medical tests in the past two years. I don't want more."

Hollister understood, then shifted his attention to designing a plan to help me. He asked if I could copy symbols on the board into my notebook even if I didn't understand them. I believed I could. Then, he advised, I should take notes, and he would ask an honors student to recite them to me, since I could understand their meaning if I heard them. He also said he would assign this tutor to read me textbook assignments and answer my questions. I was overwhelmed; in minutes, Hollister had come up with a possible solution.

For the next few weeks, Hollister's student met with me frequently. I asked scores of questions, drilling down to the most basic elements of the math. At one point, I apologized, saying he must be frustrated having to explain statistical fundamentals that most people probably comprehended with ease.

"This is great for me," he replied. "You're forcing me to learn the math at the foundation of things I've always just assumed without knowing why they were true. Teaching you is giving me a much deeper understanding of statistics."

Meanwhile, Hollister kept an eye on me in class. I frequently became lost trying to follow meaningless symbols and looked up from my notebook. When he noticed a confused expression on my face, he recited whatever formula was on the board. That often solved the problem, and I would give him a nod.

After sliding a thin needle into a vein in my right arm, Swarthmore's part-time doctor filled test tubes with my blood. I had grown to trust Millington, something of a surprise since by then I considered most doctors to be potential threats. We chatted frequently, and Millington often urged me to return to Dallas until my seizures were controlled.

"There's no point," I said. "Medications are supposed to be adjusted slowly. Naarden isn't going to do anything until at least November. If I go, I'll just be sitting around with nothing to do."

Besides, I said, what if I never got better? There was an important emotional component—quitting college would be easy; returning would be daunting if my health didn't improve, and there was no guarantee it ever would. Plus, I couldn't release the psychological mooring I had created: I would graduate with my class.

Millington listened with respect but didn't buy my argument. Taking time away from school, he said, would be best.

Magill Walk cuts through the center of the Swarthmore campus, leading from the administration building to the commuter rail stop. Smaller sidewalks cross at two points, sloping down to the path, then rising up on the other side.

On a cold night in October, I walked alone across campus toward Magill Walk, my hands shoved deep in the double-stitched pockets of my zipped corduroy jacket. At the slope, I fell into convulsions. Perhaps because of the angle, I dropped face-first into a bed of gravel. I don't know who showed up first, but soon I was surrounded by Swarthmore security and classmates.

Security officers held back the knot of students as I convulsed, my face grinding against pebbles and dirt. A friend who had been instructed on what to do during a seizure screamed at the officers to flip me over; cuts from the gravel dotted the ground with blood. But the security team ordered my friend to back off, saying I had instructed them not to touch me during a seizure. Unfortunately, I had not informed them they should ignore that rule if I was tearing up my face.

Carl and another student stumbled on the scene after the convulsions stopped but before I woke up. My jacket had torn. Multiple high-beam lights were pointed directly at me from the security vehicles. Carl knew that would cause an intense headache when I opened my eyes.

"You need to shut off those lights," he said as he kneeled down to check on me.

"Stay away from him!" a security guard snapped.

"I'm his roommate," Carl replied. "I need to talk to him when he wakes up, to let him know what's happening. Otherwise he'll panic. And he can't handle lights like that after a seizure."

The security team would have none of it. They ordered Carl to leave me alone, then phoned for an ambulance despite his protests that none was necessary. The ambulance arrived; Carl and the other student hopped in to accompany me to Crozer-Chester Medical Center. With no other intervention necessary, the emergency room doctors helped me out of my ruined jacket and left me slumbering on a gurney. After I awoke and recovered, the doctors released me from the hospital. Carl and the other classmate took me back to school and put me to bed. Large hospital bills had been racked up for nothing.

Two days after the Magill Walk seizure, I was back at the security department. "I want to start by assuring you I'm not mad," I said. "My original instructions obviously weren't clear. But I can't prepare you for every possibility."

I pointed at the cuts and scrapes on my face. "This is what happens when you don't use common sense. These injuries came because I had a seizure facedown in gravel. I know there was at least one friend there who wanted to flip me over, but one of you said not to because I wasn't supposed to be touched."

Many of the expressions staring back at me showed annoyance. "If I fall into a fire, pull me out," I continued. "If I'm banging my head on a step, put something under it or move me. If I look okay, and I'm faceup, you still should put something under my head. Don't think I'm not getting injured just because I'm not screaming. If I'm doing something that you can't get down on the ground and do with me without hurting yourself, assume I'm getting hurt, and stop it if you can."

I glanced around the room. Some of these men clearly did not like being lectured by a student. I needed to soften my tone. "But I want you to know I appreciate what you've done for me. You guys have made it so that I'm able to walk this campus. You have no idea what a gift that is. Even if mistakes happen, it's okay. I doubt there will be many times I have seizures when I'm outside by myself, so this isn't going to be a regular thing."

I shook some hands and left. A couple of months earlier, I would have cowered at their angry faces. But now it was okay. The administration had my back. So did the health center. So did my friends.

I was tempted every day to telephone Nicholson, my first neurologist, and scream at him for how wrong he had been. He had caused so much damage by warning me to keep my epilepsy secret. Because of his errors or paranoia, I had hidden for nothing. Everyone knew the truth, and no one was pushing me away.

———

The next night, Janet Dickerson, Swarthmore's dean, telephoned my brother in Cambridge, where he was attending Harvard Medical School. Eric was surprised. Why would the new dean from his old college be phoning?

"I'm calling about Kurt," Dickerson said. "We're sending him home. He's too sick to stay. We're not prepared to handle this."

An audio letter from

FRANZ PAASCHE, 1986

The seizure you had on [Magill Walk] was very traumatic for me. I felt very guilty that I was focused on my own life and I wasn't always available.

The whole experience of going through this with you for me—in the back of my mind or in my heart, I felt like in some ways I was in judgment, like this was a test of whether or not I was a good person, whether I could be sensitive enough to make things as good as I could. I really felt like I was being tested in some weird way; I don't know if it's religious or whether it's personal. I judged myself against the standard of what I thought was what you needed from me. So when I couldn't provide what I thought you needed, I really felt like I wasn't being a good person.

Being able to respond to what needed to be done became a kind of measuring rod of myself, of my moral worth. And I'm serious about this, it's true. I've thought about this a lot. And it's kind of odd, but I think that you may not have realized how deep an impact what you were going through had on the people who are close to you. And this is one way that was subtle but something you probably wouldn't have sensed.

In a conversation with

CARL MOOR, 1986

KURT: *I want to ask about our friendship after the summer in Chicago.*

CARL: *Damn, Kurt. It's never recovered. [laughter]*

KURT: *No, no, no. Come on. Be serious.*

CARL: *I was miserable junior year. We weren't getting along. It had been too intense. I was tired of it. I felt guilty for feeling tired of it. But I think there's a lot more to it than just seizures. A lot has to do with the fact that we were very good friends, and we spent a whole summer together, working together, living together. In any situation, people spending that much time together would get on each other's nerves. There's something very universal and there's something very situation-specific about the whole thing. So the blowup had a lot to do with the whole seizure thing, the whole summer, but it didn't have everything to do with it. I would say sixty/forty. Sixty percent the intensity of the health issues, forty percent just normal friend tension caused by spending too much time together.*

CHAPTER SIXTEEN

Eric called our parents to tell them Swarthmore was kicking me out. The news, coming six weeks after I had stopped hiding my epilepsy, set off a flurry of phone calls to administrators demanding an explanation. Why now? Why no warning? And why deliver the decision to my twenty-three-year-old brother rather than to my parents?

Their explanation was beyond belief. The administration had decided Naarden was incompetent and the diagnosis of epilepsy was wrong. They said Swarthmore's psychologist, Leighton Whitaker, had determined I had a brain tumor based on the way I talked.* The growth had been missed, Whitaker told them, because Naarden failed to conduct a particular type of brain scan and the Halstead-Reitan Neuropsychological Battery. These were the tests the psychologist had asked about at our first meeting.

Dickerson told my mother that, in addition to the concern about a tumor, she and a dean's committee had concluded I was too sick to at-

---

*My taped diaries, recorded at the same time Whitaker made this declaration, show that my speech patterns were no different than they are today.

tend school. At the meeting, the security chief complained that his officers, who had dealt with one seizure in six weeks, were spending "an inordinate amount of time with a single student." The health center director also protested that her team believed they had insufficient training to assist me after a seizure. The committee had concluded, Dickerson said, that the best solution was for me to go home, continue my treatment, and hopefully return when I was healthy.

At the end of that call, my mother flipped through her address book and found the number of the Dallas Epilepsy Association. She had kept in touch with the counselor we had met there years before and hoped he could help.

The moment the counselor picked up the phone, she identified herself and blurted out, "Swarthmore is throwing Kurt out of school!"

"What?" the counselor asked. "Why?"

"Some psychologist there told them he has a brain tumor."

"Why does he think that?"

My mother could barely get the words out. "Because of how he talks."

"How does he talk?"

"I spoke to him last night! The same as always!"

She rattled off the other reasons: The psychologist decided I needed more diagnostic tests. Security didn't want to deal with me. The health center nurses were scared of me. The bottom line was the school wanted me gone.

"That's illegal," the counselor sputtered. If Swarthmore received federal money—and it almost certainly did—they were violating Section 504 of the Rehabilitation Act of 1973, which prohibits discrimination against people with disabilities. I was free to leave school if I chose, but they couldn't force me out.

"What do we do?" my mother asked.

"First, don't tell Kurt. This can probably be straightened out without scaring him. The last thing we want is for him to think he has to go back into hiding."

My mother cried. If the school forced me to leave, she knew I would view it as proof Nicholson had been right—that to protect myself, I needed to return to keeping secrets.

"Listen, Elva," the counselor said, "I know lawyers who handle discrimination cases. I'll find someone to take this. But contact Dr. Naarden, and let him know what's happening."

The counselor recruited a lawyer named E. Brice Cunningham to take me as a client. He was my first attorney ever, and I didn't even know that he represented me. Cunningham instructed my mother to ask Naarden to send Swarthmore a letter about Whitaker's brain tumor claim and attesting to whether he believed I should stay in school. There might also come a time when Naarden would need to testify in court, and Cunningham suggested she ask if he would do so.

The next morning, October 23, 1981, she met with Naarden at Medical City and described what was happening. When she mentioned the psychologist had diagnosed a brain tumor, Naarden reacted with a start.

"A brain tumor? Based on what?"

"The way he talks."

"How is he talking?"

"The same as always!"

He was more bowled over when my mother recounted the psychologist's claim that the tumor had been missed because no one performed a neuropsychological test battery.

"This is why psychologists shouldn't pretend to practice medicine," Naarden replied.

The dean had made a lot of very disturbing comments about the magnitude of my health problems, my mother said, and how ill-equipped Swarthmore was to handle the situation.

Naarden stewed in anger. "What do you need from me?" he asked.

"We have a lawyer. He says you need to send a letter about the brain tumor claim. Also, if you think Kurt should stay in school, it would help if you said so."

"That's fine. Give me a name and address to send it."

"One more thing," my mother said. "We might be forced to sue Swarthmore. The lawyer wants to know, if it comes to it, whether you'd testify."

"Absolutely," he said. "I'll help any way I can."

Two nights later, the members of Sixteen Feet gathered at Mephistos, a lounge used for student shows. After weeks of rehearsals, our new a cappella group had learned a few songs but still sounded pretty raw. We decided to perform anyway—if everyone liked us, we would bow; if not, we would pretend the whole thing had been a joke.

By then, I had assumed the role of administrative manager for our singing group—I would handle workaday details, set up the performances, and obtain equipment to record our concerts. Carl ran the group, while another member was musical director.

After student jugglers wrapped up their act, we bumbled about finding our spots in front of the audience. We belted out our first tune, "Blue Moon," with me singing lead. Some friends had come to the performance certain we were pulling a prank, so they broke into cheers when they realized this was for real. I hammed it up for a photographer with a "ta-da!" pose every time there were a few beats when I wasn't singing, then playfully waved her off. We finished to raucous applause.

Carl had the job of introducing us but still cringed at the name Sixteen Feet. As he stepped forward, he flashed a grin at me. I realized what he was about to do.

"No!" I said, on the verge of cracking up.

"I guess as you've gathered by now, we're the Swarthtones," he said.

"No!" I shouted.

He smiled again. "Some disagreement over the name. Okay, we're Sixteen Feet. We got together a few weeks ago. A few months ago, actually."

In his spiel, Carl joked that we decided to perform because we had learned three songs—enough to justify an appearance, since we had an opening number, a finale, and an encore. "So we're going to do our three songs, and after that, that's it, because that's *all* we know," he said to laughter.

We broke into "A Teenager in Love." Halfway through, the lead vocalist, Neil Fisher, dropped out as the rest of us continued our "ooo-wahs." Carl stepped forward. "I just want to remind everyone, this is the midpoint in our show," he said. "So take a moment to stretch, relax.

We'll be back to finish the show in just a second, and then we'll go on to our big finale!"

Neil resumed singing about the anguish of teen romance, then on to song number three. After we finished, friends swarmed us with congratulations. As everyone mingled, I walked to another part of the room to turn off the cassette deck I used to tape the performance.

At the time, I considered the recording just a nice memento for the group. Instead, it would soon become proof that the Sixteen Feet performance had really occurred and was not a fantasy conjured by a diseased mind.

Letters from Naarden and the Epilepsy Association arrived at Swarthmore two days later. Each attacked the school's decision to throw me out. In elegant, diplomatic prose, Naarden wrote that the idea I had some undetected brain tumor was bunk. He reported that, during my hospital stay, he had conducted a complete medical history and neurological examination using the latest technologies and checked for other health problems as well. In the school's attempts to interfere with my medical care, they were demanding tests that were expensive, unnecessary, and inappropriate.

As for kicking me out, Naarden wrote that the impact could be devastating and irreparable. When young people with neurological problems interrupt schooling, he said, finding the emotional strength to return can be impossible. "Educational opportunities lost in youth cannot be made up for later in life," he wrote. "It is extremely important for students to continue their education even if seizure control is not perfect."

In its letter, the Epilepsy Association stressed that people coping with seizures struggled to be honest about their conditions because of fears of retribution. Dismissing me from college at a time when I was making significant medical and psychological progress would likely derail my nascent efforts to be honest about my health.

With that information in hand, Dickerson called a new meeting of the dean's committee that wanted me off campus. They reversed themselves and told my family I could stay. However, without informing anyone, they placed me on probation. No one ever learned what the school would consider to be a violation of probationary conditions that I knew nothing about.

Unaware of the just-completed fight over my future, I was bearing down on my studies. Most of my friends were taking midterms, but because I had started the semester two weeks late, my professors gave me time to catch up. By then, no written homework had been assigned in either class. Other than a few compliments from my professors, I had no way to judge my performance.

On the night of Saturday, October 31, I had a grand mal seizure. I woke the next morning in bed fully dressed, my body aching and my thoughts scrambled. The last thing I remembered was attending a Halloween party. No one else was in the room, and I assumed I had been alone during the convulsions. *No problem.* I decided I could handle this on my own.

In my confidence about my self-sufficiency, one fact escaped my attention. If I had woken in my clothes, that meant I had never gone through my nightly bedtime routine, when I swallowed my medicine. I gave no thought to my drugs in the morning, so I neglected to take them before heading to the library. I compounded my error by forgetting that Dilantin suppressed my appetite, leaving me with no physical reminder of hunger, so I didn't eat.

By evening, with medication and blood sugar levels crashing, I suffered another grand mal seizure in my room. I woke in my clothes once again the next morning, Monday. I had slept through my bedtime routine for the second day in a row, again failing to take my anticonvulsants. Based on the biochemistry of the drugs, by then I must have been going through barbiturate withdrawal and fallen below the minimum therapeutic blood levels for Dilantin and phenobarbital.

My decision to manage these post-seizure periods on my own was a huge blunder. Only after this episode would I realize I needed assistance in times like these to avoid dangerous missteps caused by poor judgment and confusion.

A third seizure struck Monday, this time outside. I awoke more frightened and confused than before. Security officers swarmed about but allowed friends to take me to my room. I couldn't understand why I was falling apart. I telephoned my mother in tears, telling her I was being hit by seizure after seizure. I was severely agitated and anxious— typical symptoms, I would later learn, of barbiturate withdrawal. My mother told me to stay put and wait for her or Naarden to call back. Soon my neurologist phoned. He instructed me to have someone take me to the health center immediately.

There I received my medication and slept in one of the beds. When I woke Tuesday, a nurse brought me my first meal in three days. I was still severely confused. I lamented to one nurse, "It's Tuesday; I know it's Tuesday, but it's supposed to be Saturday." I was attempting to explain that, as happened after my seizures, time had become muddled. She rushed out and incorrectly told the staff that I didn't know what day it was.

The nurses brought me three meals that day. The blood levels of my medication were coming up, and withdrawal symptoms ended. I was ready to return to my dorm, but a member of the health staff told me I needed to phone my mother first. I called from a nurse's desk.

"Hi, Mom," I said when she answered. "Don't worry if I sound bad. I'm okay."

"You sound better."

Better than what? After a back-and-forth, we realized I had no memory of speaking with her the night before.

She spoke in a decisive tone. "I'm coming to Swarthmore tomorrow."

"Mom, that's ridiculous. I'm fine. I just had a bunch of seizures. I screwed up somehow. I think I missed my medication. I'll just talk to Naarden, and we'll figure out what happened."

"No, we don't have a choice. I'm coming tomorrow."

We don't have a choice? Suddenly I knew: Either my parents had decided to bring me home, or Swarthmore was kicking me out.

"No, you are not coming!" I snapped.

She choked up. "I have to."

"I am not leaving school."

"It might not be up to us, Kurt."

I grew enraged. "It's not up to *us*? Are you telling me Swarthmore is saying I can't stay? That's *impossible*! I'm better than I've been in years!"

"We just have to—"

"No, we don't have to do anything! Everyone has to keep their word! Everyone told me, if I told the school, it would be fine. Now they're throwing me out? I've had maybe two seizures outside! Did they think uncontrolled epilepsy meant I *didn't* have seizures?"

Nicholson was right, I thought. As soon as I trusted people, they reacted in terror. Now, I thought, I would pay the price for listening to Naarden and everybody else who said that being honest was the right way to go. It took just seven weeks for those assurances to be proved worthless.

My mother and I argued until I calmed down. "Okay," I said. "Come tomorrow. But I have to leave the health center tonight."

"No, don't leave. You're too upset."

"Look, if I stay, all I'll do is think about it. If I go back to the dorm, I won't."

I returned to my room and started straightening up. As I tossed clothes into my bureau, Carl again complained about the red cloth draped on it. I knew I might be gone in twenty-four hours.

"Tell you what," I said. "I think you've just latched on to this red cloth thing. Think about it for a couple of days, and if it still really upsets you, I'll get rid of it."

I left the room to shower, something I hadn't done in four days. Standing with both hands against the wall as water streamed down my head, I relaxed.

This is ridiculous, I thought. *It's so obvious I'm doing well.* The last few days had been an anomaly. Everyone would understand. All I had to do was explain.

I left the bathroom confident this confusion would be cleared up quickly.

The next morning, November 4, I grabbed my sweat shirt and headed to the small parking area behind my dorm. My mother had taken the first flight from Dallas and checked in at the nearby Media Inn. She had called to let me know she was on the way, and I'd told her where to meet me. I had decided to keep her visit discreet to avoid revealing anything to my friends about the coming showdown with the administration.

My mother had told me we would be joining school representatives that evening in the health center to discuss my future. I agreed to attend on one condition: that Janet Dickerson, the dean, stayed away. Only she could issue a final decision forcing me to leave, and excluding her would make it harder for me to be railroaded.

After about ten minutes, a car rounded the curve. I saw my mother, distress in her face. I climbed in and gave her a kiss.

"So, this was unexpected," I said.

"Everyone is worried about you."

"Apparently. But I promise, this is really the first time in two years that no one needs to be concerned."

The last few days had been awful, she said, and I had sounded overemotional and incoherent when we spoke on the phone.

"I'm sure I did," I replied. "When I went to the health center that night, they checked my blood levels. I just got the results. I was below therapeutic on both Dilantin and phenobarbital."

She again commented on how wretched I had sounded.

"No kidding," I replied. "I'm sure it was dreadful." By the time I spoke to my mother on the phone, I had missed at least two doses of my medication.

I realized the car hadn't moved.

"Mom, why don't we go for lunch?"

We continued talking as she drove. I remained composed as we discussed the last few days. I continued to explain that this setback had been a fluke.

We arrived at the Village Porch, a nearby restaurant. I ordered a cheeseburger, which had become my staple whenever we shared a meal. She asked how I was doing in my classes.

"No way to know," I said. "I have my midterms next week and haven't had any graded homework yet. I think I'm doing well in public policy. I probably talk too much in class, but Professor Rubin keeps encouraging me to keep it up. My statistics professor has been great, and my tutor is a huge help."

She looked confused. "Dean Dickerson told me yesterday that you're doing terribly in your classes."

I laughed. "I don't know where that comes from. Probably best to wait for me to take a test before deciding I failed it."

My social life was blossoming, I said. I discussed managing Sixteen Feet, performing the concert, and my work with the Players Club.

What about friends? she asked. I replied that things were tense between Carl and me but that I was spending more time with a group of students I'd met through Harry Schulz, a member of Sixteen Feet. In fact, Harry's roommate was a talented musician, and I had already recruited him as music director for the production of *Pippin* I would be directing the next semester.

Two hours after she arrived, my mother stared at me. "You really are okay, aren't you?"

"Yes," I said. "I mean, I could be better. But this is the best I've been in a long time."

"And you're telling me the truth about everything?"

Huh? "I'm not even sure what there is to lie about. It's not like I can hide the number of seizures I'm having anymore. Everybody knows about them."

She fell silent for a moment. "Something's not right."

"Mom," I protested, "I'm fine!"

"I don't mean with you. The school is telling me things that don't make sense."

"Like what?"

"Dean Dickerson told me yesterday that you weren't functioning academically and you weren't functioning socially. They think you're falling apart and just wandering around waiting for your next seizure."

"What? That's ridiculous. They can't know anything about my grades. And I'm probably involved in more social activities than half the school. Besides, if not functioning socially was a reason to get thrown out of Swarthmore, they need to get rid of most of the people here."

She fixed her eyes on me, wordless.

"What?" I asked.

"They told me you were going to try to fool me, to pretend that you're well when you're not."

That knocked me back. "Wow." For the first time, I became angry. "So they told you if I sound and look well, it's proof that I'm not?" I shook my head. "You know, that's really despicable. That tells me they *knew* you would see I was fine. What the hell is wrong with them? Is this all just a setup?"

My mother appeared uncomfortable. She still had not told me about two weeks earlier, when Swarthmore proclaimed I suffered from a secret brain tumor and conveyed the gripes from security and the health center.

"Something's wrong," she said.

"Yeah, no kidding. But not with me."

Her reaction was delayed for several seconds. "I believe you," she said.

I shrugged. "Well, good, I guess. I mean, since there is no proof of anything they're saying and lots of proof they're wrong, I don't know why you wouldn't believe me."

We talked for another hour, then she drove me back to the dorm. She reminded me to be at the health center at six-thirty for the meeting. I promised I would arrive on time.

As she drove off, I smiled. *Just like I thought.* Everyone would see I was better. Everything would be fine.

An audio diary from

ELVA EICHENWALD, 1982

When I flew to Philadelphia in the morning and spent the afternoon with Kurt, he was fine. He was his old self or as much his old self as he's been in a very long time. He didn't look well. He was exceedingly thin, but he was happy and telling jokes. He was as well as I guess he could be. I just didn't understand it. He was not the person the school was describing to me. This idea he would try to fool me—no one's that good an actor.

I've struggled with my feelings about all of this. The whole thing was handled very badly on the part of all of us. We should have told Kurt in the beginning that the school was thinking this. And, I don't know, we have mistake upon mistake upon mistake upon mistake. It has been one big fat mistake, and it's all been against Kurt. Guilt? Yes, I have guilt. If I had to do it over again, I would hope I would do it differently.

CHAPTER SEVENTEEN

As I crossed campus that evening, lamps flicked on under a darkening sky. My right hand was thrust inside my sweat shirt pocket, holding the tape of the Sixteen Feet performance from ten days before. I hadn't brought my cassette recorder. I assumed that showing the tape would be sufficient proof that I hadn't been wandering in a daze, waiting passively for my next convulsion.

I met my mother behind the health center, and we headed inside. In a dimly lit room waited several school officials, including the psychologist, the internist, the health center director, and a member of the security staff. We took our chairs.

"Now, am I wasting my time?" I asked. "Has a decision already been made, or is this really a discussion?"

I noticed Whitaker and the center director stiffen in their seats. I reasoned that those two had been more directly involved in planning with the dean than the others.

"This is a discussion," Millington said. "Staying at school may not be the best thing for you right now. Why not just go home and get better? Why make it hard on yourself?"

"Primarily because that's my choice," I replied. "Listen, I'm sure everyone here thinks they have my best interest at heart. The reality is, most of you know very little about my treatment and what's going on."

I explained that I had been very sick for two years and spent a lot of that time hiding. But a new specialist had prescribed medications that were better controlling my seizures. I was much better physically and psychologically.

"You weren't well when you came here on Monday," the health center director said. "You were very badly off."

"I'm sure I was," I replied. "It was a fluke. I had a seizure sometime Saturday night and didn't tell anyone. I messed up my medication and forgot to eat. By the time I got here, my levels were terrible." I looked at Millington, who had checked my blood. "Right?"

He nodded to the group. "That's true."

"But all of you are missing the most important question. *Why* should I go home? The pace of adjusting medications won't change. My neurologist isn't deciding my dosage based on whether I'm at school. If I go home, every adjustment and every test will be on the same schedule as it would be if I was here."

Whitaker interrupted. "Well, Kurt, you haven't had a complete diagnosis. You haven't had the scan we discussed, and you haven't had the Halstead-Reitan Test Battery."

My mother's face went stony. "We *do* have a complete diagnosis," she snapped. "They don't have any need for those other tests. There's nothing to find."

"Well, you don't have everything," Whitaker said.

"We have everything that needs to be done," my mother responded. "And you know that."

I watched this soft-spoken but grim tête-à-tête with puzzlement. *You know that.* How would he know? He was a psychologist—he probably understood less about epilepsy than I did. In fact, neither Whitaker nor my mother was qualified to debate diagnostic tests. I assumed she was simply relaying her confidence in Naarden. I had no idea Whitaker had just revived a nonsensical argument that experts shot down two weeks earlier.

My mother and Whitaker glared at each other. Then, without a word, Whitaker stood and left the room. I glanced around at the remaining group. Everyone looked embarrassed or flummoxed.

What the hell is going on?

I wasn't sure what to say. "Um . . ."

No one spoke.

"So, are we finished?" I asked.

"No," Millington replied. "We need to keep discussing this."

I thought about asking if we should wait until Whitaker returned. Then I realized he was gone. This was the guy who had spun fantastical tales about developing sphenoidal leads, and now he was pretending to know neurology better than a neurologist. I figured his ego couldn't handle his being contradicted by my mother.

"Okay," I said. "Well, anyway, contrary to what Dr. Whitaker just said, there's nothing to be done. I'll go home, and I'll sit around. My neurologist is going to run some more tests, but not until I've been on the medications a little longer. They're scheduled for Thanksgiving vacation."

No secrets. "There's also something that might be hard for you all to understand," I explained. "From almost the beginning of my seizures, I've had this psychological commitment to graduating with my class. It's the thing I hold on to. It's my proof I can survive this, that I can live my life even if the seizures never improve. If you send me home, you're taking that from me. I'll lose a semester. I won't graduate with my class. I know it might not make sense to you, but that would devastate me. You'd rob me of what I hold on to, for no reason."

As Millington started to reply, Janet Dickerson, the dean, walked quietly into the room. Whitaker left; Dickerson came in. I wondered if they were tag-teaming this meeting.

Ambush, I thought.

"Guess we're not keeping our agreements, huh?" I asked.

Dickerson took a seat near me. "I think it's important that I'm part of this conversation," she said.

"Okay," I said. "Well, you've missed my explanation why going home won't result in getting faster medical care. You want me to start again?"

"No," she replied. "This isn't about that."

What? "I'm confused," I said, instantly fearing I'd made a mistake by uttering that word. "Then what is this about?"

"Kurt," she said softly, "you're not well. You're not functioning academically, and you're not functioning socially."

Back to this. My mother had warned me. "Okay, that's a different topic than what we were discussing."

"But that's the issue. You need to go home and get care so you can handle college."

I rubbed my forehead, trying to keep from raising my voice.

"All right, academics," I said. "I want to know how you concluded I'm not functioning academically when I haven't had a test, a graded assignment, a quiz, a paper, or anything."

"You've had midterms."

I smiled. "No, I haven't. My first midterm is Monday."

The room fell still. "So how is it you think I'm not functioning academically?" I asked.

"That's what I've heard," Dickerson said.

"From who?"

"That's just what I've heard."

I'm fighting gossip. "Have you bothered to ask the professors?" I asked in an angry, sarcastic voice.

"Would you like me to?" she said, mimicking my tone.

I picked up the phone on the desk where we were sitting and placed it in front of her.

"Yes!" I huffed. "Call them right now."

She reached for a phone book, and I told her the names of my professors. She first called Rubin and asked for my grade in his public policy class. I smiled inwardly because I knew what he was saying—he had no idea.

"Well, can you estimate what you think his grade will be?" she asked.

She looked at me as she listened. I tried hard not to look smug. Then she thanked Rubin and hung up.

"What did he say?" I asked. "An A?"

"He said you were doing well."

She again flipped through the phone book, searching for the home number of my statistics professor.

Millington broke the silence. "Kurt, we need to check your blood today. Let's do it now."

I followed him to one of the exam rooms, where he closed the door and brought out the usual equipment. As he slid the needle into my vein, he seemed tense.

"I'm really . . ." he started.

"What?"

"I'm really sorry about the way they're doing this."

That was a surprise. "I thought you wanted me to leave."

"I do, but not this way," Millington said.

When I walked back to the main room, I saw that the security officer and health center director had left. I headed to the men's room and noticed Whitaker standing in a hallway, leaning against the wall.

Is he feeding Dickerson this nonsense? I glanced at him with scorn. *What a coward,* I thought. The contempt I had for him at that moment was immeasurable.

I returned to the interrogation room, as I now thought of it. Dickerson was off the phone. "So," I said, "what did Hollister guess my grade might be when I take a test?"

"Well," Dickerson replied, "you're not functioning socially."

Jesus Christ! "First of all, that's not true. Second, if you dismiss Swarthmore students for not functioning socially, you're not going to have much of a college left."

"This isn't funny."

"No, it's ridiculous. I'm doing lots of things. I founded an a cappella group with my roommate, and we've already had a performance. I'm working with the Swarthmore Players Club. I'm already working on the spring musical I'm directing . . ."

"That's not true," Dickerson replied. "You just think you are."

Panic set in. "What do you *mean,* I think I am? What, are you hearing this from the same people who told you I was failing my classes? Is Dr. Whitaker telling you this, since he's waiting for you in the hallway? This is a bunch of lies!"

"Kurt," she replied, "you aren't doing these things."

"Yes, I *am!*" I snapped. I brought out the recording of the Sixteen Feet concert. "This is the tape of the a cappella group's performance. I sang the first song! Get a tape recorder, and I'll play it for you."

"That's not necessary."

"Well, obviously it is! I have a recording of me singing in a concert that you say never happened!"

I was losing control of myself. With each lie shot down—*you don't have a diagnosis, you haven't had all the tests, you're not functioning academically, you're not functioning socially, you're imagining everything*—another popped up.

Wait a minute. "Have any of you told Dr. Naarden this stuff about me not functioning socially and academically?"

"He's been made aware of the problems you're having," Dickerson said.

I took a few panicked breaths. If I went home with a fictional label of having had a breakdown, Naarden would change my treatment plans. He was about to start the switch of my second-line drug from phenobarbital to Mysoline that month. If he heard Swarthmore's imaginary stories, that wouldn't happen. I knew he would believe that the Dilantin was causing these fantasies that were being tossed about as fact. I needed to speak to Dickerson, heart to heart. I calmed myself, then looked her in the eye.

"Dean Dickerson . . . Janet . . . please hear what I'm about to say. I can't go home with these falsehoods. If Dr. Naarden thinks I'm flunking all my classes and wandering around school drooling, all the planned medication changes and tests will be postponed. He can't treat somebody who's going crazy. He's going to think the medicine is causing these problems, *and they're not happening*! I *have* a social life, a lot better than most of the people on this campus. I have friends. I'm doing lots of things. And you *know* I'm not failing my classes."

I saw sympathy in her face. Was I getting through? Was she reconsidering? I barged ahead, clinging to that hope, yet I couldn't subdue my anger and frustration.

"This is the first time in two years that I've started to get under control," I said. "With the next medication changes, I should get even better. But Naarden won't make the changes unless I can disprove everything you're saying about me. Goddamn it, if I can't prove this is all false, he might take me off Dilantin! This 'not functioning socially,' 'not functioning academically' is going to become part of my medical history! Decisions about my care are going to be based on lies!"

I closed my eyes. "Please don't do this to me."

Her tone hardened. "We have an obligation to the parents who paid for their children to have a normal education."

The words drove through my heart. Never had such an agony stabbed at my spirit. Tears filled my eyes. "So, what, because people see me have a seizure, I'm robbing them of a normal education?"

"This is just a very upsetting situation for students."

"Okay—okay, I'm sorry," I stammered in desperate sincerity. "I never should have started walking the campus alone. I was wrong! I'll stay in my room. No one will have to see them."

My mother cried. "Don't punish him because he's epileptic."

"We're not," Dickerson said. "But we have to think of the other students. And staying in your room doesn't solve the problem. Then you're leaving it to Carl and Franz to deal with it. They have the right to a normal education too."

Everything Nicholson warned me about was true. It was true. I'm just a thing. I'm . . .

I covered my face with my hands and sobbed. "How can you say these things to me? When you started as dean, all you talked about was diversity."

Suddenly I got angry. "Well, here I am! *I'm* diversity. How many people do you have on this campus with disabilities other than me? One? You say 'diversity,' and you want to throw half of Swarthmore's disabled students out of school!"

"That's not what I'm saying."

"That's what you just said! You guys have given reason after reason for throwing me out. Dr. Whitaker, a goddamn psychologist, says my neurologist doesn't know neurology as well as he does. Oh no, it's because of my grades! Oh, it's because of my social life! I'm imagining my social life! I'm hurting other people because they might see me have a seizure!"

My mother, still crying, interrupted. "Kurt . . ."

I stopped speaking, trying to control myself. Dickerson looked pained.

"Please . . . don't do this," I begged.

The room went silent for a moment. "Let me speak to Dr. Millington," Dickerson said.

They walked into the hallway where Whitaker waited. I wondered what role he had played. I knew he spun stories and bragged about himself all the time. Maybe I had just become a target for him so he could show off to the administration.

My mother and I sat in silence until Dickerson and Millington returned. "We still think it's best to—" she began.

"No!" I wailed. "You're wrong. You're wrong. If you just want to get rid of me, if you just want me out because of my epilepsy, then just say so—"

"That's not the issue."

"Then there is no issue! Sending me home will set my treatment *back*. It will make things worse, not better."

My mind shot to Chicago, when a similar clash over my condition had played out. A neurologist and a psychiatrist each proclaimed their diagnosis, declared the other's woefully inadequate, and then threw up their hands saying—since the other doctor was wrong—there was nothing they could do.

"If you just want me out, please just say so. But don't send me home with these false stories about failing my classes and having no social life. Please don't do this to me."

Dickerson appeared as if she wanted to cry.

After several more minutes of rambling, I ran out of words. The room fell silent. Dickerson and Millington excused themselves, then again headed out to where Whitaker was waiting. Minutes ticked by. Only Dickerson returned.

"I'm sorry, Kurt ..."

I pushed my hands through my hair as I sobbed uncontrollably. "Don't do this to me. Please don't do this to me. I can't go through this again!"

"Kurt ..."

"I'm not up to this anymore," I cried. "I know I'm going to give up. I'm not going to be able to keep fighting to get treated. I can't."

Dickerson stayed silent, appearing to consider my words.

"Please," I begged. "I can't handle this. It's going to destroy my care. It's going to destroy me."

A pause. "We're willing to take that risk," Dickerson said.

The dean ordered me to leave campus directly from the health center. She promised I could return the following semester if I wanted, but I felt certain she was not telling the truth.

I was crushed, beaten. I knew I would be forced to combat these falsehoods, to once again prove my sanity, for Naarden to continue my treatment plan. I could barely move, much less talk. My mother and someone else helped me to the car. We drove to the Media Inn. Back in her room, I asked about returning to school to collect my things and say goodbye to my friends.

"We can't, Kurt," my mother said. "You're not allowed on campus."

Something cracked—my resolve, my fortitude. Nothing made sense. I grabbed a plastic box off a table and threw it against the wall, smashing it to pieces.

"What the *fuck?*" I screamed. "I can't go back on campus? What am I, fucking Hitler? I'm so fucking horrible, if anybody even sees me they're going to fall over dead?"

"Kurt, stop!"

"Nicholson was right! He told me if I didn't hide, I'd get destroyed. All of you told me to be open! Look what *fucking* happened! I can't go back to school! I can't pack my clothes! I can't say goodbye to my friends!"

My rage knew no bounds. I ranted, threw more things, and collapsed on the floor in tears. My mother stroked my hair as she told me she was going to call my brother at Harvard. She needed help. This was more than she could handle alone.

I dozed off in one of the beds but awakened with a start the next morning, my mind throbbing with rage. Eric arrived and tried his best to calm me. My mother knew I trusted Millington; I had already told her that I believed Whitaker had deceived him. She called Millington and asked him to come to the hotel.

He showed up quickly. Pacing, I launched into the same plea from the night before, my voice cracking with fear that, if I returned home labeled as nonfunctioning, my treatment would be disrupted forever.

"Kurt!" he snapped, stopping me short. "It's over! Just leave, and come back next semester."

Next semester. I knew there would be no next semester. I believed Millington thought it was true. But based on what had already happened, I knew—even if I survived the lonely months at home until the first half of the school year ended—Swarthmore had no intention of letting me return.

"It's—" I began.

"Kurt!" Millington said sharply again. "You need to go."

With that, I hit psychological overload. My emotions shut down. I stopped crying. My muscles relaxed. I sat down on a bed. My thoughts cleared.

I ran the situation through my mind. Someone had told my mother that I would try to fool her into believing I was doing fine in class and in social activities. I needed to confirm I wasn't imagining things. Then there was Carl; he had been pretty rough on me. If I disappeared and never returned, would he get hit with the same self-recrimination I felt for what I had put him through? I couldn't let that happen.

"All right," I replied calmly. "I'm leaving."

"That's good," Millington said.

I looked at my mother and Eric. I felt nothing. "But I'm not leaving until I get a chance to go back and say goodbye to my friends," I said.

The room exploded with shouts of anger and disbelief. I sat stoically, saying nothing as everyone around me fell apart. Someone threatened to have me sedated.

"I suppose you could try that," I replied, "but I'm not going to swallow any pills. That leaves an injection. You can try that, but you're going to have a fight on your hands."

More shouts. Millington stormed out. My mother headed to the bathroom in tears. I approached my brother and sat in front of him.

"Eric, I'm not asking for much," I said. "It doesn't make sense that they won't let me pack or say goodbye to friends."

I noticed he was tearing up.

"Eric," I said, "I have to go back to school."

A moment passed as he looked me in the eyes. I could tell he saw something; he understood. My mother returned.

"Mom," he said, "he has to go back to school."

A flurry of phone calls ensued. Finally, the administration compromised. I would be allowed to return before I left, but I could not speak to anyone other than a few friends in my room.

I would be given one hour. If I tried to stay longer or to speak with anyone else, I would be physically removed from campus by Swarthmore security officers.

An audio letter from

CARL MOOR, 1986

We started hearing rumors that someone had seen your mother and she was in town and then started to think, Well, Jesus, something's up and he's really sick. *I had been walking down Parrish Hall toward the mail room, and I saw Mrs. Eichenwald.*

I said, "Mrs. Eichenwald, what are you doing here?"

And she goes—she just turns to me, and she starts to cry. She says, "Kurt has something to tell you."

And I said, "What is it?"

And she said, "I can't tell you. Kurt's going to tell you."

And so I went rushing back to the room, and Franz and I were waiting around there, and we knew at that point that you were gonna die. We thought, Death. This is it.

CHAPTER EIGHTEEN

Carl and Franz waited nervously in our room. As part of my agreement to leave, I refused to allow anyone to give them details of what was happening. I feared they would be fed lies that I was imagining a social life and failing my classes. That could undermine my attempt to prove to myself I *was* active on campus. If I was delusional, I wouldn't know; a conversation with Carl and Franz—if no one else had spoken to them yet—might give me the information I needed to be certain the administration was lying.

I arrived with my mother and brother. I didn't know where to start. How to explain that going home, supposedly to allow me to get better, could instead set back my care—potentially forever—if Swarthmore's falsehoods came with me?

"I've been thrown out of school," I finally announced.

Instant relief for the roommates. I wasn't dying. My mother filled in some blanks, and from their perspective, this meant I would spend a couple of months getting better. I'd be back soon. They couldn't understand why I considered this such a big deal.

I had thought a lot about how to confirm to myself that the school was inventing falsehoods. I wasn't going to ask, *Didn't I really do this? Didn't I really do that?* Instead, I talked about Sixteen Feet, the concert, my work with the Players Club, *Pippin*, and friends. They never contradicted me. When I expressed concern about leaving the a cappella group in the lurch, Carl assured me others could take over the administrative details and sing my leads.

That was all I needed to hear about Sixteen Feet. The school's assertion that I imagined my role and fantasized a concert was a lie.

"Dickerson also said I've been disrupting campus life, that I've been a bad influence for other students."

Franz interrupted. "No, you haven't. Don't think that. More people know about your seizures, but no one cares."

I rambled. I didn't know how to explain that the school's false allegations were going to delay my treatment. I had never even told Carl about the dueling diagnoses between the Chicago neurologist and psychiatrist. Laying out my fears of reviving that battle in Dallas required a history lesson, and the clock was ticking; if I spent too much time on the past, I risked being dragged away by security before confirming everything I needed to know. I stumbled over some words and broke down again. For a moment, the room was silent.

"Well," Carl said, "at least you've got your health."

Everyone laughed. Carl's reliable sense of humor got me back on track. I laid out the allegations that I was failing my courses but quickly moved on; I remembered my professors had disputed those claims the night before.

The end of my allotted hour approached. My brother grabbed a few shirts from my closet and stuffed them in a bag. I put on a heavy jacket; it wasn't particularly cold, but I would need it in December. We didn't have time to pack anything else. We left behind jeans, most of my button shirts, T-shirts, underwear, and socks. I said my goodbyes and walked toward the door.

I stopped, numb with realization. As soon as I passed through that doorway, I would be plunging back into the fight, begging my neurologist to treat me as I struggled to convince him that Swarthmore had lied to get rid of me. How could I convince anyone these tales from college officials were fictions? It was hopeless. My treatment, my life, was over.

"I'm not going," I announced.

I walked to a bed and sat down. Eric cried, and my mother became hysterical; she knew security would show up any minute. She begged my roommates to help.

Carl stepped forward, grabbed me by the jacket lapels, and slammed me against a closet door. "Kurt," he said, "go home. Go home now and beat this thing. If they're so wrong to send you home, prove it. Don't whine. Go home and beat it."

I didn't know what to say. I could beat epilepsy, even if it was uncontrolled. I couldn't beat other people's reactions and decisions. But Carl was right. I had no choice.

I hugged my roommates and walked out. Three minutes before the deadline, we notified security I was leaving. They had already been preparing to come get me.

A few hours into the flight home, I went into convulsions. The blood tests from the night before showed that my medication levels were still low, and the stress of the previous twenty-four hours likely served as a trigger. I bit my lip, and blood seeped from my mouth. My mother assured the crew I would be fine, and the pilots stayed on course to Dallas.

One of my best friends, Jason Kinchen, was waiting at the airport. We had been close since middle school, and I had told him about my epilepsy in the summer after freshman year. Jason attended Dartmouth College, which had a flexible study plan allowing students to take off the fall semester. He knew I had been traumatized by my abrupt expulsion and wanted to assure me that I had a friend at home to stand by me.

The plane arrived, and Jason watched EMTs rush on board. I was wheeled off, and he walked alongside my mother as they brought me to a room in the airport. My emotional collapse after my dismissal had been so strong that my mother now believed there was a good chance Swarthmore had been telling the truth, that I had been nonfunctional, and that I had lied when I told her at lunch about my school activities. Despite witnessing Dickerson's phone calls with my professors, my mother had also become convinced in her panic that my supposed academic failures were real.

I woke up disoriented and confused but stayed silent. I remember thinking I was in danger but not knowing why. My mother hurried out of the room every so often, then burst back in a few minutes later. She called Naarden and arranged for me to be taken that night to Medical City. At some point, I heard her on the phone speaking to Talbot, the rehabilitative psychologist. "So far as he knows, it will be a medical admission," she said.

Was she talking about me? Were they planning a psychiatric admission? Things were falling apart faster than I had anticipated.

Jason noticed my eyes had opened. He stood beside me.

"Hey, buddy. How are you doing?"

How did Jason get here? No matter. I needed to speak to him before anyone else did. "Jason, you need to listen. They are going to make it out that I'm crazy—"

My mother appeared. She told me that I was at the Dallas airport and had experienced a seizure on the plane. I was rolled outside in a wheelchair while Jason fetched his car. Someone loaded me into the backseat; my mother sat up front.

"We're taking you to Medical City," she told me.

"Yeah, I heard," I said, my speech slurred. "As far as I'll know, it will be a medical admission."

My mother sighed. "I don't know why I said that."

"Because you believe them, Mom! Because Swarthmore ripped my legs out from under me, I can't control my reactions, because I'm not some fucking robot, and so you think they're right and that I'm crazy!"

"That's not true," she said.

We both knew she was lying.

Jason drove to the Medical City emergency room. I didn't know why I was there. I'd had a seizure. What was an ER going to do?

My mind was jumbled and no one explained what was happening. I lay on a metal table. A woman came over and said, "I know this is going to hurt, but just . . ." The rest of the memory is gone.

Someone put something in my mouth and told me, "Bite." I did but didn't know what I was clenching in my teeth or who had put it there. I started putting pieces together.

I took the thing out of my mouth. "Are you about to do electroshock therapy?" I whimpered.

"No," someone said. "That would cause a seizure. No one wants that."

A woman again warned me that something was about to hurt. Suddenly I was in agony. The pain stopped, then I heard a voice. "We have to do it again." My memories shot back to the biopsies in Chicago, but this was completely different. Then the severe pain returned. I woke up with a nurse taking my blood.

I was wheeled to my room. My father arrived, and he was walking with my mother. I saw Jason on my left.

"Don't leave," I pleaded with him.

"I won't. I promise, I won't."

In the hospital bed, I thought through the events I could remember from the emergency room, trying to figure out what had happened. Why hadn't anyone told me what they were doing?

Naarden appeared. I remember being impressed; I knew it was nighttime, and he had come to the hospital. He had his usual broad smile.

"So, Kurt, I understand you were having some trouble with your thinking," he said.

I knew it. Swarthmore had told him their fabrications. But I wanted him to be explicit.

"What do you mean?" I asked.

"Well, that you weren't functioning socially and you were having trouble with your classes—"

I bolted up in bed. "Dr. Naarden, *it is a lie!* They're lying to you! I was functioning . . ."

I stopped. My voice rang in my ears. Desperation made me sound unstable. This, I knew, was my only chance to convince him that he could continue the treatment plan, that—other than the math issues— the Dilantin hadn't harmed my ability to think.

Calm, calm. If you don't sound calm, he won't believe you.

No use. I was too scared of losing everything. I couldn't control myself. "It's all a lie!" I exploded.

Naarden listened silently.

"I promise you, it's not true! I've been doing so well. I have lots of friends. I've been coming together for the first time in years! At worst, I've been too self-reflective, trying to understand everything that's happened to me. I'm not taking a full course load, but you and the dean told me not to!"

He responded in a relaxed tone. "Yes, okay."

I knew he was patronizing me. "This 'not functioning socially' stuff isn't true! They made it up!" Once again, I listed everything I was doing—Sixteen Feet, Players Club, the musical.

I rubbed my forehead. "I'm not imagining these things. They happened. Please, if you don't believe me, call my friends at Swarthmore; call my professors!"

Naarden tried to reassure me with a few soothing remarks, then asked my parents to accompany him into the hallway.

Jason walked to my bedside and started to speak. I held up two fingers. "Shhh!"

·I heard Naarden. "I think that is what he really believes was happening, but . . ."

I stopped listening and grabbed Jason's arms, pulling him closer so I could speak softly.

"Jason, I have been set up," I said, desperation in my voice. "There are a bunch of lies about me. Anything you hear, don't keep it from me. Anything I say, don't repeat, because I have to have someone to trust!" I placed a hand over my eyes. "Please, please believe me."

"I believe you," Jason replied in a tone of horror. "I believe you."

I looked at him again. "If you think I'm crazy, tell me, and I'll talk with you about it. But don't keep anything back! If someone tells you something, don't believe it until you talk to me. Please promise me."

"I promise," he said.

The next morning, Naarden checked on me. My mother was sitting in a chair. I stayed silent out of fear I might start yelling in anger.

Suddenly, I realized: It was early November. Naarden had told me long ago that, if the seizures weren't controlled by around this time, he would be adjusting my anticonvulsants, starting the switch from phenobarbital to Mysoline.

I spoke before he did. "You said you'd be changing my medication about now. When does that start?"

"Well," he said, "before we start any adjustments, we have to figure out whether the Dilantin has been causing your cognitive problems at Swarthmore."

"I didn't *have* any cognitive problems!" I shouted.

"Kurt—" my mother started.

"No, *shut up!* The Dilantin was working! I had a social life. I was doing well in my classes!" I stopped and thought for a second. "Jesus Christ, I'm lying as easily as Swarthmore is," I said softly.

"That's—" Naarden started.

"No, that's not what I mean. I'm not lying. I can't say I was doing well in my classes any more truthfully than Swarthmore can say I was doing badly. There's no way to judge."

I stopped speaking. My mother was crying. I apologized for snapping at her so rudely.

"Please, Dr. Naarden, stick to the treatment plan," I said. "I know I seem crazy. If you just tell me these lies aren't going to cause my treatment to be changed, I'll be fine. I promise."

Naarden struck a thoughtful pose that I knew masked his alarm at what must have seemed like paranoia. I realized he couldn't imagine that whoever had spoken to him from Swarthmore—Dickerson? Whitaker? Millington?—would fabricate a story. I was telling him that a college administration was conspiring against me. Even I thought that sounded insane.

"I'm not going to make any decisions right now," he said. "There's a lot of conflicting information. Before we make any changes, we have to figure out what's going on."

"Okay, well, there were those diagnostic tests you wanted to do over Thanksgiving. That's just a couple of weeks from now. Are you still doing them?"

"We need to work out some things. I'd like you to see a psychiatrist. He'll help determine what's going on."

"I know what's going on!" I cried. "I'm going to have to keep having seizures because everyone believes the school. I might have the only medication that's ever worked taken away because I can't convince you they're lying."

Naarden put a hand on my shoulder. "I told you from the beginning, I'm not going anywhere. I'm going to work with you to get the best control possible. We just need to take a break right now and reassess."

Despair gave way to fury. "Fine! Take a break! But if you all *ever* figure out what's really going on, don't come to me and say, 'Sorry we delayed everything. Now you need to stay home another semester to do the tests we were planning for November.' I will *not* stay home longer because everybody's too stupid to understand what's happening!"

Had I seen the movie *Rashomon?* Naarden asked. What that film shows is that different people can have conflicting interpretations of the same events. "So there's your perspective, there's Swarthmore's perspective, there's my perspective, and there is the right perspective."

"Fine," I replied. "And mine is the right perspective."

Proof. I need proof.

An hour later, I was alone in my hospital room. Right then, it was my word against people with job titles. I asked my parents and Naarden to phone my professors, but no one would. I couldn't produce papers or tests. I glanced at the clock. Franz worked a main desk in Parrish Hall about this time. I grabbed the phone beside my bed and dialed. Seconds later, he was on the line. He asked how I was; I'm sure I sounded terrible.

"I need help," I said. "Could you send a letter to my doctor? All it needs to say is what I was doing at school, whether I had a social life, whether I was doing things."

Hesitation. "Okay," Franz answered, sounding tentative.

I closed my eyes. I knew—there would be no letter. Carl and Franz both thought it was good for me to be home; the idea of writing this letter would make them uncomfortable because they didn't understand what was happening. They couldn't know circumstances were derailing my medical care, that the switch from phenobarbital to Mysoline scheduled for that month had already been put on hold. Franz and I spoke for a while longer, then I hung up.

This is hopeless. I thought of Arizona again. Run away. Lose the past. Start with a new neurologist who wouldn't know about Nicholson or Craddock or Strauss or Whitaker or anybody, who wouldn't know about Swarthmore's fictitious stories. I wept. It wouldn't work. I was trapped.

Dr. White, my hematologist, walked into the room. "How are you doing?"

"Awful," I replied sharply. "You have to listen to me!"

He looked shocked. "What about?"

Again, I recounted the story of how Swarthmore's fairy tales had come to threaten my medical progress. "I don't know if it was about liability or if someone was lying to the administration, but now I'm fighting a fiction that is putting my treatment at risk."

White stayed silent until I finished. "Oh God," he said.

A flutter of elation rushed through my chest. "Do you believe me?"

"I have no reason not to," he replied.

I clasped my hands and brought them to my mouth. Perhaps I had found another ally. White accepted my word because he had never heard Swarthmore's distortions. My story made sense, so long as no one spun yarns I had to disprove.

We spoke for twenty minutes. By the time he left, I felt invigorated and ashamed. I had been weak and begging. No more. I needed to gather my strength.

"Goddamn it, I've fought too long," I grumbled to myself. "I am not going to let you bastards win."

I glanced out the window. *They sucker-punched me*, I thought.

"I am going to beat you," I said.

Each time I tried to explain my fears, no one understood. It seemed simple to me—my hope of gaining control was gone because I couldn't disprove the claims against me; because of my fears, I raged in shouts and abuse, reinforcing the perception that I was unstable.

Eventually, the chaos and tension overwhelmed my mother. "If you're so well, why are you yelling?" she said. "Maybe if you controlled yourself and stopped being so angry, it would be easier to believe you!"

She was right. I couldn't talk about this nightmare and stay calm. My only hope for winning them over was to feign serenity.

A metaphor occurred to me. I understood how to convey the paradox I faced. I would stop talking about me and concoct stories of fictional people to drive home my points. My parents and Jason were in the room. I looked at my mother.

"I want you to imagine two men. One is on fire. The other is a blind man who has never heard of fire but who's holding a bucket of water.

The burning man yells to the blind man, 'Throw the water on me!' And the blind man replies, 'But I'll get your suit wet.' The burning man screams, 'I don't care; throw the water on me!' And the blind man says, 'I don't think you know what you're talking about. You don't want to ruin your suit.'

"So the burning man says, 'Please throw it! I'm on fire!' And the blind man replies, 'What's fire?' The burning man screams, terrified of dying as he tries to define fire. And the blind man says, 'Calm down! I'm not going to do anything so long as you're so emotional!' And the burning man tries to be calm but can't, because he's terrified, knows he could die, and knows the blind man doesn't trust him. He shouts and screams, and the blind man repeats that he must calm down. So the burning man is left wondering which will come first: death or the blind man finally listening."

I glanced around the room. "I'm the burning man. All of you are the blind man. I'm telling you why I'm scared, why I'm emotional. I'm begging you to throw the water. But you're not hearing what I'm saying."

My parents both grew extremely upset. "What are you talking about?" my mother said. "That doesn't make any sense!"

"Yes, it does," I replied.

Somehow that was the breaking point. Both my mother and father left, emotionally wrung out. Jason walked over to my bed.

"Did that make sense to you?" I asked.

He exhaled a single exasperated breath. "It makes perfect sense."

"What's the water?"

"Having everyone stop listening to Swarthmore and just go back to the original plan they had for treating you."

I nodded. "Yup. That's it."

My mother drove me past Medical City down a winding road. About a mile ahead, I saw a high-rise building of dark glass encased in what looked like a concrete helmet open on each side.

I had been released from the hospital a few days earlier. Neither my pleas nor my newfound metaphor tactic succeeded in allaying anyone's skepticism. My diagnostic tests that had been scheduled for Thanksgiving were canceled, adjustments to my anticonvulsants postponed indefinitely. I accepted that I would have to put up with the seizures as they were, with no hope of improvement, until I convinced more people I was functional.

Jason tried his best to persuade the others I was fine, that everyone was confused by the intensity of the situation, and that I made sense. His opinion was dismissed; by then, my family bought into Swarthmore's warning that I would manipulate people into believing I was well. Jason, they thought, had been fooled by my tricks.

Naarden had urged me to see a psychiatrist to determine if my anger, desperation, and supposed thinking problems were the result of an underlying mental disorder. He recommended Dr. Richard Roskos, who maintained an office in the helmet building.

I considered Roskos to be my last chance. If I couldn't convince him that the school was lying, I would run out of options. This, I knew, would be tough: I would be telling a psychiatrist that my college was plotting against me.

Just because I sound paranoid doesn't mean people aren't out to get me.

After I spent a few minutes in his waiting room, Roskos appeared and invited me into his office. He was tall, with glasses, an inscrutable face, and a gentle tone. After some preliminary chitchat, he asked why I had come to see him.

"What do you know?" I asked.

"Just that Dr. Naarden referred you to me."

"You've spoken to no one else?"

"No."

He's got to already think I'm paranoid. In for a dime . . .

"When it comes to talking to people, do you have to do what I tell you?" I asked.

"Yes, I'll do whatever you ask."

I shifted in my seat. "Okay, here are the rules. If anyone calls you about me, you don't talk to them. If you bump into someone who wants to tell you something about me, you walk away. You speak to no one about what I tell you, you let no one talk to you about me."

Roskos nodded. "Fine."

I launched into my story, starting from my first seizure and continuing to the day I was told my medication changes and diagnostic tests were being postponed.

Shortly after I finished, Roskos glanced at the clock. "We're out of time for today. When do you want to come back, and how often do you want to see me?"

I prepared to leave. "Five days a week until we get this freaking nightmare straightened out."

Roskos appeared surprised. "All right," he said. "Let's get you a regular daily appointment, starting tomorrow."

An audio diary from

ELVA EICHENWALD, 1982

In the weeks after he was thrown out of school, emotionally he was in a very bad place. I had great concern for my son. I thought that he was finally breaking under the strain from all those years of chaos. A human being can take so much before they give up. Emotions are a very funny thing. And I thought that he had reached the breaking point.

I don't know, Kurt, even if at this listening you would agree with that. But we ... the experience of seeing other people who have had breakdowns ... He appeared to me to be having a breakdown. I was so frightened. And there is nothing else one can do at that point but to force the individual to get the care that is needed.

CHAPTER NINETEEN

A worker at the United Way handed me a black notebook listing not-for-profit groups in Dallas. With my treatment plan on hold, I had nothing to do after my morning sessions with Roskos. Boredom set in, so I decided to take on volunteer work.

Positions that required driving were out. So was anything involving children or animals; a seizure might hurt them. Then I saw a job title: "media contact." That sounded perfect. Not only would that kind of volunteer role give me the chance to phone reporters, but it would also burnish my résumé for future job applications in journalism.

But the group's name gave me pause: the Association for Individuals with Disabilities. If I joined, would my doctors conclude I considered myself disabled, then add that to my psychological profile? I explained my worries to my mother, who agreed not to tell anyone if I worked with AID.

I called the number, and a man named Ovid Neal answered. Five minutes into our talk, he offered me the job. AID directors were meeting that night, he said, and he invited me to attend.

They gathered in a large conference room, and Neal introduced me to the impressive group. There was Stuart Couch, a counselor who worked with the Dallas County commissioners; Tom Morrison, a supervisor for Region 6 of the Department of Health and Human Services; as well as contingents of lawyers, social workers, and other professionals. Many had disabilities, but they had not allowed those to impede their success.

I spent the evening listening until Neal spoke about a discrimination case involving a doctor named Donald Balaban who worked for the county health department. Confined to a wheelchair because of multiple sclerosis, Balaban had been fired three times despite positive employment reviews; each time, state and federal commissions ordered his reinstatement. Following the second dismissal, the department had removed him from his senior post and assigned him to a jail where he was ordered to do nothing. He had no access to a bathroom. His coffee arrived filled with roaches. When he was thirty minutes late, he was fired a third time. Calls to his wife went unanswered, so an official phoned the sheriff; Balaban was carted out, placed in a paddy wagon with no air-conditioning during a heat wave, and driven home.

Not long before, I would have dismissed the story of this man's abuse as too ridiculous to believe. But after my recent run-ins with Swarthmore, I wasn't so quick to doubt. Just because people had fancy job titles didn't mean they weren't capable of terrible things.

I held up my hand. Someone laughed. "You don't need to raise your hand. We're not in school."

I smiled in embarrassment. "Okay," I replied. "Listen, I worked with an organization called the Better Government Association in Chicago. They deal with the news media to expose cases like this. One thing I learned from them is, if you want government to act, you need publicity. I could call them and ask them to handle this case."

After a short discussion, the directors agreed: They would let me consult the BGA on the Balaban case.

The next day, I telephoned John Laing, who ran the BGA internship program, and told him about Balaban. He apologized but said the group couldn't help.

"We focus on Illinois," he explained. "We don't have the staff to conduct an investigation in Texas."

I thanked him and hung up. I considered the situation for a moment and decided to try another tactic.

The AID directors met the next night to deal with a separate issue. When I showed up uninvited, a few appeared surprised, but everyone was welcoming. After they wrapped up their discussion, I started to raise my hand, then brought it down. *I'm not in school.*

"I'd like to make a proposal about the Balaban case," I said. "I called the BGA, and they won't take a case in Texas. But I have another idea."

I hesitated, eyeing the group. These people were at least twice my age. I had no idea how they might react to my next words.

"Let me do the investigation," I said. "The BGA allowed me to handle a case when I was an intern. I know how to do this. Once I've finished the work, I'll find a reporter to write about it."

Neal was skeptical. "I've tried to interest reporters. They don't do anything."

"That's because it sounds unbelievable," I said. "Asking them to invest time on something just because we say it's true won't work. If I do the investigation *for* them, write the findings, and turn over the documents, no one will turn us away."

They made another snap decision. "Okay, Kurt," said Couch. "You do the investigation and try to interest the media."

After three days as a media contact, I had talked myself into a new job: investigative reporter with an advocacy group for the disabled.

Jackpot!

I located my recording of the Sixteen Feet performance in my sweat shirt, exactly where I left it on the night Swarthmore threw me out. I was into my second week with Roskos and had told him several times about the school's claim that I imagined cofounding and singing with an a cappella group. When the time came for my morning appointment, I pocketed the cassette and grabbed a portable recorder I'd purchased soon after returning to Dallas for taping my daily diary.

I entered his office bursting with excitement and started speaking before I sat down. "Remember Sixteen Feet? The group that doesn't exist? The concert that never happened?"

"I know that's what the school said," Roskos replied.

I slid the tape into the recorder. "Here's the imaginary concert. I sing lead on the first song."

"Blue Moon" filled Roskos's office. I wondered what the reaction might be in the waiting room to this serenade.

"You've got a good voice," Roskos said.

"Uh . . . thanks." *Not the point.*

The song ended. "Okay, listen!" I said.

Carl's and my voices played.

> *"I guess as you've gathered by now, we're the Swarthtones."*
> *"No!"*
> *"Some disagreement over the name. Okay, we're Sixteen Feet . . ."*

I clicked off the recorder.

"There! Sixteen Feet! I *did* cofound the group, and there *was* a concert a few weeks ago."

"Well," Roskos said, "looks like Swarthmore was wrong."

"They weren't wrong," I replied. "They're making it up."

I threw myself into investigating the Balaban case, starting by interviewing the doctor and copying all of his records. I called officials at Dallas County Health Department but got the brush-off each time. I realized I was too eager, too pushy. I remembered my telemarketing techniques—establish a relationship, speak slowly, find out the other person's needs before asking for anything. Why not do the same now?

Five calls later, I reached a department employee who stayed on the line with me. I gave my name and put her at ease with small talk. We discussed her background and her children. After the conversation, I raised the Balaban case. She told me she couldn't discuss it without risking her job.

I considered her words. She hadn't said no, she didn't invoke rules prohibiting disclosure. She was worried about being fired. She wanted to help but was scared. *Telemarketing.* What did she need? An assurance there was nothing to fear.

"I understand," I said. "I don't want you to discuss it. But I know there have to be internal documents about this."

"I can't give those to you."

Time for the sales pitch, based on what I had learned about her in the last few minutes.

"Karen, you've told me about your work with the church. You care about people. And sometimes when bad things happen, and people are hurt, we have a responsibility to do the right thing, to ignore rules that allow wrongdoing to continue. Do you think anyone would do this to Dr. Balaban unless they thought they could count on those rules to keep it secret?"

She didn't reply.

"I'll never reveal how I obtained any records. But if it's as bad as I think, we can stop this, you and me. If this was my parents or your children, I know we would both be praying that someone would turn over the documents, regardless of the rules. Help me stop it. I promise, no one will ever know you did."

She said nothing for almost thirty seconds. From my telemarketing days, I knew to stay silent no matter how much time passed.

"Okay," she replied. "It will take me a day to pull everything together. I can meet you tomorrow after work."

For dinner, my mother cooked spaghetti, my favorite. Spending days reporting calmed me significantly, as did my daily sessions with Roskos, so mealtime with my parents had become quite enjoyable.

I found I repeated myself a lot, and my behavior that night was no different. As I devoured the food, I told them again about playing the Sixteen Feet tape for Roskos and how he agreed the a cappella group was real. I laughed, saying how bizarre Swarthmore's argument had been. Eventually, I said, the truth would have come out.

"It's like when they said you had a brain tumor," my father commented casually.

I put down my fork. "What are you talking about?"

"They tried to kick you out earlier in the semester," he explained. "They said you had an undiagnosed tumor."

I looked at him, then at my mother. I scarcely knew what to say. "Are you serious? Why am I just finding this out now?"

My mother spoke. "Everything was so frenzied when you got home; we just didn't want to throw that into the mix too."

"So how did they decide I had a brain tumor?"

"Dr. Whitaker said so, based on the way you talked."

The school psychologist? "Are you kidding me? Does Naarden know?"

"Yes," my mother said. "He was involved in stopping them and telling them it was impossible."

Stay calm.

"So are you saying that you knew, *before* they made up these stories about me having a breakdown, that they made up stories about me having a brain tumor?"

Neither answered for a moment. "It was easy to prove the tumor wasn't real," my mother said. "But that night in the health center you were so upset, and none of us knew what was true."

I rubbed my forehead. "Jesus Christ," I muttered. "They made up something to get rid of me, and it failed. So you believed them when they made up something else? How much time between the two stories?"

Silence again. "A few weeks," my mother said.

I absorbed this news. "Okay, so here's reality." I sighed. "They wanted me out. I don't know why. Maybe they're afraid of liability. They made up two stories. Everybody knew the first one was bogus but trusted the second one. So now my treatment is on hold even though all of you knew they lied once before."

My mother's words were soft. "Let's wait to hear what Roskos says."

I detected hesitation in her voice for the first time since my dismissal. Maybe she was starting to believe me.

I was on the phone with another member of Sixteen Feet, ripping into Whitaker, calling him incompetent, and saying he had been trying to get rid of me all along.

"I think Whitaker's talented," he responded. "Apparently he was able to diagnose a brain tumor in a student that all of the doctors missed, just based on how he talked."

For a moment, I was speechless. "Are you fucking *kidding me?*" I exploded. "That's me! Except he's lying! There's no fucking brain tumor! That son of a bitch is lying to students to impress them? What kind of ego does that take?"

I remembered. *I was on the research team that developed sphenoidal leads.* And he had walked out of the health center meeting when my mother contradicted him, choosing instead to lurk in the hallway.

Things started to make sense. If anyone was lying, I felt certain it was Whitaker.

The past summer had been full of great movies. John Landis's *An American Werewolf in London* had been released in August, but I missed it because of time spent on my medical care. Landis directed one of my favorite movies—*The Blues Brothers*—and this new film, a horror comedy, sounded great. I was flipping through the newspaper when I saw *American Werewolf* was playing at a nearby theater. I begged a friend to take me, and soon we were munching popcorn and drinking Cokes as the picture began.

I watched as two actors playing college students backpacked through England when suddenly a wolf attacks, killing one man and mauling the other. The survivor, David, is taken to the hospital. After his release, a full moon rises, and he falls to the ground, beginning a painful transformation into a werewolf.

A thought popped into my head. *I wonder if that's what I look like during a seizure.*

The hospital, the doctors, the loss of control. Everything cut too close. Then came a scene when David wakes up after resuming human form, in a place he doesn't recognize, with no idea how he got there.

I was David. Michael was the monster. Michael was me. I was the monster.

The film tore at me as the dialogue took on meanings no screenwriter could have intended. I grew increasingly uncomfortable as I watched a scene where David goes to a movie theater. I was in a movie theater. He sits down surrounded by people he killed as a werewolf. Jack, his friend who died in the original attack, is a decaying corpse in a chair near him. The others with him are the undead who cannot rest until David has perished.

"What shall I do?" David asks.

"Suicide," Jack replies.

One of David's other victims chimes in. "You must take your own life!"

David asks Jack why he is tormenting him. "Because this must be stopped," Jack replies.

The suffering faced by the people around him starts to convince David to end his life. "How shall I do it?" he asks. A dead woman suggests sleeping pills, but that method comes with the risk that someone might save David before he died.

"I could hang myself," David says.

"If you did it wrong, it would be painful," Jack replies. "You'd choke to death."

Another corpse breaks in. "So what? Let 'im choke."

"Do you mind?" Jack replies. "The man's a friend of mine."

I stood, spilling my popcorn on the floor as I hurried out. I was the monster. I destroyed friends. Carl was Jack. I destroyed strangers. *They all want me gone.* Who could blame them?

It took me days to recover from the image of damaged people urging David, the character I associated with myself, to commit suicide. I never saw the end of the movie. I could not bring myself to ever watch it again.

After weeks of reporting, I had gathered hundreds of pages of documents—from the woman at the health department, Balaban, and state and federal agencies. The story was indisputable, the mistreatment worse than I'd heard. The material showed that county officials had lied to government investigators in writing. Balaban had been placed on the defensive, forced to disprove falsehoods. The parallels in our cases did not escape me. While Balaban's mistreatment was far crueler, it proved that reputable people would fib when they wanted to rid their organization of someone with a disability.

Anger built inside me—not involving shouting or drama, but a commitment to expose people who abused power. From then on, my taped diaries included contemplations on the wrongs that permeate society. I devoured books about injustice and law—*A Theory of Justice* by John Rawls, Plato's *Republic*, and even works of fiction like *To Kill a Mockingbird*.

I changed. For so much of my life, I'd focused on myself—my challenges, my problems, my desires. Now I saw the shallowness of self-absorption. As I reported the Balaban case while also fighting for myself, I developed a conviction toward championing the powerless. This spawned a contained, controllable rage that has stayed with me ever since. I could direct it, target it at whatever injustice I uncovered. While I have often regretted my inability to overcome this intensity of indignation, it became the foundation of my career as a reporter, driven by an almost unhealthy obsession with exposing the powerful who preyed on the weak.

Balaban was my first war. Once I had gathered the information I needed, my mother brought me to St. Mark's, where she still worked as the nurse. I lugged my documents to the library, preparing to start typing up my findings there.

On December 8, I finished two memos describing my evidence about Balaban. The first, a narrative of the events, filled 17 single-spaced pages. I attached another 823 pages of proof. The second, titled "Reasons for Investigation," described the situation's hopelessness, the need for exposure, and the resonance these revelations could have on society—an appeal for justice that added five thousand words to the tome.

That night, I presented my memos to the AID directors and answered their questions. I explained that I would circulate the information to any reporter who would speak to me.

After the meeting, Stuart Couch from the county commissioners' office and Tom Morrison from Health and Human Services asked to speak with me. By then, I knew Couch worked as a counselor and Morrison handled investigations of discrimination against the disabled. I had drawn the broad outlines of my personal situation for them, and they had expressed sympathy.

Couch had told me that he also had epilepsy and went through similar struggles after his first seizure at nineteen, with doctors casting doubt on his condition because of his normal EEGs. They acknowledged their error only when a new test detected seizure activity. For obvious reasons, we bonded over our shared stories.

I sat across from him and Morrison. Couch spoke first. This wasn't about Balaban.

"Kurt, I'm a counselor. And I can tell you, there is nothing wrong with you psychologically." He fumed, his voice laced with anger. "God-damn it, what is wrong with those people? I mean, you have seizures, and you get emotional because of it. If they want someone who's not going to react like that, they're going to have to find a dead person with epilepsy."

I appreciated his support, but I knew no one was going to accept his opinion as definitive. "Thank you," I said.

Morrison cleared his throat. "In my work, I have seen the types of things Swarthmore did lots of times, involving many schools trying to get rid of disabled students. You need to know, their action was illegal."

That stunned me. I didn't know they had broken the law. While the counselor at the Epilepsy Association had told my mother long before, no one had ever informed me.

"It violated Section 504 of the Rehabilitation Act of 1973," Morrison said. "I work on discrimination cases involving that law." He leaned in. "I am here to help, any way I can. And if you want to file for a federal investigation of Swarthmore, tell me, and I'll reach out to someone to get the paper work ready."

I thanked them and agreed to consider bringing in the government. That was not a decision to be made lightly.

When I arrived home, I found mail from West Virginia University College of Law waiting for me on the kitchen table. I tore open the yellow envelope and found a letter from a law professor inside. She wrote that she had heard about what Swarthmore had done and explained how their actions violated Section 504. I had never heard of this law before, but now I had received lessons about it twice in one day. She offered to represent me for free if I sued the school.

Back at Swarthmore, Carl and Franz were worried. For years, my choices had put them under incredible pressure. While I had finally ended the secrecy, now I was blaming that decision for my getting thrown out of school. With me at home, the rest of the semester had been one of the calmest periods for them in a long time. If I returned and again started trying to hide the state of my health, the responsibility would fall on them. They worried about our friendship, they worried about their ability to hold up if the chaos returned. The two of them sat down to discuss what to do. Carl was particularly frightened.

In 1986, Franz spoke with me about that moment and the anguish both of them felt. "Carl and I were really scared that the friendships were really in danger, because we were feeling so conflicted about everything," he said. "We decided that the healthiest thing was to have some distance. And it's not the type of thing I ever thought I would tell you. But I think it's something good for you to know."

"Kurt, I believe you."

It was two days later, December 10, and I was at my daily appointment with Roskos. I had seen him about twenty times before he finally reached his judgment about my mental health.

I tried to contain my excitement. "So you don't think I have a psychological problem?"

He chuckled. "You're a normal neurotic."

Overwhelmed, I didn't know what to say.

"But," he continued, "I can't help you if you don't let me talk to anybody. Dr. Naarden is waiting to hear my conclusions. He's not going to change anything until he does."

Irrationally, I thought it would be best if Roskos stayed quiet. *Maybe I should put up with the seizures in exchange for having someone know I told the truth.*

"I'm sure you're worried this is going to be like Chicago. It's not. It won't end up with me saying you have epilepsy and Naarden saying you don't. That's never been an issue. You're past that. But if you want things to get better, you have to give me permission to talk."

I closed my eyes and thought. "Okay."

That afternoon, Naarden called me at home.

"I heard from Dr. Roskos," he said. "He tells me you'll be fine if I treat you like any other patient. So I want you to come by tomorrow. We'll need to start the switch from phenobarbital to Mysoline . . ."

He mentioned something about the drug, but I wasn't listening. I didn't care. We were back on the treatment plan, five weeks later than if Swarthmore had never intervened. I had missed the diagnostic tests originally planned for November, and we couldn't reschedule them before school started. Too bad. I had warned everyone—I wouldn't miss the second semester to catch up on delays caused by their refusal to believe me.

The fight was over. Dickerson had promised on the night of the dismissal that I could return, and whether she meant it or not, now my doctors were ready to tell Swarthmore there was no medical or psychological reason to keep me out. I knew the college had broken the law. A contact at HHS was ready to do battle. My mother finally revealed she had hired a lawyer, E. Brice Cunningham, when the school tried to get rid of me over the imaginary brain tumor. And then there was the West Virginia law professor.

I spoke with Carl and Franz every so often, occasionally mentioning the coming semester—how I was looking forward to seeing friends, attending classes, directing *Pippin*. During one call, as I chattered about my return, Franz interrupted.

"Are you sure you're coming back?" he asked.

"Yeah, absolutely," I replied. "Why?"

He and Carl had heard from Nancy Orr, the dean of housing, Franz said. From the sound of it, the school was planning to put someone else in my room. *These people are so disorganized*, I thought. Dickerson had said long ago I could come back. Orr was confused.

"That's just a mistake," I said. "I'll fix it."

As I hung up, my mother called to me. She was headed to St. Mark's, which I was still using for work on the Balaban case. I told her that I needed to contact the housing office at school, and she offered to let me phone from her office.

Twenty minutes later, standing next to my mother's desk as she filled out paper work, I reached Orr. I liked her; she had been helpful over the years and always spoke to me in a friendly manner. I expected this would be quick.

"I heard from Franz that there is some confusion," I said. "I want you to know, I'm coming back next semester."

Orr's voice was cold. "Kurt, I don't think that's your decision."

"Of course it is."

"No, it's up to Janet Dickerson and the dean's committee."

What? "That's illegal," I blurted out. "And that's completely changing what Dean Dickerson said. She told me it was up to my doctors. She told my brother I could return any time."

"Look," Orr said. "Let me get you in contact with Janet."

Orr placed me on hold, and my mother asked what was happening. I recounted the conversation.

"That's got to be a mistake," my mother said.

Minutes ticked by. I asked my mother for a pen and paper; Morrison from HHS had told me to keep records of my conversations with the school. Now, unexpectedly, what should have been a routine phone call had escalated into something more.

Orr picked up. "Okay, what Janet says . . ."

I wrote a note to my mother. *JD doesn't have guts to speak to me.*

". . . is that there's going to be a dean's committee meeting and they'll decide whether you're coming back."

"How are they going to do that?"

I wrote down Orr's answer as she spoke the words. I could sense the fury building in my mother as she read them.

"*They'll make the decision based on what's in your best interest and in the best interest of the school.*"

The call ended, and my mother's face reddened in anger.

"They're not letting you back in!"

MARI COSSABOOM, 1981

A longtime friend

I really understand what's going on with you and with Swarthmore and how hard this has been for you. You've had to fight every step of the way. I know you must be really tired, but you've got to keep fighting. If you don't fight, you've lost. If you don't fight, then you might as well just give up and live in a padded cell.

CHAPTER TWENTY

That night, I paced anxiously in the living room, staring at my feet as I strode past my father's expensive stereo system. His collection of Asian antiquities—small Buddha statues and hand-carved wooden deities—filled the room, and in some part of my psyche, I wanted to throw one against the wall in anger. Focusing on my Nikes kept that thought at bay.

My father sat in an orange chair and my mother on the couch as they waited for me to speak. I stopped my march.

"I want to sue," I declared. "Enough people have gotten away with hurting me. I want lawyers to handle this."

"That's not a good idea," my father said. "Swarthmore hasn't committed to any decision. If we push, they might lash back. We should try the soft approach."

"What do you mean 'the soft approach'?" I shouted. "A soft approach isn't going to work! They *lied* to kick me out! Do you think now we're just going to persuade them to let me back in out of the goodness of their hearts?"

My mother had a thought. She hurried to the kitchen and returned with a copy of the St. Mark's student directory. She remained standing as she flipped through it.

"Don Lloyd-Jones is on the board at Swarthmore," she said. "He's the father of one of our seniors."

"Are you kidding?" I asked.

"No," she said. "I'll call and ask if we can meet with him."

She returned to the kitchen and placed the call. My father and I stayed in the living room; he listened patiently as I seethed about my college. Minutes passed before my mother returned with a triumphant smile.

"He'll see us tomorrow," she said.

My mother and I arrived at the Lloyd-Jones residence at about 11:00 A.M. By then, I had learned he was second in command at American Airlines. I figured that for such an important executive to invite us over on short notice, my mother must have helped his son a lot during his years at St. Mark's.

Lloyd-Jones brought us into his living room. Everything about him communicated gracious amiability, from his mannerisms to his tone of voice. My mother opened the conversation by summarizing my history of epilepsy and my dismissal from school.

I interrupted. "They did it twice. The first time they blamed it on a brain tumor I don't have. The second time they said I was failing my courses, which I wasn't, and had no social life, which I did. Janet Dickerson herself said I could come back. Now they're saying, if it's not in the best interest of the school, they'll keep me out!"

I caught myself. I was talking too loudly and too quickly. My mother resumed her narrative with no more interruptions from me. I had expected Lloyd-Jones to be outraged by the school's actions, but he showed no outward signs of distress. The story was too complex, with too many conflicting currents.

At the end of the visit, Lloyd-Jones promised to discuss the situation by telephone with Theodore "Dorie" Friend, Swarthmore's president. My mother thanked him.

I wasn't as polite. "When you speak to President Friend, give him a message from me: Swarthmore broke the law when they threw me out. I have a letter from a West Virginia University law professor willing to represent me in suing the school. I've already spoken to someone with the government, and he says Swarthmore broke the law."

Lloyd-Jones maintained his placid demeanor. "I understand," he said. "I'll speak to Dorie."

Lloyd-Jones called my mother on Sunday. He had contacted Friend, who spoke to Dickerson. She assured Friend any problems would be worked out.

"So deal with Janet," Lloyd-Jones told her. "She'll take care of everything."

My mother relayed his comments to me. I did not find the news encouraging.

Late on Monday, January 4, I called Swarthmore and spoke with Dickerson for the first time since leaving school. I asked if I would be allowed to return and, if not, what reason they had for refusing.

"Call tomorrow or Wednesday, and we'll have a decision," she replied.

I had an appointment scheduled with Naarden the next afternoon at three-thirty. Before we left for the checkup, I phoned Dickerson again. Her secretary told me that she was in a meeting, so I left a message and hung up. I told my mother what the secretary had said.

"She's lying!" my mother declared forcefully. "It's a lie!"

"Mom, give her a break." I laughed. "She's probably in a meeting. She *is* the dean."

Thirty minutes later, my parents and I were seated across from Naarden in his office. He asked if I was having trouble on my new drug combination. I slept more easily, I replied, but that was nice.

Then the conversation changed direction. "We need to discuss what you're going to do about school," Naarden said.

"What about it?"

"We have to consider whether it would be better for you to stay home for another semester given the problems you've had."

I was stunned. "What are you talking about?"

"The academic issues you were having."

I thought this was over.

"Again, what are you talking about?"

"I received a call this morning from Dr. Millington, who spoke with the dean. And she had told him it was a matter of school record that you withdrew from one course, were failing another, and were doing flashes of A work in another but mostly poor work."

"Wait a minute—" I barked.

My mother touched my arm. "Shh, let him finish."

I nodded.

"Since your performance was poor in the first semester, it's probably the medication," he said. "So it might be best if you stay home and get everything straightened out."

I stayed silent until I was sure he had finished.

"Dr. Naarden," I said, "they are *lying* to you. Yes, I dropped a course, right off the bat, because Janet Dickerson *told me to*! I *had no grades* in my other classes. They are just trying to stop me from coming back!"

"It's true," my mother said. "It is absolutely true. They are trying to get rid of him."

I put my hand on his desk. "They don't want me because I have seizures. They don't want the liability. They don't want anything to do with it."

My new sense of targeted rage kicked in. I assessed what Naarden had just told me and the school's relentless efforts to keep me out. *What are they planning?* I had called Dickerson just before this appointment. Based on her commitment from the day before, they had less than twenty-four hours to give me a final decision. That meant . . .

"They're trying to trick you!" I blurted out. "They want you to tell them it would be in my best interest if I didn't return. That way, they can kick me out and blame you!"

Naarden looked at us as if we were all insane.

"You're going to get another call from Millington," I insisted. "I bet they're tricking him too. He's going to ask for your recommendation on if I can return to school. They want to trick you into repeating back exactly what they told you!"

Minutes later, the phone rang. Naarden picked up, covered the mouthpiece with his hand, and said, "Speak of the devil."

It was Millington. I stayed silent. As Naarden listened, his smile disappeared. For the first time, I saw anger in his face.

Then he spoke. "I am an adviser to Kurt and his family, nothing more," he said in sharp, clipped tones. "If you want to know if Kurt is returning to Swarthmore, I suggest you call him. Otherwise, we have nothing to talk about."

Naarden hung up and looked at me. "I think I'm beginning to understand what you've been saying this whole time," he said.

My head drooped. I was amazed. What was the probability we would be there right between Millington's two calls? If my appointment with Naarden had been at any other time, my chance of returning to college would have been over.

Amid the tumult, I received a call from Peter Applebome of *Texas Monthly*. I had left him a message, hoping to spur interest in the Balaban story, and was excited to hear back. I explained the case and told him I had compiled documents proving everything. He said that the story sounded great, but he had just joined the *Monthly* from the *Dallas Morning News*, and this seemed like a better article for the newspaper. He offered to put me in contact with a reporter named Christy Hoppe.

Hoppe listened as I described the Balaban situation and asked plenty of questions. I told her I could get the documents and memos to her as soon as possible. She suggested we meet the next day at Kip's Restaurant, not far from my home.

Dorie Friend, Swarthmore's president, called a meeting of school officials to review my case. The group included Dickerson, the security chief, the head of the health center, Whitaker, and Patricia Whitman, Swarthmore's equal opportunity specialist.

Friend asked a series of questions. Then Whitaker took the floor. Gone were the stories about the brain tumor, the academic failure, the lack of a social life. This time he proclaimed a new diagnosis.

He had reviewed one of my EEGs, Whitaker said. "And what it shows is," he continued, "not only does Kurt not have epilepsy, but he is mentally ill."

As Whitaker prattled on, Whitman listened in disbelief. Unknown to Whitaker, she also had epilepsy. She understood EEGs, what they could show, and what they could not. She knew this psychologist was delivering impossible interpretations.

She interrupted. "Lee, as I'm sure you know, many people with epilepsy have normal EEGs. You can't say the EEG shows epilepsy doesn't exist."

Then Whitman dropped the bomb. "Also, I have no idea how you're saying the EEG proves Kurt is mentally ill. An EEG can't show anything like that. It just measures electrical activity. How are you concluding it shows mental illness?"

Whitaker mumbled a few replies, then stopped speaking.[*] The discussion resumed. Whitman listened to the rationalizations for my dismissal with increasing dismay. She couldn't believe that they were bringing her in on a case directly related to her job only at this point. None of them understood the law.

The meeting ended, and everyone gathered their things. Whitman approached Friend.

"Dorie?" she said. "Can we speak?"

Whitman waited until everyone else left the room to say more.

"I want to tell you, if Kurt sues the school, he will win," she said. "And not only that—I'll testify on his behalf."

Friend's eyes held steady. But the color drained from his face.

Dickerson's self-imposed deadline came the day after we witnessed Millington's call to Naarden. I phoned her office, still grateful at having been with him at that exact time. The secretary placed me on hold, and I waited beside the kitchen table. I expected this would be short. There wasn't much for her to say other than "You're back in."

Dickerson picked up.

"Hi, Dean Dickerson," I said. "So, what's the decision?"

---

[*] A year later, Whitman told me this story. I immediately called my parents to share the amazing tale. My father exploded in anger. He reminded me that I had never authorized any of my doctors to send an EEG to Swarthmore and the school had no equipment to conduct one. Whitaker had never had possession of, nor could he have lawfully reviewed, any of my EEGs.

"Well, your neurologist and Dr. Millington had a telephone call yesterday . . ."

Yeah, I know, I thought smugly. *I was there.*

". . . and Dr. Naarden said it was up to your psychiatrist whether you should return and that your psychiatrist should call the school psychiatrist to discuss it."

Don't speak. This was fiction, and I had witnesses to prove it. If I blew up then, the outburst could be used against me.

My voice hardened with contained rage. "That's odd," I said. "Why would my neurologist want my psychiatrist to speak with your psychiatrist? If anything, I would think he would just ask my psychiatrist to send a letter."

"Dr. Naarden recommended that the psychiatrists speak to each other."

This is unreal. "Okay, but that makes no sense. I was dismissed from school because of my seizures. Why does a psychiatrist have to call for you to let me back in?"

"Well, your neurologist told Dr. Millington that you don't have epilepsy. In fact, he said your problem is psychological."

I sank into a chair, stunned. Whitaker knew about the misdiagnosis in Chicago; had he used that to manipulate Millington, to trick Dickerson? Millington knew the story too—was he lying? Or had administrators finally figured out they had broken the law and started grabbing any rumor they could to make the problem go away?

Something worse occurred to me. Why the hell was some dean telling a student that his neurologist was blabbing to near strangers that he was insane? Had she considered the damage that might be caused by suggesting my neurologist was lying to me yet letting some college internist know the *real* story?

We rambled on, with Dickerson making a series of statements that contradicted things my parents had already been told. Five minutes after the conversation ended, Naarden called. My blood tests showed my Mysoline level was too low, and he gave me instructions to increase the dosage.

"Okay," I said. "Listen, I have something else to talk about. I just spoke with the dean of Swarthmore. She said you told Dr. Millington I don't have epilepsy and that my seizures are psychological."

"*What?*" I could almost picture his mouth gaping. "That is a fabrication. You heard my call with him. I said no such thing."

"Yeah, but I had to ask."

I could hear anger in Naarden's voice. "Kurt, I just told you to start taking a higher dose of a very powerful drug. And you're already on Dilantin, *another* powerful drug. I don't throw anticonvulsants around like candy. You have epilepsy."

I sighed. "Yeah, I know. They're just lying again."

I asked my mother to join me later that day for my appointment with Roskos. Since Naarden resumed my treatment plan, I had cut back on my visits with the psychiatrist. But that week's events were so breathtakingly preposterous, I decided he might need my mother to confirm that my account of Swarthmore's outlandish behavior was true.

I told him about Dickerson's insistence that he speak to the school psychiatrist about me. "No way I am doing that," Roskos said. "That violates the ethical rules of my profession."

"I know," I said. "It seems like they're saying to return to school, I have to waive doctor-patient confidentiality."

"That's exactly what they're saying."

I asked Roskos if he should send a letter giving his judgment on whether I was fit to return. He advised we wait to see how things unfolded—with everything Swarthmore had done so far, he said, there was no telling how they might react to correspondence from him.

My parents asked to speak with me in the living room that evening. They looked somber. I knew something bad had happened.

"I called the school," my mother said, her voice faltering. "They said Janet Dickerson never said the things you attributed to her. They said you're making it up."

I didn't know whether to laugh or cry. "Don't tell me. You believe them."

My father spoke. "Kurt, it's just so crazy. Why would they tell you things like this? Why would they say your neurologist says you have a mental illness or you have to let them interview your psychiatrist?"

I sat down. "I can't believe we're back to this. *They are doing whatever they can to keep me out.*"

"They're claiming you're making up these stories about what Janet Dickerson is saying," my mother said, "and they say that this is proof you shouldn't be coming back."

Unreal. Even after everything they had seen, my parents still couldn't believe that the college administrators would say anything to get rid of me. The second semester was about to start. And now everyone doubted me again. I could think of only one way to bring all the doubt to an end.

The next day, January 7, I was alone in the house carrying my portable cassette recorder and some Scotch tape. I walked into my parents' room and went to the phone on their bedside table. After placing the handset on the bed, I strapped the recorder onto it with tape, placing the microphone against the earpiece. After pushing the plunger button to reset the dial tone, I pressed RECORD and ran to the kitchen phone. I dialed Swarthmore, hoping my amateurish wiretapping efforts would work. I asked for Dickerson's office, and the call was transferred.

Dickerson answered the phone herself with a cheery "Good afternoon."

"Ah, hi, this is Kurt."

She told me she was just writing a letter to my family. "What can I do for you?" she asked.

"I was just calling to find out what was going on."

She explained that Dr. Millington had sent her a letter, and then she moved on to discuss one of the conditions of my return. "I realized in talking to you the other day that there might be some concern in your psychiatrist talking to us," she said.

"The only concern I had was that I didn't see why my psychiatrist had to talk to the school psychiatrist when I had never seen him."

I stopped. I was getting off track already, making an argument. I needed Dickerson to repeat things she had already told me, statements that my parents would know were false.

"There's one question I have, which is that, when I left, you told both my mother and me that I would be returning next semester, seizures or not."

"No, I didn't," she said.

My mom will be interested to hear that. "You did not tell us that?"

"No. Absolutely not."

"The thing is that my mother remembers the exact same thing being said."

"Well, I know that I didn't say it," Dickerson replied. "I would be very careful not to."

Moving on. What was the problem with me returning? I asked. How was I different from other students? I hoped she would reply by citing my seizures. No such luck.

"All I can say is this: We need to have some recommendations from reputable doctors that—well, apparently whatever is going on is as much psychiatric as it is medical."

There it was. She had repeated that they believed the seizures were psychological.

"'Apparently' based on what?" I asked.

"Based on what I have heard in writing from Dr. Millington," she said, "and what I have not heard in writing from Dr. Naarden, but what I have heard reported from Dr. Millington, is that there is no structural cause for your seizures."

That was jumbled. I knew what she was saying, but I had to think of a way to get her to repeat it more clearly. "Mm-hmm," I said.

"Is that right?" she asked. "They have done everything, that all the tests confirm that there is nothing structurally wrong?"

"Yeah."

So, she said, the same way I would want to protect myself, the school wanted to be protected too. I had no idea what she meant and asked her for clarification.

"Well, if there is a problem, i.e., if you have a bad accident," she replied.

The more we spoke, the more confusing the conversation became. I decided I needed to push back, to tell her that Millington—by thinking "nothing structurally wrong" meant the seizures were psychological—was showing his ignorance of epilepsy.

"There's a couple of things that I think you should know," I said. "First of all, the fact that there is no structural problem—I guess this is something that Dr. Millington does not understand."

"Why?"

Because I had told Naarden that the school used this explanation, I said, and he had told me that the absence of a structural problem in the brain did not mean the epilepsy was psychological. He had told me that Millington was absolutely wrong.

"Seizures do not show up as a structural problem necessarily," I continued. "They *can* be caused by a brain tumor. They *can* be caused by calcification. But there is something called idiopathic seizures. 'Idiopathic' means no known cause."

I decided to point out the illogic of the school's position. What *difference* did it make what the cause of my seizures was? The episodes would be no different if Millington's misinformed position were correct. So what was the point of this debate?

I stopped. I was arguing again. *Not the goal of this call.* She had mentioned before that she was acting under professional advice. I reminded her that she had told me that.

"What advice was that?" I asked. "I keep hearing that, and I really want to know who said it."

"Well," she replied, "you were not passing your courses."

Wow. That was the fastest topic change since this had all begun. Okay, on to my academic performance.

"Now, that's the second question I've got," I said. "How do you have that information?"

"From your professors."

Time to remind her. "I didn't take a test, I didn't have a paper, and I didn't have a homework assignment done yet. We hadn't done anything in my courses."

"All I know is that I spoke to your professors."

"They said I wasn't passing?" I asked.

"Well, that's the impression I got. Well, he didn't say that you weren't passing but that you were not performing well."

He. One professor. *Probably Hollister,* I thought. I'm sure he must have told her that I needed a tutor, and she took that to mean I was failing. I wondered if he had told her about my medically induced inability to comprehend symbols.

The conversation meandered on as I lured Dickerson into repeating many of the things she had said to me before. I decided to find out, once and for all, who was behind one of the strangest events in the whole saga of my battle with the school.

"Why did you call my brother at medical school?" I asked, referring to the first decision that had been made to dismiss me. "Why did you not call my family, meaning my parents? It wasn't until my brother called my family . . ."

She mentioned something about Naarden, who I knew had nothing to do with her call, and the fact that she knew my brother well. Someone had also shared with her that my father had been in denial about my epilepsy, which had not been true since August. I immediately knew where that bit of information came from: I had told Whitaker in our first session when I was recounting the whole story. Within a second, Dickerson confirmed my convictions.

"It was my advice, frankly, from Lee Whitaker, that if we were thinking about this, that, well, frankly, thinking about this, that, not asking you to leave but that . . ."

Her words were becoming confusing again. Whitaker had told her something. "Yeah?" I said.

". . . it might be better to call Eric to find out whether it might be better to approach your parents or not," she said.

The insanity of the whole situation captured in one sentence. A psychologist had told a dean information straight out of a counseling session. He had told the dean to call *my brother*—a kid in his early twenties—to ask whether they should notify *my parents* that they were planning to kick me out. I would have laughed at the absurdity of it all if it had not been part of a deeply traumatic experience.

Dickerson mentioned that Naarden had said the seizures were the consequence of a psychological problem. I was sure he had discussed the psychological challenges of having epilepsy; he had done so with me many times. Stress brought on by fear could trigger a seizure. But this interpretation—either it was a lie or a grotesque misunderstanding.

"Can you think what it would be like to be having epileptic seizures and not have a psychological effect?" I asked. "That there's a difference between cause and effect? Now, what Dr. Naarden is talking about is effect. There is, however, the fact that the effect can be a trigger. That does not mean that there is something psychologically imbalanced."

I raised Millington's calls to Naarden and mentioned that I had heard the last one. Dickerson said Millington had reported to her that Naarden's behavior had been significantly different in the second call.

"Now, we don't know what the cause of that is," she said. "I mean, it could be that, ah, Dr. Naarden is your father's colleague and that—"

"Dr. Naarden did not even know my father before August."

"Well, all I know is that Dr. Millington was surprised at Dr. Naarden's response."

What Naarden had said, I told her, was that if school officials wanted to know whether I was returning to Swarthmore, they should call me.

"But the point is that Kurt doesn't make a decision as to whether Kurt is coming back to Swarthmore," Dickerson said.

"Really?"

"That's right."

"Why not?" I asked.

"And that it is Swarthmore's decision as to whether, as to whether Kurt may return, and that's why he—"

Time for the killer question. "Swarthmore has the right to dismiss me because I have seizures?" I asked.

"That's what we did," Dickerson replied.

After she hung up, I ran to my parents' bedroom, removed the recorder from the handset, and rewound the tape. The call had gone perfectly; I could only hope the recording had worked and was audible. My heart beat fast as I pushed PLAY.

The opening seconds were a dial tone, then some clicks. I heard the line ring. Dickerson answered. Every word was clear. I listened for a few minutes with angry satisfaction. This might not have been usable in court—for all I knew, I had broken the law by taping her—but no one could doubt what she'd told me. Then I heard the crucial statements, the one from her that I knew was a confession to violating antidiscrimination laws.

> *"Swarthmore has the right to dismiss me because I have seizures?"*
> *"That's what we did."*

I listened a second time, hit REWIND again, then clicked off the recorder. Afterward, I headed into the family room to watch some television. I wanted to stop thinking about Swarthmore.

As soon as my parents arrived home, I grabbed my tape recorder and stormed into the kitchen. I didn't say hello.

"If you don't believe me," I said, "maybe you'll believe Janet Dickerson."

I pushed PLAY. My parents listened to the conversation with growing horror. People at the school had lied to them directly, pretending I was making up stories.

The tape ended. No one spoke.

"Well?" I asked.

"I'm calling your lawyer," my mother finally said.

"And," my father added, "let's call your friend at Health and Human Services."

He shook his head, a fury on his face unlike any I had ever seen. "We're going to destroy this school," he muttered coldly.

In a conversation with

DR. ALLAN NAARDEN, 2017

It was life-changing. You were a young college kid. You wanted to do whatever you wanted to do with your life. I also knew, parallel to all of that, that there was so much prejudice against people who had a seizure disorder, that this was just another example of that. How they had put you in a category, a box if you will, and they weren't treating you like a person. They were treating you like a thing, and that really bothered me that that had happened because the goal of giving you medication was not to tick off a little box saying "I gave you medication." The goal was to try and get you to the best place that you could be with regard to seizure control, and not have it be the center of your life. That getting on with your life, doing what you wanted to do, was really the most important part of this.

It really angered me that they were using epilepsy as a weapon. If you want to talk about weaponizing epilepsy, that's what I thought they did.

CHAPTER TWENTY-ONE

My mother drove me downtown the next afternoon for a two o'clock appointment with Morrison at HHS. I'd told him that morning about the recording, and he wanted to hear it right away.

A few hours earlier, I met with my lawyer, Cunningham. He had assured me before that he could use the law to force Swarthmore to take me back, but after listening to the recording of Dickerson, he changed his advice. "You have to leave that college," he said. "They're going to get you. They're going to do something." Once I settled in at another school, we could sue Swarthmore for discrimination.

Before I made a final decision, though, I wanted to hear from Morrison. He listened to the tape with a faraway look. None of us spoke until the recording finished.

"That psychological evaluation she's talking about is a setup," Morrison said. "There's no way you pass it."

"I know."

He seemed to replay the words he'd just heard. "Get the hell out of that school," he said finally. "You can go to any school in the country, but not Swarthmore and not one in that area."

"Wait, not even on the East Coast? Why?"

He leaned forward at his desk.

"I'm sorry, but this is the way the world works," he said in a matter-of-fact tone. "I can get you back in, but there's no law that says they have to like that. They can pull anything on you. From what I have heard on this tape and from what I have seen, they *will* pull anything on you. Transfer somewhere else."

"Why are they fighting this so hard? What's the big deal?"

"Several possibilities. One is, they're just uncomfortable around epileptics. Or maybe their psychologist or internist is lying to the decision-makers. Or they've got a lawyer who told them how badly they screwed up."

I thought for a second. Franz had mentioned that he'd heard from Dickerson. She told him the school knew I was looking into laws regarding my dismissal and they had consulted a lawyer. I relayed that to Morrison.

"The dean is talking to your friends about the school's legal activities?" he asked. "Why?"

"No idea."

Morrison considered this new information. "Okay, then here is what we have to assume. You're in a legal Catch-22."

The standard under law, Morrison explained, was that disabled students could be dismissed if they no longer qualified for the school program—for instance, if they flunked out. But the strongest proof that a college had broken the law was if a disabled student was readmitted.

I raised my hands in exasperation. "That doesn't make any sense!"

"Yes, it does," Morrison replied. "If they let you back in, they're conceding that you're qualified for the program. That means they're confessing the original dismissal was illegal. If they're consulting a smart lawyer, they know if they let you back in, they have no defense if you sue them."

This is insane! "So, they can't let me back in because throwing me out was illegal, and letting me back in proves that?"

Morrison nodded.

"Oh my God," my mother mumbled.

A pause. "How are your seizures?" Morrison asked.

"What does that matter?" I snapped.

"Just an idea. Maybe if we can tell them your seizures are under control, we can craft some way for them to back out gracefully, like telling them you're better because you stayed home and thanking them."

"Well, I'm not better! In fact, my doctor delayed my treatment because of their lies! I'm having a grand mal seizure about once every two weeks."

My mother interrupted. "That's not quite right. They have gotten somewhat better since Dr. Naarden increased the medication."

"Okay, fine," I said. "I'm still having seizures, but I'm better. The changes that were going to be started in early November, but were delayed until December, are making me better. But I'm not going to crawl to them and apologize because I'm still having seizures!"

Morrison urged me to relax. "Don't misunderstand. I'm trying to come up with another approach. Because without one, it's really too dangerous for you to go back to school."

"But if I'm back in . . ."

"They know you can sue at any point. So if you flunk out after you return or do anything else that warrants dismissal, they can use that as proof you were never qualified for the program and the forced readmission was in error. That would eliminate the danger that you could win a lawsuit."

"I won't flunk out."

"Unfortunately, it might not be up to you," he replied. He described a case where a university had illegally dismissed a disabled student. Lawyers got him readmitted. Suddenly, after previous semesters of good grades, he flunked several courses. He was tossed out a second time for poor academic performance.

"I won't flunk," I said.

"Neither did he," Morrison replied. Years later, some professors revealed to HHS that the administrator behind the dismissal had threatened their tenure if they let the disabled student pass once he returned. The administrator had wanted to eliminate the dangers of a lawsuit.

I didn't believe the story. "You're kidding!"

"I wish I was, but no. That happened. This is not a fight you want to take on. They can flunk you; they can trump up charges, anything to end liability. Whatever they do will go on your record, and any other school you apply to will see it."

I stayed silent.

"Kurt," Morrison said, "if you go back to Swarthmore, you might end up never getting an education."

There has to be a way. "Do you know people that have returned, that fought it?" I asked. "I'm not talking about fighting in court right now. Court's down the line. But do you know people that fought it and won?"

"I think there are about five that I know of," he replied. "That's not in this area. That's nationwide."

Five. So it's not impossible.

"Okay, then I'm going to fight it."

My mother responded first. "Kurt, *why?* You might never graduate from college! Swarthmore has been terrible to you! Why do you want to go back?"

I stood and grasped the back of a chair.

"Because the administration isn't Swarthmore," I argued. "If I go back to school and I have a seizure in front of people, then I'm just Kurt who had a seizure. If I go somewhere else, within two weeks, I'll be 'the epileptic.' If you think Swarthmore is scared of seizures, imagine how strangers will feel! I'll always be alone. I'll have no friends. I'll be pitied. I'll be defined by epilepsy."

I started pacing. "And I am *not* going to let this goddamn school transform me into 'the epileptic.' I'm going back to my friends, back where I want to be, *because that's where I want to be!* I have that right!"

I stopped to think of my next words; Morrison and my mother remained silent. They seemed to know I wasn't finished. "More important, Tom—you say you see this every day. Okay, so let's say I give up, I let Swarthmore chase me away because I'm scared of what they'll do."

My voice rose. "What about next time? What do I do if another school gets rid of me or I get fired from a job? Run away again? I either fight now, or I will hate myself for being a coward, for saying, 'Maybe I'll have the backbone next time.' There *is* no next time!"

Morrison started to speak, but I interrupted.

"This stops now!" I barked, jabbing my finger down with each word.

A metaphor popped into my head. "Look, Swarthmore got in a sucker punch and knocked me to the mat before I even knew the bell had rung," I said. "I could say, 'I'm just going to lie here, because I don't want to get hit again.' But maybe if I get up, maybe if I punch back, I'll find out they have a glass jaw. Maybe I'll knock them out in one punch. If I don't *try*, I'll never know. I'll just be the guy who wouldn't get off the ground because I was afraid. For the rest of my life, I'll be miserable because I won't know if I could have won."

Morrison took a long look at me. "Okay," he said. "Then I have to put you in contact with my counterpart at Region 3 in Philadelphia. If you want a federal investigation of Swarthmore, it falls into his jurisdiction."

He was all business now. The first step, he said, was for me to fly to Swarthmore and occupy my room. The school would either leave me there or force me out. Both responses would be helpful evidence in the looming war.

The intensity of the past few days transformed my father. Whether he had been consumed by discomfort over my epilepsy or by guilt about my mismanaged care, he experienced an extraordinary metamorphosis into my strong advocate. The Dickerson tape convinced him— Swarthmore had tricked him into turning against his son, and now the school was hunkering down, preparing to deny me an education.

Taking charge, he told us to tape every call with the school. Then we could compare recordings and verify what each of us had been told. We also would send letters from my doctors attesting, in one sentence, that I was medically and psychologically capable of returning to college.

While my mother and I were at HHS, my father picked up the doctors' letters and sent them by certified mail to Dickerson. I called to let him know that HHS had recommended I occupy my room at Swarthmore despite the possibility that the school might have me arrested for trespassing. After we spoke, my father dialed the dean's office with a tape rolling.

"Dean Dickerson, this is Dr. Eichenwald. We need to know what decision you have made."

She replied that they had sent a letter and it would arrive at our house the next day.

"What does it say?"

"It simply says that Kurt may return when we have evidence that he is ready to return and be a fully functional student."

My father swallowed his anger; he knew Swarthmore could have asked my doctors that question long ago. But the school had already labeled Naarden and Roskos as unreliable based on the falsehood that they were his colleagues.

He told her that letters from the doctors were on the way. Dickerson said she hoped everyone understood Swarthmore was acting only in my best interest.

No one believed that, my father replied—not the family, not me, and certainly not the doctors. "It was their impression that there are two things going on," my father said. "One is [to] somehow label Kurt as having a psychiatric illness and not true seizures, which of course is ridiculous. He wouldn't be on two toxic or potentially toxic drugs if that was a thought. And the other consideration is, there really is an attempt to keep him out."

"I don't want to keep him out ..."

"That's fine. Then we both agree."

"I am not trying to make a *specific* attempt to keep him out."

She mentioned Swarthmore's insistence that I be evaluated by a college psychiatrist. While Naarden and Roskos said there were no psychiatric or medical issues that would interfere with my attending college, Whitaker and Millington maintained there were. My father couldn't believe it—Dickerson valued the opinions of a college psychologist and internist who barely knew me over those of a renowned neurologist and psychiatrist who had spent time with me, diagnosed me, and treated me?

In fact, she explained, the school doctors believed the experts were wrong. "What they say is that the cause of Kurt's seizures is not just physical—"

"No, that's quite incorrect. I don't know where Dr. Millington got this information from," my father replied. "Like Kurt told you, both of us and Mrs. Eichenwald were in the office with Dr. Naarden when Dr. Millington called. So we know exactly what Dr. Naarden said."

He recited my experiences in Chicago with the toxic medication. "Dr. Naarden put him on a second set of drugs. You see, there is no way that Dr. Naarden, who I respect very much as a physician, would expose Kurt to drugs that can potentially kill him on the basis of just thinking, 'Well, maybe it's epilepsy.'"

Dickerson started to speak, but my father interrupted.

"He can register on Monday morning with the registrar. Is that correct?" he asked.

No, Dickerson replied, first I would need to be screened by a psychiatrist chosen by the school. My father insisted he would never condone that examination, which clearly—as everyone knew—would be a setup.

"I really don't want to get the feds into this, but that condition is not acceptable, and if the college insists on it, we are going to have to go the legal way," my father said.

Well, she replied, the school was ready to defend itself. "Our college counsel believes that we will be found not guilty. But I don't want to get to that. I want Kurt to be in school."

But first, the conditions had to be met. She maintained that the school was being reasonable by allowing an outside psychiatrist to conduct the evaluation since we had made it clear no one trusted Whitaker.

"To put it mildly," my father responded. "In fact, Dr. Naarden feels he may well report Whitaker to his professional organization. I don't know if you are aware of the fact that Dr. Whitaker has been telling students, without identifying Kurt, that he was able to diagnose a brain tumor—"

"Diagnose what?"

"A brain tumor in an individual where the physicians had felt there was no such thing."

"Are you kidding?" Her astonished tone was real.

"We have this from four different sources."

"Oh my goodness."

"That's all right," my father said. "If he wants to be a damned fool, that's fine, because obviously the students who made the connection, when they see Kurt again, are going to know he still has all his hair and his skull is still intact, so he didn't have a brain tumor."

Back to the law. "We're not keeping him out because he has a sei-zure disorder," Dickerson said.

My father considered telling her that he had heard a recording of her saying the opposite. "You can't keep him out for any reason, and you can't bring in something else and say, 'That is why we are keeping him out.' That also is illegal."

Dickerson brought up our recent conversation—the one I taped—saying I had yelled at her. Again, my father felt tempted to tell her he had heard the call and that, while I sounded angry, I never raised my voice. Instead, he kept his counsel.

Despite the finality of my vow in Morrison's office, I remained unsure if I was making the right decision. Carrying on the fight might rob me of a college degree; the future that I had envisioned could slip away. Morrison, Cunningham, and Roskos all advocated leaving Swarth-more. Naarden agreed, urging me to make a strategic retreat; I would be under a microscope there, and the stress could make gaining seizure control harder, he warned.

That night, I called Franz. Skipping the sordid details, I explained in general terms that the school was fighting to keep me out. "Why am I trying so hard?" I asked him.

"Because we're family," Franz said. "Because you love us. You have too strong a sense of right and wrong to let this go."

After hanging up, I walked to my bedroom, picked up my tape re-corder, lay down on the bed, and pressed the red button.

I described the day's events and pondered whether to take on the college. "So what I was told at HHS is that the possibility existed that I would not get an education because in fighting Swarthmore, they'd label me a troublemaker," I said in a tense voice. "If I slipped, I'd be thrown out. To transfer, I have to get a recommendation from the dean's office, or I would not be admitted anywhere else. So I have a choice. It comes down to: If I do this, I might not get an education at all."

I turned off the recorder, then later switched it back on. I had about forty-eight hours to decide. "It's getting down to the wire. I've got this real bad feeling in my gut, like I ought to have an ulcer, but I don't," I said. "I'm just torn. I'm scared, maybe because everyone has told me that I should be. I am just so scared. 'You might not ever get an education, or you might get everything you want. What choice are you going to make?' I haven't decided yet. It's hard to decide."

I rambled a bit, then wondered how I must sound. "I'm getting philosophical because I'm scared," I said. "But there is a principle. I'm fighting for principles. That sounds ridiculous sometimes to some people. There is a justice, and there is an injustice. That's what the fight is for. That is what my emotions are. If I deny myself the right to have what I want unjustly, I don't think I'd ever be able to like myself again. Other people keep saying, 'You can fight it once you're gone. We'll all fight it once you're gone.' I don't think I could do that. I can't turn tail and run."

The words spilled out until I noticed the cassette was almost finished. "This is the complete end of this particular tape," I said. "See you in the next installment for our future excitement."

ELVA EICHENWALD, 1982

Somewhere around Christmas, I finally began to hear and to understand what Kurt was saying. And I have reached the point where I can allow this young man his right and his privilege to be himself. It has taken a long time. No, it hasn't. It has taken a lot of work during this time to finally reach the point of opening my hand and wanting my son to become the person he's meant to become.

During that time that he was at home, I went from being constantly afraid he was going to have a seizure to not worrying about it or at least not worrying about it a lot. I am aware that he can have a seizure at any time. I look where we are just simply so that I'm aware of what I can do to make things easier for him.

But I am encouraging him to be at the school and to do whatever it is that he wants to do. I needed to know that his goals were healthy goals. I needed to know that he was fully aware of everything that might happen to him while he was here. I wanted him to know the consequences of his actions. And I think it was the only thing I could do as his parent while letting him go. And if he was not fully aware, I would have had to let him go anyway. He must reap the benefits of his own actions at this point.

I would rather be going anyplace else but Swarthmore at this time.

CHAPTER TWENTY-TWO

Traces of red spotted the pocket of my button-down shirt. I noticed, then glanced at my aching hand; I had bitten my nails until two fingers bled. *Damn.* This was one of the new shirts I'd bought in Dallas, since most of my clothes were still in my dorm room. Now bloodstains caused by anxiety may have ruined it.

It was Monday, and I was traveling with my mother to Philadelphia. As I asked a flight attendant for a napkin, my mother saw the bleeding. She brought a tissue out of her purse, and I wrapped it around my fingers.

I had announced my decision the previous day: I was going back to Swarthmore, and if forcibly removed from campus, I would head to HHS in Philadelphia to sign the paper work for an investigation. Over the weekend, we received a Mailgram from Swarthmore dictating conditions for my return. There was, of course, meeting with a psychiatrist named Silas Warner, an associate of Whitaker. I was forbidden from using the health center, I was required to retain a new neurologist, my grades would be under constant review, and so on.

After we received the Mailgram, I spoke with Paul Cushing, the

HHS investigator who would be handling my case. Like Morrison, he warned that challenging the school might wreck my future. After I read him the Mailgram, he again urged me to skip confrontation and file for the federal inquiry. I repeated what I'd told Morrison. I wasn't going to abandon my rights out of fear; I would not accept losing if I did not first try to win.

My parents and I debated which of them would accompany me to Swarthmore. I said I needed someone there only to drive and possibly bail me out of jail if I was arrested for trespassing. And I imposed a rule: No one but me was allowed to speak to any official at the school.

"If I screw this up, I can live with it," I said. "If someone else screws it up for me, I will never forgive them."

By that point, my father was so angry I feared he might hit someone at the school. Mom was the choice by default.

After landing, we drove to the Media Inn, the site of the chaotic night when I had staged a sit-in until I was allowed to bid my friends goodbye. I called Cushing, my lawyer, and my psychiatrist. Roskos was key; based on the advice of my lawyer and HHS, I could never accept Swarthmore's demand that I speak to their psychiatrist. Roskos needed to be available for my planned compromise.

My mother drove me to school. In our dorm room, Carl and Franz told me they had decided they would share the double and I would stay in the single. This seemed like a healthy way to address the mental exhaustion I was sure they must be experiencing. While I worried about being alone in a bedroom, I told them the arrangements were fine.

After unpacking, I went down the hall to a phone for on-campus calls. I dialed Dickerson's office and left a message that I was back in my dorm and wanted to meet the next day.

On Tuesday morning, I walked to the registrar's office. Although Cushing knew the ploy was a long shot, he advised trying to sign up for classes, which would make it harder to evict me. I filled out the documents, then handed them to the woman behind the counter, who promptly reminded me I needed approval from my academic adviser for my schedule.

I headed to Trotter Hall and sat outside the office of Professor David Smith from the political science department. About an hour passed before he showed up and invited me in.

"I know I've arrived late, but I wanted to get your approval of my schedule," I said, handing him the schedule card.

He didn't look at it. "I'm sorry, but the dean has told me not to sign your registration records."

I nodded and took the card back. The gamble had failed, as expected.

Hours later, Dickerson sat in front of me, looking nervous. With my mother beside me in silence, I tried to get a read on the dean. Until now, I had perceived her as someone who had slipped into error by originally engaging in "benevolent discrimination"—denying me my rights for my own good—but who then transformed into a monster, willing to destroy my future to cover up the mistake.

Now as I studied her face, I softened. This was her first year as dean—maybe she had been deceived by advisers. The security department wanted me gone, the health center feared me. Millington was badly informed—thus his call to Naarden about my fictitious academic problems—and ignorant of the nature of epilepsy. But at the center of it all, I believed, was Whitaker, who started this ordeal with his brain tumor theory before pushing on to false declarations about my emotional health. Deans and internists would rely on a psychologist for assessments of a student's mental state. They had no basis for challenging him.

Perhaps, I thought, this amalgam of ill will, incompetence, arrogance, and error might have confused a novice dean who wasn't experienced enough yet to recognize she was being fed bad information by others with undisclosed agendas.

If my assessment was right, then I might be able to persuade her, to become a gentle force pushing back on her doubts. *Persuade.* I had learned that skill as a telemarketer. *The last thing I should do is hit her with demands from the get-go.*

I spoke before the first question was asked. "I spent most of my time off in a really interesting job," I said.

She appeared disarmed by my words. "Yes, I heard that from your father. You were working with disabled people?"

"Sort of. I mean, it was for a group of people with disabilities, but really what I was doing was investigating a situation involving a doctor. In fact, it looks like there will be an article about what I did in the local newspaper."

She smiled. "That's great!"

After a few more minutes of chatting, I moved the conversation to the topic at hand.

"The job was a lot of work," I said. "Truthfully, I don't think a lot of students here could have done it. I think that alone demonstrates there's no reason to keep me out."

Like clockwork, Dickerson reverted to the stock response: No one wanted to block my return, but I had to meet six requirements. When she mentioned my grades would have to pass minimum standards, I stifled a laugh.

"Well, I assume if I'm failing my courses, I won't get to stay," I said.

I accepted other conditions without argument: I would not use the health center for seizure-related problems. I would obtain a neurologist in the area. However, I insisted, Naarden would be in charge; the other doctor could consult with him. Then it was on to the requirement I meet with a school-selected psychiatrist. I refused.

"Dean Dickerson, that's a ridiculous requirement, and it's not going to happen," I said. "I've seen a psychiatrist since I left—not because I'm mentally ill, but to help me deal with the emotions of having epilepsy."

"I understand that."

"You should already have a letter from him saying I'm fine. The idea that some guy who has never met me is going to speak with me for an hour and determine what's going to happen over the next few months is absurd. Unless he's breaking out a crystal ball, he's going to be guessing."

I wanted to make sure I chose my next words carefully. "And let me be honest, any psychiatrist who thinks he can assess a patient in one session is incompetent."

Dickerson interrupted. "Dr. Warner is highly qualified."*

"That doesn't matter. If he thinks he can determine whether I'm able to return in a single session, he's either incompetent, thinks I have schizophrenia or something, or has already been fed a bunch of nonsense by Dr. Whitaker."

My expression went hard. "And the last thing I want is another fool diagnosing me with a brain tumor based on how I talk simply so he can brag to students that he's smarter than real doctors."

Dickerson appeared uneasy but repeated: The requirement that I see Warner was not negotiable.

"Then we're at an impasse," I said. "And if we don't find a compromise, this is going to become a legal case."

"I know that's what you think," she replied. "But we've consulted with college counsel." That lawyer, she said, had assured them the decision in the fall was legally bulletproof.

I crossed my arms on the table and leaned forward. "And let me ask, how many cases has that lawyer handled involving Section 504?" I intentionally didn't define what I meant, implicitly communicating this was more complex than she might think.

"You have a college counsel who handles faculty contracts or something. I have a civil rights lawyer who says you broke the law. And I have a law professor who specializes in 504 cases who has offered to represent me for free in suing Swarthmore."

I considered mentioning that federal investigators were ready to pounce as soon as I gave the word but decided to keep that card hidden.

"So if we're playing battling experts," I said, "I like my position, backed up by people who go to court over this law all the time, compared to the opinion of some college lawyer who probably thinks 504 is a time of day."

I had metaphorically slapped. Now I needed to soothe.

"I don't want this to be ugly," I said. "I just want to come back to school."

---

*I later learned that Warner instructed gay patients they could not be mental health professionals and argued that watching professional sports was dangerous because it inflamed "macho" attitudes and taught men they could succeed by breaking rules.

Dickerson wouldn't budge. Finally, I said I would accept the original proposal: Warner, the school's psychiatrist, could speak with Roskos, nothing more. To my surprise, she agreed.

The following morning, after his discussion with Warner, Roskos reached me at the hotel sounding flabbergasted. "You *never* would have passed that exam," he said.

When Warner called, Roskos had followed my instructions and kept his words mostly limited to stating that there was no psychological reason to keep me out of school. Repeatedly, the Swarthmore psychiatrist asked for details; Roskos replied that the questions were outside the scope of what the school needed to know and answering would violate doctor-patient privilege. Warner mentioned mental problems I might have, and Roskos pushed back: Given that Warner had never met or spoken to me, Roskos said, he was not in a position to make a diagnosis.

Round and round they went, with Roskos parrying each of Warner's thrusts by repeating his one-sentence conclusion.

Warner ended the call in exasperation. "I'm sorry," the man retained by Swarthmore said. "I just don't believe that Kurt doesn't have a severe psychiatric problem."

We had all been right—the requirement to meet with the school-hired psychiatrist had been a setup. He diagnosed me with an array of psychiatric issues without ever having heard my voice.

By Thursday, my fourth day back, I began to believe I might win. I had been attending courses I wanted to take that semester, and no professor had realized I was not actually enrolled. The only one I skipped was a seminar taught by my academic adviser. If I showed up, he was sure to report to the administration that I was going to classes.

From my mother's hotel room, I phoned Cushing at his HHS office. With glee, I described my second meeting with Dickerson. After Warner struck out with Roskos, the dean renewed the demand that I speak directly to their psychiatrist. No way, I retorted. I had kept my side of the bargain. The only reason anyone would push me to meet with Warner now, I said, was because they didn't like Roskos's answer.

"Besides, we already know Warner's diagnosis," I had said. "He told Roskos he had no doubt I had a mental illness. Good luck arguing in court that your psychiatrist can diagnose someone using telepathy."

Despite my amusement, Cushing did not find the story funny; instead, he insisted that it proved I needed to file for a federal investigation of Swarthmore. The psychiatrist gambit had been a fraud, and now the school was trying other tactics. The charade would never stop. Even if I forced my readmission, he said, administrators would find a way to drive me out.

My upbeat attitude ended that afternoon. After my father heard about the Roskos-Warner call, he could no longer control his fury and dashed off an injudicious letter to Dickerson. I heard through an ally in the administration that the missive had been ugly, setting back our progress considerably. I decided not to call my dad—there was no purpose. Instead, I asked my mother to contact him and communicate a message from me: no more contributions from the peanut gallery.

That afternoon, Dickerson and I met again. She was furious and mentioned my father's letter. I explained I had no idea what he had written and didn't want to know, because he was not speaking for me.

She looked at me angrily. "I'm not going to lose my job over this!" she snapped.

An opening. "Dean Dickerson, I don't want you to lose your job," I said. "I just want to come back to school."

Later that day, without asking for my permission, Cushing telephoned Swarthmore, identified himself, and asked to speak with a particular senior administrator.

"I'm calling because, against my advice, Kurt Eichenwald wants to return to your school," he started.

That evening, Cushing reached me at the Media Inn to discuss his call to the school. He refused to identify whom he had contacted.

"I was very clear with him," he told me.

Him? Dorie Friend? Who else?

He recounted the opening of his call. He informed the person that HHS had been following the case after being alerted by me. He told the official that he had urged me to authorize a federal investigation, but I refused. However, he advised, he could tell my resistance was waning.

"I ended on a strong note," Cushing said.

"What did you say?"

"I told him, if I finally did persuade you to file, the question is not whether Swarthmore has broken the law," he said. "The question is, how many times?"

I woke the next morning elated. I had been on campus for five days, met every term of readmission, and now the school had received a direct warning from the federal official who would be conducting an investigation if I authorized it.

With a new sense of power, I went to an on-campus phone and called Dickerson. My face fell. There was no decision; the issue still had to be resolved by the dean's committee. That was the same bunch that had thrown me out the first time.

That's it. Exultant a moment before, I now felt defeated. If even Cushing's call could not budge them, the fight was pointless. I'd already missed classes, and I couldn't turn in homework for courses I was surreptitiously attending. The school could drag this out, then refuse readmission or create such a delay that I could never catch up. Then they would have the bad grades they needed to get rid of me again.

I called my mother at the hotel and filled her in on the developments. "Come pick me up," I said dejectedly. "We need to go to Philadelphia so I can file for the investigation."

In the car, my mother could see I was devastated. She assured me that I would get into another school, but I knew it was a promise beyond her power to keep. From the hotel, I called Cushing and told him that hardball had failed and that I was coming to sign the paper work.

During our drive, we passed the off-campus office of Millington, Swarthmore's part-time internist. *Maybe he doesn't know everything that happened*, I thought.

"Mom," I said, "that's Dr. Millington's office. Pull in there. I'm going to try one last thing."

To my surprise, Millington met with us almost immediately. My anger built as we marched toward our chairs. There was no purpose in holding back. No reason to be polite. This was all or nothing.

"I don't know if you're aware of what's gone on," I began.

I launched into a monologue. The brain tumor charade, delays in my treatment and cancellation of diagnostic tests caused by the school's incompetence, the lies, the attempts to keep me out, the diagnosis by a school-hired psychiatrist who never spoke to me, the taped phone calls, my civil rights lawyer, the West Virginia law professor, and HHS investigators begging me to set them loose on Swarthmore.

"Now, here is where things stand," I said. "I don't give a *damn* about president's committees. I don't give a *damn* about dean's committees. I don't give a *damn* about who wants to meet with who or who wants to talk with who."

I held up two fingers. "Swarthmore has two hours. And if I am not readmitted by then, then I am going to Philadelphia and filing for a federal investigation. And then I am going to *The Philadelphia Inquirer*, bringing all the paper work and all the tapes. So either I get back in, or all of you can look forward to seeing your pictures in the paper."

Without giving Millington a chance to respond, I pushed back my chair. "I'll be in my dorm room."

My mother drove us to a restaurant for an early lunch. I picked at my food while she expressed pride in everything I had done. Whether I returned to school or not, she said, I'd fought for my beliefs. Even when people lost, they should be proud of taking on the challenge.

I murmured thanks for her words, but they rang hollow. Without readmission, I would lose another semester. Transfer deadlines had passed long ago. I would miss my junior year, then be forced to explain why to my next school. If I lied, I would be caught; if I told the truth, I would probably be rejected.

After lunch, she dropped me at school, where I could wait until my two-hour deadline passed. About forty-five minutes remained.

I walked into my dormitory, and headed up the stairs. Turning right, I saw the front of my door at the end of the hall. There was a message scribbled in blue on the attached whiteboard. The words—and a punctuation mark indicating confusion—became clear as I approached.

Janet Dickerson called to say welcome back (?)

"Yes!" I screamed, punching the air.

An email from

JANET DICKERSON, 2017

I have been thinking about you continuously since you wrote . . . I am incredibly pained and sorry to learn of your traumatic experiences at Swarthmore. Most of your testimony about your interactions with Dr. Whitaker and Dr. Warner was completely unknown to me, and that which I thought I knew has been put in a completely different context.

I was aware you had been diagnosed with epilepsy and that you were on medication that needed to be managed appropriately. At that time, my knowledge of epilepsy and the potential for seizures was relatively limited. I found it helpful to have a professional colleague in the administration who had epilepsy who could inform us laypersons about the condition. She coached us on how to respond when she had seizure activity, and she was an effective advocate for students who had epilepsy or related medical conditions. At the very least, as you say, she successfully challenged Dr. Whitaker in a meeting [about] you. But I know—now—that was not enough. That was not nearly enough.

The doctor had asserted that you were not managing your medications. I regret that on the night I was called in to deliver the decision to you that you would be required to withdraw until you were medically cleared to return, in accepting the recommendations of our health professionals, I contributed to the trauma that has so greatly affected your life. At the time I thought I had no reason to question their judgment.

Today, I think deans and campus health professionals have a much greater understanding of the causes and potential effects of epilepsy. Professional development opportunities are more routine, and the Americans with Disabilities Act (1990) requires that campuses accommodate students with chronic medical conditions.

. . . I view you as a role model for how to carry on and have an extraordinary life while dealing with a chronic, potentially debilitating condition. As I stated in my last message, I am—perhaps undeservedly—very proud of you.

Kurt, I have tried to be forthright in my response. I'm very, very sorry, and you have my heartfelt apologies.

CHAPTER TWENTY-THREE

The next morning, I awoke deeply depressed. It made no sense to me; after months of fighting, I had beaten Swarthmore. I was on my treatment schedule. I likely would graduate with my class. Yet my joy had lasted less than a day.

I lay in bed, contemplating these confusing feelings. Then the answer came—despite the tumult since my dismissal, I'd recovered only what I'd lost. So much effort and anguish, and all I accomplished was to stay in place. My seizures were better, but that had almost been an afterthought to me since November. I still lived with them. Now, with no target to battle, I was too wrung out to easily resume confronting the difficulties posed by epilepsy. I had learned a frightful lesson: I might face these conflicts—with jobs, coworkers, associates—for the rest of my life.

Stop feeling sorry for yourself.

I climbed out of bed to shower. The senior hired by the school to supervise our area of the dorm stopped me in the hall to ask about my state of mind and health. He may have been trying to be supportive, but I knew his job entailed reporting to the deans, so I lied. Everything was great, never happier.

I didn't feel guilty for the subterfuge—Swarthmore had made deceit a condition of my return. I was forbidden from revealing details of our confrontation. If I discussed what they had done, I could be deemed in violation of the terms of readmission. The administration also required that I see a psychiatrist, which was fine with me. Talking to a person would be more helpful than speaking into my tape recorder.

Things remained tense with Carl, but there were fewer arguments since we spoke far less. In my diary, I expressed concern that I may have caused long-term damage to his emotional health. To clear the air, I asked Carl and Franz to dinner that weekend, but neither showed up. Instead, I went back to spending time with Harry Schulz and the new friends I'd met through him.

On Monday, I returned to the office of my academic adviser, David Smith. For the second time, I produced my class schedule. No one had informed him I was back in school, and he repeated that he was forbidden from approving my courses.

"No, I've been readmitted," I said. "You can sign now."

To my surprise, he took my word and reviewed the card. For the first time, he saw I wanted to join his constitutional law seminar. That concerned him. He asked about my seizures—frequency, type, aftermath. I could feel it coming: He was going to reject me from taking his class.

"What medications are you taking?" he asked.

"Dilantin and Mysoline," I replied.

He leaned back in his wooden chair, its springs squeaking. "Whew!" he said. Then he sat up. "I don't think you're going to be able to handle the work necessary for this course."

Here we go. "Why not?"

"Those medications are pretty heavy stuff."

He explained that he knew someone treated with Dilantin, and it had slowed her thinking. From his description, it sounded as if his friend had been incapacitated. I wanted to say only an incompetent neurologist would leave a patient in that condition but held my tongue.

"I can handle the class," I replied. I described everything I had done related to law—debate, BGA, Balaban, other classes. He asked a number of questions, and I answered them all.

After pleading my case for forty minutes, I begged. "Please. Don't make a decision before you've even seen me in class."

He stared at me, then turned to his desk and signed the card. "Well, we'll see," he said. "I guess I'll take the chance."

I thanked him and retrieved the card. At the registrar's office, I marked that I would take the seminar pass-fail. I feared becoming a professor's self-fulfilled prophecy.

As required under the conditions of my return, I set an appointment with a neurologist, Dr. Guenter Haase at the University of Pennsylvania. Swarthmore had urged me to use a doctor at nearby Crozer-Chester Medical Center who had been recommended by someone at the health center. HHS, my lawyer, my family, and I all considered the suggestion absurd—I wanted my neurologist as far away from Swarthmore as possible. I feared I might stumble across a doctor who would serve as a pipeline of information back to the school.

The college demanded I let an official contact Haase to confirm that I was seeing him. I agreed, but only after telling Haase to say nothing beyond verifying my appointment. I instructed him to end the call if they asked for details or tried to provide any information about me.

My first consultation lasted forty-five minutes. I recounted my history and, to explain the rules I gave him regarding the college, launched into a tirade about my dismissal. He drew blood for testing. Then he asked about my diet. Did I eat a lot of sugar? How did I feel afterward? Did I ever notice an association between consuming sweetened foods and seizures?

Thinking he was heading down a path of nonsense, I lashed out. "I don't have sugar seizures or whatever it is you're talking about," I snapped.

The neurologist, a kindly and gentle-looking man, was taken aback by my vehemence. "That's not why I'm asking. I'm wondering if you've been tested for reactive hypoglycemia."

"I don't even know what that is."

"That means after you eat something sweet, your blood sugar rises and crashes quickly. That can serve as a seizure trigger."

I was about to argue, but he interrupted. "I'm not saying you have seizures from sugar. A sugar crash can be like stress or lack of sleep.

It can lead to a seizure in someone with epilepsy. Since you're still having seizures, we should run a test to see if there are any sugar problems."

No way. "Contact Dr. Naarden. I'm not doing anything without his approval."

Haase called the next day.

"I don't know how you're still standing," he said. He explained that Mysoline breaks down into phenobarbital. The blood tests showed my levels of that drug had hit seventy-two milligrams per milliliter.

"Is that high?"

"Like I said, I don't know how you're still standing. The upper therapeutic range tends to be around forty."

I thought for a second—I *had* been wobbly, short of breath. I had fallen over once, but I had ignored it. That made me angry at myself. I knew my Mysoline dosage had been increased, and amid all the school-related commotion afterward, I never bothered to have my blood levels checked as Naarden recommended. Haase told me he had already informed Naarden. I thanked him and called Dallas.

Naarden instructed me to reduce my Mysoline and added that I probably would not feel well as the levels dropped. Then he mentioned Haase's suggestion about a glucose tolerance test.

He expressed skepticism about my having reactive hypoglycemia. "Lightning doesn't strike twice in the same place," he said.

Still, he said, he didn't know everything. We discussed the test. I insisted that he review the results.

The phone rang in the hallway as I assembled my stereo in my room. Someone let me know the call was for me. On the line was my high school girlfriend, Mari Cossaboom; we had remained close even after our breakup years before.

"Kurt!" she exclaimed. "Your story is in *The Dallas Morning News!*"

I panicked. "About me and Swarthmore?"

"No, about Balaban!"

My heart raced. I had been taking calls to answer questions from

Hoppe, the *Morning News* reporter who had accepted documents and memos about Balaban. But I had feared the story was going nowhere despite the mountain of evidence I had uncovered.

"Read it to me!" I shouted.

"Okay. The headline is 'Ailing Doctor Fights for Job.'"

"Nice!"

My excitement grew as Mari recited the first paragraph.

> *In the four years Dr. Donald Balaban has suffered from multiple sclerosis, he has battled the bureaucracy three times to keep his job at the Dallas County Health Department. Now, he is paid $1,200 a month to do nothing.*

As she kept reading, I slapped the wall in delight at certain words and phrases. "Harassed," "threatened," "intimidation," "barren office," "growing mold," "caged paddy wagon," "struggle," "uncontroverted evidence."

I wanted to cry. *Justice won again.*

I thanked Mari and phoned Balaban. He told me fifty people had formed a group to fight for him because of the article. In a series of calls, I told members of AID that they needed to call local television stations and even national media organizations such as the Associated Press and United Press International. Then, as the story spread, they should pressure the county commissioners to hold hearings.

AID held a meeting to discuss strategy, and afterward, a director called me. They loved the plan, but no one in the group believed they could handle it. They asked if I would do the job from Swarthmore.

I leaned against the wall and thought. *Classes, Sixteen Feet, rehearsals for* Pippin, *hanging out with friends, seizures.* I didn't have the time. I just didn't.

"Okay," I said. "I'll do it."

Two days later, time opened up: I was asked to leave Sixteen Feet. I'd performed poorly at a recent rehearsal, probably because my drug levels had been soaring. Now another member of the group and Carl were in our dorm room, telling me I needed to go.

The other member spoke. "What if we're singing in Philadelphia, and you have a seizure during the performance—" he started.

I exploded in anger before he finished. Carl and Franz, who sat nearby, shouted in unison for the other singer to shut up. That was not the issue at all, Carl said. He asked everyone else to leave the room so he could talk to me alone.

He spoke in a quiet, supportive tone. "You're putting too much pressure on yourself, and you might hurt a lot of other people because of it. You're doing *Pippin*, you've got classes, you've got Sixteen Feet. You *know* stress causes seizures, and you're setting yourself up for more."

If that happened, everything could fall apart. "Sixteen Feet might die," he said. "You won't be able to direct the musical. You might flunk out. Stop trying to prove you're invincible. If you're not going to think about yourself, think about everybody who's going to be hurt if you load yourself up with too much responsibility."

I took in his words. Carl was speaking from the heart, expressing a pragmatism based on his knowledge of my health. Even though the conversation was about my leaving the group, the tension between us was gone, at least at that moment. He was talking to me as a friend, one with a greater sense of reality than I had. He was right. I was still being self-centered.

"Okay," I replied. "I'll drop out of the group."

"It's just time off," Carl said. He looked pained. "I feel really bad about this."

"Don't," I said. "You're right. I was being selfish. I wanted everything. I can't do that anymore."

Carl thanked me. "You'll be back."

Within four days of the *Morning News* article, I persuaded Dallas's ABC affiliate to broadcast a piece about Balaban and convinced a UPI reporter to write an article.

Later, my mother called with news. After the UPI report appeared, Balaban's story had been picked up by CNN. I decided the time had come to start pressuring the Dallas county commissioners. I phoned one, Nancy Judy, and left a message. On my second attempt, I reached her colleague Jim Jackson. I explained that I was calling about the Balaban story in the *Morning News*.

He chuckled. "You can't believe everything you read."

"Usually that's true, but not this time," I replied. "I reported that story. I gave my information to Christy Hoppe."

A second passed before he replied. "Who do you work for?"

I'm a nobody college student.

"Who I work for is irrelevant," I said. "I'm a reporter from Dallas who now lives on the East Coast and who's embarrassed for my hometown. I'm trying hard not to let this lead to a national scandal. That's why I'm calling. What are you going to do about Dr. Balaban?"

On the other end of the hall, another phone rang. A classmate called out that Nancy Judy was on the line. I knew he had yelled loud enough that Jackson must have heard.

"So here's where we are," I said. "I'll keep talking to commissioners, pushing for you to hold hearings. And if you don't, I guess Dallas will have to have a national scandal."

It was a pure bluff.

My hall mates discovered what I was doing with the Dallas politicians. While Carl and Franz found the undertaking bizarre, others considered it hilarious. I told each commissioner to call me on "my direct line," which was the number for the pay phone down the hall that never received incoming calls. When it rang, my hall mates knew to either be silent or simulate the noise of a newsroom. A student once started typing near the phone to lend realism with sound effects.

Stuart Couch, the member of AID who was also a counselor with the county, phoned to let me know that the commissioners were planning to bury the case. They suspected that this Kurt Eichenwald guy couldn't bring in more national news media.

I decided to go all in. I telephoned Jim Jackson and castigated him, saying I had heard about the plans. "I tried to protect Dallas," I said, "but if this is the path you want to take, I guess the commissioners and the city deserve the terrible publicity."

After a short back-and-forth, I hung up. I had done everything I could for Balaban. I could only hope my last tirade proved effective.

Couch called me two days later. "Did you arrange for a *60 Minutes* advance man to come here?" he asked.

"What?" *How would I know anyone from* 60 Minutes?

"Yeah, we're hearing from *60 Minutes.* Jackson is blaming you. He said you threatened to bring them in."

I chortled. "I never said anything about *60 Minutes.* And no, I had nothing to do with it."

"Well," Couch said with a laugh, "however it happened, everything has changed. They're scheduling hearings for March 1."

I hung up and told the story to my neighbors. This was total victory. With public hearings, the politicians would have to find a solution. Balaban was safe.

Weeks later, my mother forwarded a letter from the mayor of Dallas that had been addressed to me at my parents' home. I was rushing to lunch, so after fishing the envelope out of my mailbox, I ran to the dining hall, waiting to open it until I picked up my food. I found a table with some friends, then opened the letter. I broke into laughter.

"The mayor of Dallas is appointing me to his new task force for handicapped employment!" I exclaimed. "They still have no idea I'm a college student!"

The Balaban case drove my reporting for the rest of my career. I learned never to dismiss even the most unbelievable story. I discovered that the skills for persuading people to cooperate matched those for successful telemarketing: Never lie, assess character, appeal to principles, answer every question, and determine what impediments might keep them from speaking. Reporters need persistence, not the name of some major publication behind them, to crack a story. The next call, the next document, the next confrontation, might provide the information that exposes truth.

Dickerson stopped me in a hallway in the administration building and asked if I had seen my new neurologist yet.

"Nope," I lied. "But I have an appointment."

When she asked for the date, I told her I didn't remember but had it written down in my dorm room. She then discussed the seizures I had experienced since returning to school—she knew when they'd happened, where, and even that Carl had helped me back to my room after one occurred.

"Well," I said, "I've never denied I have poorly controlled epilepsy."

A few days later, my parents received a letter from Dickerson that they found unnerving in its detail. I had not seen my new neurologist, she wrote, then added out of nowhere that the school refused to assist me in traveling to Philadelphia for appointments. Instead, she again suggested I consult a neurologist near the school who had been recommended by the health center. None of us understood the travel condition. The University of Pennsylvania was walking distance from the commuter rail station; I had always planned to use public transportation. The repeated urging that I see their recommended neurologist convinced us all that the administration was up to something. Otherwise, why would they care who treated me?*

The letter also reported specifics of my seizures—including when and where they had happened—and described them as occurring at the same rate and intensity as in the first semester. She mentioned that the security department had never been contacted about these episodes and griped I was not keeping the health center staff informed, a strange complaint given that cutting off their involvement had been a condition of my return. She also disclosed she was checking my attendance—fortunately, I hadn't missed a single class.

She ended the letter with these words: "I have promised Kurt that he will be informed first, and consulted fully, if any new recommendations are made or decisions reached."

My parents sent the correspondence to Morrison, Cushing, my lawyer, and me. Cushing called me after reading it.

"Like I warned you, they've got you under a microscope," he said. "Be careful."

---

* Little blocked a friendly doctor from sharing information with the health center, even if I instructed the physician to keep it secret. The center maintained a relationship with me since they were technically responsible for all students, despite the restrictions on me. The stringent federal medical privacy rules that exist now were not yet in place, and even under those, doctors can share information without patient authorization.

As required under my readmission agreement, I searched for a psychiatrist, again making sure it was someone with no connection to Swarthmore. I found one in Philadelphia, and we discussed my history, my fears of injury, my confrontation with the college. Then the conversation sputtered. After our third session, he called it quits.

"You don't need a psychiatrist," he said.

Not only were my emotions—fear of seizures, anger at the school, guilt about hurting friends—normal, he said, but it would be worrisome if I didn't experience them. Our conversations had become repetitive, and he didn't want to waste our time trying to talk me out of rational feelings.

He suggested I find a support group for people with epilepsy or maybe a counselor. Obviously, he cautioned, I should stay away from Swarthmore's psychologists. But he promised, if the school called, he would only say that he could not discuss a patient. He would not tell them our sessions had ended.

I left the appointment amused. Weeks earlier, Swarthmore had argued I was so mentally ill that I could not return to school. Now a psychiatrist insisted I was too well balanced to need his help. I looked up the name of a counselor and wrote down the number. I would call him if I needed him.

As increasing numbers of Swarthmore students learned about my epilepsy, a bizarre and unexpected reaction set in: anger and hatred directed at Carl and Franz.

Despite the tensions between us, I understood that my bad decisions and medical mistreatment had left them overwhelmed with complex emotions—guilt, love, anger, exhaustion, helplessness, frustration. I believed our close friendships would recover if they were given enough time and distance from me. Yet they continued to come to my aid after a seizure, whether it occurred in our suite or if someone called them for help. At times, they were amazed that other students seemed unable to think rationally when confronted with a seizure. Once Carl was summoned to a classroom where I had gone into convulsions and was stunned to see that I had been left twisted inside a student chair/desk combination. He knew my contortions inside the metal rungs would likely leave me hurting when I awoke. *How much sense does it take to get the furniture off the person who's caught up like that?* he thought.

Despite their lack of knowledge, others who had learned about my epilepsy only weeks or months before began lecturing Carl and Franz. Although I didn't learn of this until years later, many of these new-comers treated me as a delicate victim while I was unconscious, and angrily castigated Carl or Franz when they spoke to me after a seizure with their typical ribald, teasing humor. Such joviality, these students insisted, demeaned the seriousness of a condition that they thought should be managed with gravity, not jokes.

Classmates I barely knew lashed out at my roommates. Once I went into convulsions in Mertz Hall and someone called Carl and Franz to help. I was near the entryway, and both of them were con-cerned that passersby would see me looking disheveled and injured while I was unconscious. "We were very conscious of your dignity," Franz told me years later about the Mertz seizure. "We didn't want you to be lying there with your shirt hanging out and your face sideways in front of people. We wanted people to know you as the Kurt that you were. We didn't want to expose you."

Most people agreed to leave me alone when asked. One student, Anna, was drunk and started asking innumerable questions that my roommates considered invasive of my privacy. Franz told her that I was fine and that I just needed to be left alone.

Anna exploded. "You two guys are such assholes!" she shouted. "You think that you're the only ones who know anything about this. You act as though this is your own personal problem. Well, why don't you two go fuck yourselves!"

She stormed away, leaving Carl and Franz behind, stunned. Years later, Franz still described that moment as traumatic, because no one had ever spoken to him with a voice laced with such hatred.

My roommates protected me by not disclosing that I had become the object in some tug-of-war, with them on one side and, on the other, near-strangers eager to join the excitement. Carl likened it, years later, to members of a platoon returning from years at war and being lectured by soldiers who had never seen a battlefield.

Only once did I witness this kind of behavior myself. We were in our suite and a friend named Shelly was visiting. Carl was in a bad mood and yelled at me about something. Shelly in turn angrily demanded that he treat me better because of all I had been through. Before I could intervene, Carl jumped up and scrambled for the door.

"Fuck you!" he shouted as he rushed out of the room.

"Fuck you too!" Shelly roared back.

She turned to me, the anger still visible in her expression. Before she said a word, I brought my index finger close to her face.

"Don't you *ever* talk to him like that *ever* again!" I snapped, making no effort to hide my fury. She appeared stunned that I had turned on her for what she saw as rising to my defense.

"You have *no idea* what he has been through," I said angrily. "No one—*no one*—has any right to criticize him."

I took a deep breath. "If anyone owes *anyone* an apology, it's me! To him!"

Naarden was wrong. Lightning struck twice; I failed the glucose tolerance test. In addition to epilepsy, I had reactive hypoglycemia. When I ate anything sweet, my blood sugar rose and then crashed. He sent me a letter with the details, saying that the test suggested I was prediabetic.

I traveled to an appointment with Haase, my Philadelphia neurologist, who reviewed the results. He told me that the sugar crashes could be serving as a trigger for seizures, just like lack of sleep or alcohol. Haase instructed me to change my diet—I could no longer eat or drink anything sweetened.

I took the news in stride; choosing between syrup and seizures was easy. In fact, discovering this second medical problem excited me. Maybe this would be key to improved control.

That night at a rehearsal for *Pippin*, I told friends about the finding. They asked if I was upset and were reassured when I said no. Later that evening, a student who walked the campus selling Dunkin' Donuts arrived in the theater. Absentmindedly, I purchased a cream-filled donut and brought it toward my mouth.

"Kurt, *no!*" screamed Jocelyn Roberts, the *Pippin* choreographer and Carl's new girlfriend. "Don't eat that!"

I looked at the donut. *Sugar.* I had been so close to taking a bite, and I really wanted it. A cast member took it out of my hand and walked away eating the sweet snack.

For decades, I would crave that cream-filled donut.

Pippin was a big success. On the last night, after the crowds left, I jumped off a chair and screamed, "*Fuck you,* Swarthmore!" The celebratory reception of the musical boosted my prominence on campus. Swarthmore could never again label me as nonfunctional.

The number of seizures lessened throughout the second semester, but they never stopped. Around that time, I experienced the nighttime convulsion that led to my being buried in snow. After my rescue, which led to my screaming on the staircase as I stared at my injured hands, Franz turned up and brought me to my bedroom. My clothes were caked with ice and frozen urine, and I was trembling from the cold. Franz took off my pants, put me to bed, and covered me with a quilt. The next day, I woke on my bedroom floor. The room smelled from the urine that had melted overnight. Harry dropped by later, and the two of us followed my trail in the snow, eventually finding my books and glasses at the spot where I had dug myself out.

A month later, I informed Carl and Franz I would not be living with them our senior year. Their relief was obvious. Harry and I planned to room together, but an official at the housing office refused to allow it; Harry would be a resident assistant, and so could not room with another student. Speaking only to me, she said I had guilt-tripped Harry into offering to share a double with me. When I told Harry about her comments, he exploded. I told him it didn't matter; I had experienced worse. Besides, I would just take a single on his hallway and, except at bedtime, would leave my door wide open whenever I was inside. I would be fine.

As the end of junior year approached, Carl, Franz, and an assortment of their new friends planned a picnic. I wasn't invited—no surprise. Even though I would not be living with them anymore, I believed the damage I'd caused to our friendship was irreparable.

The day of the event, the crowd gathered in our suite, then headed out. I was on my bed, reading a book. Carl returned and appeared in my doorway.

"Are you coming?" he asked.

I was confused. "To what?"

"To the picnic."

"I wasn't invited."

"Of *course* you were invited," Carl protested.

I laid the book on my chest. "Carl. I wasn't invited."

He sighed, then paused.

"Okay," he said. "You're right. You weren't invited. Now *I'm* inviting you. Will you come?"

I smiled and sat up. "Absolutely."

And that was it. There was no further discussion about our troubled year, no recriminations. Apparently, my decision to move out had been effective. From that moment on, my friendship with Carl and Franz was restored. We remain close to this day.

Although I still experienced convulsions every two weeks or so, I managed to load up on classes in my senior year. By taking one extra credit each semester, I reached my four-year goal of graduating with my class.

Carl invited me back to Sixteen Feet and reappointed me administrator. I joined the college newspaper to write pieces mostly about mismanagement of the college. To my astonishment, my best sources were school officials who knew I had kept quiet about what they had done to me.

As graduation neared, I visited the registrar. She was aware of my health problems, and I asked if I could attach a letter to my transcript explaining what had occurred. That way, if anyone ever reviewed my grades, the correspondence would clarify how sick I had been throughout college. She dug up my records and returned to the counter.

"I don't understand," she said.

"What?"

"Why do you need a letter?"

"Well, to explain—"

"Kurt," she interrupted, "don't you know? You're graduating with academic distinction."

I ran to the office of Professor Al Bloom, who had advised me in my freshman year to ignore my grades and focus on understanding what I was taught. I excitedly told him the news.

"Not a surprise," he said. "I always tell students, if you just worry about learning the material, the grades will come."

I gave him an enormous hug.

Two days before graduation, I visited Gil Stott, an associate provost with the reputation as one of the kindest people in the administration. He knew nothing about what had happened to me.

I recounted the story of my dismissal, the legal violations, the fight to return. My family had been robbed of a semester of tuition, I said. The school's assertions about my inability to survive Swarthmore had been proven false: I was prominent in my class, graduating with distinction. I had made an impact, despite seizures. I had been thrown out on the basis of lies, discrimination, and ignorance. I wanted our money back.

Stott looked sympathetic. "I'm sorry, but there's nothing that can be done about that," he said.

"Okay," I replied. "But I need to make this clear."

I stood, ready to walk out on this point. "No matter what happens in the future, no matter what I become, I will never return here. I will, however, contribute ten dollars a year by deducting it from what Swarthmore owes me. Which means I'll be long dead before the school gets a dime."

"I'm sorry you feel that way," Stott said. "And I'm sorry this happened to you."

I choked up. Stott, uninvolved in my dismissal, was the only person at Swarthmore to have ever apologized.

"Thank you," I whispered before leaving the room.

A light sprinkle fell on the morning of graduation. The school announced that, for the first time in its history, ceremonies would move from the beautiful outdoor amphitheater to the ugly, hot gymnasium.

The rain stopped an hour before the scheduled time, but the school refused to reverse its position. Our class would break the more-than-a-century-old tradition. To me, this was another example of administrative incompetence, fortified by arrogance, and it triggered my focused rage.

As students lined up outside the gymnasium, I called for revolt. "Don't walk in!" I yelled. "If we don't go, they can't have graduation. Demand we have it at the amphitheater. Don't let us be the ones who end the record."

Someone objected, worried we might get in trouble.

"What are they going to do?" I asked. "Throw us out?"

My rabble rousing won some converts, and soon the new president, David Fraser, faced a potential uprising. He marched the class to the amphitheater, telling us to gather in front of the stage.

"So you understand, you don't graduate when you're handed your diploma," he informed the group. "It's when the president announces that you are graduates."

With that, Fraser uttered the magic words. "Congratulations," he said. "You are all graduates of Swarthmore College."

Now, he said, the class needed to return to the gymnasium, where families and friends waited. When the time came to receive our diplomas, we lined up as we had practiced doing the day before.

The moment arrived when I was the next to be called. I stood beside Janet Dickerson, who was there to direct each student onto the stage.

I heard my name, and before I took a step, I looked her in the eye.

"I told you I'd make it," I said.

She shook my hand. "Congratulations," she replied.

An audio letter from

FRANZ PAASCHE, 1986

It's hard enough to excel at Swarthmore, but it's virtually inconceivable that someone could graduate with distinction while having so many seizures over a period of years. Somehow, you just had a tremendous will to continue your life and to continue to strive to do all the things you wanted.

It's funny how something that was so painful could at the same time lead to such rich emotional fulfillment and friendship. I guess that's something that I've known about you. I don't know, I guess I've told you that, because you've experienced such agony, I think you're also much more able to have joy. The depths and the heights go together.

That's how I think about the whole experience. I never use the word "epilepsy." In describing what you have to someone else, I guess I use epilepsy, but when I think about you I never think of you as "an epileptic"; I never have and I don't think I ever will. I think of you as Kurt, who has this problem that came on suddenly and unfairly and that I'm sure you will conquer someday. "Epilepsy" just sounds so clinical and distant. What you have is very personal, and separate, and part of us.

CHAPTER TWENTY-FOUR

Brightly colored pins dotted a map of the United States on my bedroom wall. Each represented a form of transportation: red for subways and trains, green for buses, and yellow for taxis. The results weren't encouraging. The main cities where I could work at a newspaper were Washington, D.C., New York, Chicago, and maybe Philadelphia. Yet getting hired in those locations, I thought, was possible only for journalists who cut their teeth in small towns, places where I would have to drive.

It was the summer of 1983. I shared a small house with three others in an Arlington, Virginia, neighborhood built after World War II. I had been hired for a three-month unpaid internship at the *Washington Monthly*, a small political magazine housed at a brownstone in Adams Morgan, the center of Washington's Hispanic immigrant community. Fortunately, I could forgo a salary; the remaining savings from my telemarketing days could cover a few months of expenses.

My choice of the *Monthly* was part of a plan I had pursued for more than a year. To obtain a reporting job after graduation, I would need a collection of news or magazine articles I wrote in the past; the best chance for getting into print would have been through a summer newspaper internship after my junior year, but no publication hired me. I'd also applied to be a volunteer at *Chicago Lawyer* magazine that summer. The year before, while living with Carl in Chicago, I made contacts who could introduce me to staff at the magazine. During spring break of my junior year, I traveled to Chicago for summer job interviews and met with the editor, Rob Warden, but he rejected me as well. I thanked him for his time and, as I headed toward the door, saw a pile of advertisements on the typesetting machine. Somebody had to click away at the keyboard for hours so the ads could be printed in the magazine.

Necessity gave me an idea, one that I knew might backfire. But if I'd learned anything from fighting Swarthmore, it was the value of pushing boundaries by taking risks.

I accepted an unpaid summer job at a nonprofit in the same building as *Chicago Lawyer*. Without realizing that I might inflict the same damage as I had on Carl the previous summer, I persuaded my friend Harry—who by then knew how to handle my seizures—to try his luck in Chicago and share an apartment with me. Fortunately my health stayed mostly steady, with only four or five convulsions during those two and a half months.

Every weekday, I headed to work at the nonprofit. During lunch, when Warden wasn't around, I took the elevator downstairs to the magazine's office. I introduced myself to the managing editor and offered to typeset ads if he taught me how to use the machine. He never asked if I worked there, and within twenty minutes, I was banging away at the keyboard. I started arriving at the magazine early in the morning, leaving for my real job at 9:00 A.M., returning at lunch, heading back upstairs at 1:00 P.M., then typesetting after 5:00 P.M. until the office closed.

I soon learned that working late in a city posed risks that had been unknown to me at school. One night, I woke up after a grand mal seizure when someone kicked me in the stomach. I heard voices, laughter, and taunts. A group of teenagers was beating me, enjoying the chance to terrify a defenseless person. I tried to see where I was. Pavement, in a lighted area. I heard a train. An "L" station. The teens stopped tormenting me when the train pulled in, perhaps fearing they would be caught. I stood, stumbled onto the train, and dropped into a seat. Later, an "L" employee woke me, possibly at the end of the line, and I took a taxi home. In the immediate aftermath, I felt nothing about the event; I just wanted to push it out of my mind, to ignore my vulnerability that the assault revealed. I finally discussed the attack many months later, and then only with a counselor. I at first waved it off as insignificant, just a consequence of living in a city. Only after he pressed me did my true feelings—of violation, weakness, fear, embarrassment—finally emerge.

Weeks passed at *Chicago Lawyer* with no one ever asking who I was or why I was there. The managing editor—assuming I had been hired as an intern—assigned me a story as a reward for my typesetting work. I reported and wrote a lengthy article. The night the editors were closing that issue of the magazine, Warden reviewed each story after they had been laid out for printing. He studied mine, remembered who I was, then looked toward the typesetter where I sat entering last-minute ads.

"Kurt! I told you that you couldn't work here!" he shouted.

I shrugged. "Yeah, I know. I decided to ignore you."

Warden shook his head. "Goddamn it. That means you wrote this as a freelancer and not an intern. We have to pay you."

I smiled at him.

Pause. "Okay," he said. "Now you're an intern. And I'm giving you a new assignment. And *this* one doesn't pay."

"Fine by me." I chuckled.

As I'd hoped, my *Chicago Lawyer* articles helped me land the *Washington Monthly* internship after college. The magazine seemed a promising career launching pad: The founder, Charlie Peters, hired inexperienced young editors, most of whom went on to major publications such as *The Washington Post*, *The Atlantic*, and *The New Republic*. I thought that if I worked hard at my internship, I'd have a chance of being hired as an editor, giving me entrée to a newspaper in a city with mass transit.

Just as at *Chicago Lawyer*, boring chores at the *Monthly* had been ignored. Letters and packages sat in piles in a makeshift mailroom, and I saw an opportunity. I arrived early every day and stayed late, opening letters, tossing out junk, and taking anything that looked useful to the editors. I fetched coffee and became something of an errand boy. I stayed at the office as much as I could, fearful of missing an opportunity for real work.

One day, I got my break. A friend of Peters had written an article about a politically connected bank, but editors found it weak. One of them, Jonathan Rowe, asked if I could beef up the story with additional reporting. I jumped on the assignment, digging through records at the Library of Congress and conducting phone interviews. Eventually, I returned to Rowe with my conclusion: The piece had missed a bigger story about banking regulation. Rowe asked if I would be willing to do the rewrite, and I eagerly agreed. My version had little relation to the original story, and Rowe thought I should have the byline.

A few days later, I arrived at the office and heard a loud argument upstairs. Tim Noah, another *Monthly* editor, explained that Peters's friend was angry and still wanted the byline.

"That's fine," I said. I would rather have the editors think they owed me a favor than just add another article to my clips.

Rowe edited the piece, asking me to stay nearby in case he had questions. Eventually, he switched to working on a small accompanying piece—known as a sidebar—that he had written. He removed his byline and typed in mine.

"Wait," I said. "I didn't write that."

"Kurt, be quiet," Rowe replied amiably.

That was my first article after college graduation: The one I wrote did not have my byline; the one I didn't did.

I loved the *Monthly*. The best part was that no one cared about my epilepsy. If I had a seizure, people nearby followed the instructions I had discussed earlier with them, then they returned to their jobs. If I arrived at the office struggling from a recent seizure, the editors asked after my well-being, then told me to get to work. For the first time in years, I didn't fear someone might upend my life because of my health.

As my internship neared its end, I asked Peters to consider me for an editor position when one opened up. He wanted me to continue writing for the magazine, he said, but I could never be on staff. Finances were tight, and a longtime employee suffered chronic health problems; because of that, Peters often tussled with the company that provided group health coverage. If he hired me, the insurer could cancel the policy or raise rates beyond the magazine's budget. Given my preexisting condition, no company would sell me individual coverage that I could use to avoid being on the *Monthly's* group policy. Under my father's insurance with the medical school where he worked, I could retain coverage till the age of twenty-five, but I hoped my job would last longer than that. I would eventually need the *Monthly's* group insurance, and that could lead to everyone at the magazine losing their coverage. Charlie apologized for telling me that because of insurance, I could never be hired.

"That makes sense," I replied. "Thanks for being honest."

Afterward, I visited Rowe to discuss job prospects. He mentioned that he had previously worked for the Center for Study of Responsive Law, run by consumer advocate Ralph Nader. An old colleague had told Rowe that the group was looking for someone to write a book about state governments. Rowe promised to contact his friend and urge him to interview me for the position.

The prospect struck me as promising. Working as a consumer advocate was not a path to a newspaper job, but writing a book certainly could be.

In recommending me for the job, Rowe never mentioned my health, and neither did I. Despite the Nader group's reputation as a fighter for the little guy, I trusted no one when it came to applying for work.

One of my first interviews for the job was with a young woman who chatted with me in her cubicle about my background. She asked how I would approach writing the book, and I gave a detailed response based on some intel from Rowe.

Then a voice called out, "Does anybody know anything about seizures?"

I stopped midsentence. "I do," I shouted.

I was brought outside, where an older man was having convulsions. This was only the second grand mal seizure I ever witnessed; I had been too frightened at Swarthmore to reveal my epilepsy when a kitchen worker needed help during his convulsions. Not this time.

A passerby was pinning the man's shoulders down, and I told him to let go. Then I slipped off my jacket and slid it beneath the man's head before checking his pockets for a bottle of medicine or a medical-alert card. I looked up at the terrified faces in the crowd, expressions I recognized, and was surprised that they found something so minor to be so shocking.

Someone approached with a spoon to put in the man's mouth. I explained why that was unnecessary, and the onlookers relaxed. Eventually, the man woke up extremely disoriented. I explained what was going on and where he was. Two people helped me take him to the Nader office, where he gradually became more coherent. Soon he said he wanted to go home. I told the staffer who had been interviewing me that I would return in a few minutes; I wanted to accompany the man to make sure he was not heading out too quickly.

Walking down the street on that sunny day, I asked if he wanted me to stay with him until he reached his destination. He declined but seemed uncomfortable. I told him not to feel embarrassed. I understood that emotion, I explained, because I also had seizures, but we had no reason for shame.

We reached the corner. He took my hand and squeezed it. "We're both gonna be all right," he said.

I watched him slowly cross the street, and for the first time, I believed that was true.

My interviews with the Nader group continued for days. While in the office, I met other staffers and engaged them in conversation. One, named Russ, relayed the organization's history. I noticed many filing cabinets labeled with the words "American Automobile Association." I asked Russ if someone had written a book about the AAA.

"Not really," he told me. There had been a report about a decade earlier, but it was fairly inconsequential. "The AAA has been an obsession of Ralph's for years. But there's no story there, so it just keeps getting assigned to people they want to push into quitting."

That seemed cruel. *If they want to get rid of employees*, I thought, *they should fire them, not waste their time on a pointless assignment.*

My final interview was with Nader's top aide, John Richard, and took place in a side area of the cluttered offices. Supposedly, the meeting was a formality. Again, I discussed how I would handle the book, and then he told me the salary. To a recent college graduate, the awful pay sounded like a fortune.

Richard asked his last question. "If we offered you the job, would you take it?"

"Absolutely," I replied.

Wait a minute. Medical bills.

"Um, hold on. Does the job come with group health insurance?"

Richard gave me an odd look. "Yes."

"Okay," I said. "Then I'll take it."

We shook hands, and I left the building, ecstatic that I was a leading candidate for a position that ultimately could help launch a newspaper career.

The next day, my home phone rang. On the line was John Richard calling with good news. "We've decided to offer you the job," he said.

"That's great!"

He again told me the salary. "But, rather than putting you on a group policy, we're going to pay you five hundred dollars more so you can buy private insurance."

Oh God, I thought. *As soon as I'm off my parents' policy, I'll be uninsured.*

I was about to reply, then stopped. I'd screwed up the day before—my question about group insurance had revealed I probably had a health problem. Now I had to tell the truth.

"I can't get private insurance, John."

"*Why not?*" he asked rapidly. He sounded almost proud to have trapped me into answering the question raised by my response the day before.

"You could have asked me yesterday," I answered. "I have epilepsy, and my seizures are poorly controlled. No insurance company will sell me a policy. Most don't cover preexisting conditions or don't kick in to cover chronic health problems for almost a year."

He drilled me with questions about my epilepsy, each more pointed than the last. None were about how to handle a seizure; instead, he focused on the severity of my convulsions and how they might affect the staff.

Richard suggested no solutions for the insurance problem, which concerned me. If I wasn't included on the group policy, my employment would always be tenuous. My job there could only last until my twenty-fifth birthday, the day I would be off my parents' insurance. I couldn't gamble that I would immediately find a job with group insurance at that exact time. I would have to walk away from the organization whenever I found an employer—any employer—with the insurance I needed to protect myself from the destruction of my finances, my credit, and my health.

When he finished, I said I would see him in the morning. Afterward, I sat on the couch, worn-out. *This could be bad.*

I strolled down a treelined street near Dupont Circle the next day, anxious but ready for what I hoped would still be my first day of work. When I arrived in the Nader offices, a woman approached.

"Hi, I'm Kurt Eichenwald. I'm starting here today."

"Hello, Kurt! Welcome aboard. Let me get you set up."

Her bright smile relieved me. She gave me some forms to fill out, then handed me keys for the building and office doors.

"I'm sorry. We don't have much room," she said. "There's a cubicle about to open, but until then all I have is a storage area."

She showed me the space. There was a desk and a phone, more than enough for me to do the job. "This is great," I said.

"Well, I'll move you to the better spot as soon as it's available."

She told me where to find office supplies, wished me luck, and headed out. I fetched a pen and a yellow pad so I could get to work. My panic had been for nothing. *I have to stop being so easily frightened,* I thought.

Over the next hour, a few staff members dropped in to welcome me to the organization. Then John Richard appeared.

"Kurt, could I speak with you?"

"Sure," I said. I followed him across the office to a spot where we could talk alone.

"We reviewed your résumé again, and we're worried you might not actually have enough experience to write a book . . ." he began.

Oh God. Here it comes.

". . . so we think it's smarter to give you a freelance assignment, then decide if you're up to the book."

"I don't understand," I said. "You have clips of my freelance articles. What is one more going to show?"

"You haven't written anything for us," Richard said. "We don't know how much of your articles was written by you and how much was the editors."

I protested—by that standard, no one could be hired without first taking a freelance assignment for the Nader group. But I quickly gave up. *What kind of outfit, I asked myself, would hire someone after weeks of interviews, then take away the job a day after discovering the new employee has a chronic health condition?* They had known everything about me when they offered me the job—everything except my epilepsy. This wasn't about skills.

Richard trotted out conditions: I was off staff with no salary. Instead I would be paid five hundred dollars when the article was published. Plus, I was forbidden from working in the offices.

The last rule hurt the most. Just like Swarthmore, the Nader group wanted me out of sight. Still, I masked my disappointment. I had learned from being thrown out of school: Gather information, assess, then plan a response.

"Okay," I replied. "What's the assignment?"

"It's something that's important to Ralph," Richard said. "We want you to investigate the American Automobile Association."

Say nothing. I remembered Russ's words: Everyone knew there was no AAA story. That was the assignment given to anyone they wanted to force out.

I accepted the project and gathered my things to leave. As I walked onto the street, I shoved my hand into my pocket: Yes, I still had the keys I had been given that morning. I remembered the lesson from Health and Human Services. I would ignore Richard; instead, I would return in the morning to occupy the Nader offices every workday, for as long as I could. If they wanted to get rid of me, they'd have to throw me out.

The next day, after using my keys to let myself into the offices, I hurried to the storage area where I had set up shop, hoping to avoid Richard's watchful eye. The spot was perfect: It held filing cabinets stuffed with more than a decade's worth of reporting about the AAA. I opened the top drawer of one cabinet and pulled out some records.

I had a plan, driven by my rage. If Richard ordered me to leave, he would have to explain his logic for denying me access to the AAA documents. Of course, I knew there was no AAA story in those files. I had a different idea. I would give them an article, but not the one they might expect.

My strategy for fighting against discrimination had evolved. Now if someone tried to deny me my rights, I would strike back hard. I expected—or at least hoped—that my plan would teach the Nader organization a very rough lesson.

I contacted Rowe at the *Washington Monthly* and told him what was happening; I had no doubt Richard was trying to drive me out because of my health problems. Rowe insisted it must be a misunderstanding and advised I speak to Nader directly.

Days passed with nobody ordering me out of the office. Either Richard didn't know I was there, or he wanted to avoid a confrontation. Eventually, I saw Nader arrive in the office. I approached him and described how I had been hired to write the book, only to have my job changed after I revealed my epilepsy. I watched him as I spoke; he didn't look at me.

"Talk to John Richard," he said as he walked away. "He'll take care of it."

Sometime later, the phone rang at my desk. On the line was Sidney Wolfe, a physician sometimes called "Ralph Nader's doctor" who headed the Health Research Group, a Nader organization. I braced for another discussion about my health.

Wolfe's questions were reasonable and informed, not like the ones Richard had posed. After a few minutes, he wrapped up the call. "Ralph's just being a hypochondriac," he said.

I hung up more anxious than before. Now I had reason to believe the aversion to my seizures might be from Nader himself. I had to find a new job and get out of there fast.

About a month earlier, I'd attended a party at the invitation of a *Washington Monthly* editor. The event had been a soirée of the capital's political and media power players. I introduced myself to some people, and now I needed those contacts to help me find a new employer before I turned in my AAA article. So I stayed home one day, phoning everyone I had run into at the get-together. I called former *Monthly* editors, such as Michael Kinsley, who ran *The New Republic.* I received invitations to write freelance articles for various magazines but no job offers.

Then, some luck. I reached a young journalist named Tina Rosenberg whom I had met at the party. She wrote for many magazines and struck me as brilliant. To my surprise, she remembered me. I told her I was in a bad situation and needed a job.

"Actually," she said, "I'm about to quit mine."

She had joined the speech-writing staff of Walter Mondale's presidential campaign, she told me, but hated the work. She was a journalist, not an advocate, and wanted to move on. The chief speech writer, Ross Brown, needed someone for Rosenberg's slot, and she offered to pass on my résumé.

Working as a speech writer seemed like a step backward. Then again, it would get me out of the Nader organization and possibly grow my contacts in journalism. My current situation was untenable, and the longer I stayed, the more my career would veer off track. Any option was better than that.

I met Ross Brown a few days later at Mondale campaign headquarters in Georgetown. She radiated the demeanor of a political junkie— stressed, with a rat-a-tat-tat speaking style but friendly and no-

nonsense. After I met with one other person on the staff, Brown told me the job was mine. This time, though, I wasn't going to accept immediately.

"Thank you," I said. "Now I want you to withdraw your job offer."

A puzzled look. "What?"

"Withdraw your offer. I have something to tell you. In the past, after hearing this, some people have chosen to push me out. I'd rather be turned down for the job than work in a place where I'm not wanted."

"Okay," she said hesitantly. "The job offer is withdrawn."

"Thanks. I have epilepsy. It's poorly controlled, and I still have grand mal seizures. That means that I might have convulsions in the office."

Brown glanced toward the wall in front of her desk, appearing to be deep in thought. Finally she spoke. "I don't want to be the kind of person this matters to," she said.

"Then don't be," I replied.

She nodded and turned to face me again. "I'm not," she said decisively. "The job is yours if you want it."

I completed my AAA article. The Nader group wanted something explosive, and I delivered just that.

Rather than exposing wrongdoing at the AAA, the piece detailed the secrets behind Nader's obsession with the auto club, based on the consumer advocacy group's own files. I found documents dating back to 1969 and 1970 in which Nader demanded that AAA officials work with him as consumer advocates for car buyers. The letter Nader had received in response was, to say the least, not complimentary. The records showed that AAA's missive and its refusal to join his cause had enraged Nader; he'd ordered an investigation of the group, assembling a twelve-member team to dig up dirt.

Nader publicly announced the project in 1971, and the AAA agreed to cooperate. The internal records showed that the Nader researchers planned to feign objectivity and utilize the auto club's assistance to advance preconceived attacks. While there was no indication Nader knew, one investigator stole a pile of the AAA documents out of its headquarters. Nader followed up weeks later with a demand that the association release all of its financial records, and soon, AAA ended its cooperation out of a belief that they were being set up. In August 1971, Nader announced his report would be ready by winter and demanded to speak at the AAA annual meeting the following month. After the association refused this demand, the investigators picketed the conference while the AAA president assailed Nader for harming the cause of public safety. That angered Nader more. The report promised for the winter of 1972 took three years, and it landed virtually unnoticed. The investigators found almost nothing. Nader demanded more digging.

My article chronicled these events as they'd played out over more than a decade, casting the undertaking as a relentless, biased pursuit of AAA primarily because it had insulted Nader personally. In the last paragraphs, I disclosed that this was my final day working for Nader and that I had been hired as a speech writer for Mondale's presidential campaign. I included my new office phone number, where they could reach me for questions.

Once I finished the final draft, I slid the article into an envelope labeled for John Richard, dropped it at the front desk, and walked out the door for the last time.

A few weeks later, a thousand-dollar check from the Nader group arrived at my home, twice the amount the group had offered. By paying that money, the Center for Study of Responsive Law had purchased the rights to my article, meaning I was not allowed to sell it anywhere else.

The story was never published.

If you can, let all of the pain of the last few weeks go. Try to start over. Evaluate for yourself, take your destiny in your own hands. Without risk, we cannot live life, only exist. We all must accept that, and then you get on with living your life to the fullest of your potential. You could have chosen the easiest way out by choosing to live here at home, a non-productive human being. I could have tried to force you to stay—wrapped you in cotton batting—and kept you safe. However, we both chose the risk of your living a full and productive life. Was there a choice? Again, Kurt, I am sorry for all the confusion and hurt. Now get on with it! I love you always.

An audio letter from

FRANZ PAASCHE, 1986

I remember my personal compassion and anger at what had happened with your health and I remember the pain that comes from that. Then I watched a whole other thing, which is this whole other pain that can come from people that don't understand. You were such a bright, capable person going through those problems, problems with insurance and people screwing around with you. It just made me angry. It was just incredibly ironic that these liberal institutions—and you were working for solidly liberal, politically correct institutions with politically correct people. In the abstract they could be compassionate about minorities, and the oppressed, and the handicapped, but when they were faced with you straight on, with somebody who had a problem, and it wasn't so much an abstract societal responsibility but their responsibility to do something to make it livable for you at their job, to ensure you some kind of security through insurance, people just didn't measure up. It's very ironic that people who say one thing politically can't deliver.

CHAPTER TWENTY-FIVE

The streets of Washington around Union Station bustled with pedestrians and traffic. I watched the commotion through a window at a table in The Dubliner, an Irish pub favored by lobbyists, politicians, and journalists. When I arrived, the greeter urged me to sit at the bar; during busy lunchtimes, they likely preferred holding tables for parties of two or more. But I declined. Barstools scared me—collapsing in a seizure from that height could cause a serious injury when I hit the floor.

A waiter placed my hamburger and fries in front of me, and although I was hungry, I felt in no mood to eat. My job at the Mondale campaign started the following week, and I had decided to spend the day sightseeing. I'd passed men and women dashing about in power clothes, rushing to important jobs or critical meetings. After hours of meandering, I realized something was wrong—I was incomplete. I had wandered into The Dubliner not so much for a meal as to think.

I sipped my diet soda. Suddenly, that night at Northwestern when I had planned my life flashed into my mind, accompanied by an unformed sense that I had lost my focus.

As my food cooled, I revisited the questions I had contemplated during those hours. What did I want from life? What was I fighting for? I watched people walk by a window near me, many of them probably so caught up in work that they barely noticed the world around them. *Any of us could be dead by morning.* If this was our last day, would we have fully lived our lives? Or would we all have frittered our time away focused on the inconsequential?

Working at a newspaper isn't enough. That was just a job. It was important, but it didn't *matter.* We live, we die, and somebody else takes over our spot at the office. I accomplished my goal of graduating with my class, but building a life based on employment seemed a shallow self-betrayal. I had envisioned so much more at Northwestern but had since ignored most of it. If I became a newspaper reporter, would I feel complete? If I still had seizures, would I have nothing else of value, no objective to pursue to prevent my epilepsy from assuming a vast role in my day-to-day existence?

I needed a more important purpose. I stared at the empty seat across the table. Then he appeared in my imagination. A young man, healthy and strong, happy with life. He was my someday son, a child from my marriage to a woman I'd never met.

A new touchstone emerged, one within my control. I made my plans, establishing a new goal to take the place of my obsession about graduating with my class. In a few decades, I decided, I would return to The Dubliner with my oldest child. My wife and I would have dedicated ourselves to raising our children to be good people. That would be the most important thing in my life: my family, not my job. And if I managed to reach that future, if I never gave up, I would be at this same table, in the same chair, and he would sit directly across from me.

And then I would tell him I was proud of him.

At the Mondale campaign, I specialized in sermons. Otherwise, as the junior-most of three speech writers, I just helped out the others and was lucky if I wrote a sentence or two for Mondale's important appearances. But his talks at church services somehow fell to me.

Speech writing is nothing like what people imagine. We were no Svengalis, spinning words that Mondale slavishly recited. We wrote, then listened to tapes of his appearances to learn which phrases he liked. But the stump speech rarely changed; mostly we put new powder on the same old face.

I was appointed liaison to the travel and schedule meetings, putting me at the heart of the operation. I was a nobody, the cat watching the queen, but from my perch against the wall, I saw the inner workings of a presidential campaign. I listened as officials planned articles for the next day's newspapers based on leaks and "exclusives" that were actually just strategic manipulations by the staff. Without fail, newspapers carried stories planned at that meeting, including "dirt" whispered to reporters about fictitious infighting, fed to provide the designated leakers with future credibility.

Anything could be faked, and reporters often fell for it. Mondale gave a speech where he claimed to be so mad about a development that he was tossing aside his prepared remarks. The news reported Mondale's angry action. In fact, the statement that he was no longer going to use his prewritten speech was part of the prewritten speech.

The most bizarre part of the job, though, was joke meetings where we crafted humorous lines for Mondale. From those, I learned how history can be manipulated. I was on a joke-meeting conference call when someone came up with a hilarious zinger. Mondale recited the line that day to wide acclaim. (That was the first time I realized that reporters cared more about good jokes than about important policy speeches.) Later, a campaign official who had not participated in the call took credit for the joke, a false claim that was reported as fact in a history of the 1984 election.

The staff in my section of the headquarters knew about my seizures. One day I woke up on the floor of the research room after a convulsion. I feared this would be the day I was fired, but nothing changed. It was a relief to discover that the reaction resembled the one I had seen at the Washington Monthly and not what I had experienced at Nader's group.

For the most part, though, I never discussed my history with colleagues. If I wanted to avoid being considered "the epileptic" rather than a worker with epilepsy, I had to treat my condition with the same nonchalance I sought from my coworkers.

I broke that rule for the first time with a young staffer assigned to women's issues, who had been talking to me about the emotional impact on an individual from discrimination. I described my belief that, while people should fight bias they face in their lives, they must avoid letting it dominate them. She responded with annoyance, saying that, as a white male, I could never understand the corrosive pain inflicted by prejudice. Without a word, I stood up and shut the door.

"Let me tell you why I understand discrimination," I began.

I spoke for twenty minutes—I'd been thrown out of school, lost a job, lost friends, known I could be fired and blackballed from future employment if I fought back. By the time I finished, the certainty in her expression gave way to a look of embarrassment.

She apologized. "I made assumptions I shouldn't have."

"That's okay," I replied. But now, I said, she should reconsider my point: If people subjected to discrimination allowed it to consume them, they had surrendered control of their lives. Fight back, sure, but never forget to move forward.

One afternoon at about three o'clock, Franz flagged down a cab on Capitol Hill. Both of us had ended up in Washington, both in political jobs. He worked on the staff of New York's senior senator, Patrick Moynihan, and remained on my medical-alert card as a contact. He'd received a phone call a few minutes earlier from someone at the Mondale campaign who sounded terrified. I had gone into convulsions, and the person on the line wanted to know if Franz could come to the campaign's Georgetown office to help.

The cab dropped Franz off at the headquarters on Wisconsin Avenue. He had been told to head to the back, and as he walked, he was surprised to see every office was empty. Finally, he saw me asleep on the floor, partly under a table, surrounded by my frightened coworkers. He noticed some nickels, dimes, and quarters lying beside me; he figured they fell out of my pocket during the seizure. He moved the table away, but even with him taking charge, the fear in everyone's face had not eased. Time for a joke to help everybody calm down. He started scooping the coins off the floor.

"You know," he said. "We have a free change rule: Anything that falls out of his pockets, you get to keep."

Everyone laughed and seemed to relax. As always, humor defused the tense situation.

"It's all right," Franz said. "There's no problem, he's fine."

Thanks to the joke, everyone believed him.

By spring 1984, my interest in speech writing had waned. I made a terrible advocate, often finding myself typing things I didn't believe. Once I played what I assumed was a recording of Mondale and thought he made a lot of strong points. Later, I read the cassette label—I had been listening to Senator John Glenn, one of my boss's opponents for the nomination.

Then there was health insurance. The campaign provided me with none. While I had two years left before I would age out of my parents' policy, the fear of losing coverage continued to weigh on me. I often awoke in emergency rooms where I had racked up huge bills. Uninsured, I could be bankrupt in months; even if I later found group insurance, I would be unable to obtain a mortgage because of a history of bad credit. If I didn't solve this problem by June 1986, I might never own a house.

I announced my plans to leave the campaign and asked a few friends for leads on journalism jobs. A man on the scheduling desk told me that television networks were hiring for the elections, and he gave me contact information for a producer at the CBS News Washington bureau.

I telephoned the next day, but the producer told me she had nothing available. She suggested that instead I should contact Wally Chalmers, the political editor at the CBS Election and Survey Unit in New York, to find out if there were jobs there.

When I reached Chalmers, I told him that the producer I just contacted had recommended I call him. I purposely used the producer's prominent name and the word "recommended." I hoped Chalmers wouldn't ask me if the producer was actually recommending me or if she even knew who I was.

Chalmers also told me he had no jobs available. Still, he offered to meet with me at the CBS offices at West Fifty-seventh Street the next time I was in New York.

"Actually," I said, "I'm going to be there the day after tomorrow."

"Don't make a special trip. Like I said, I don't have anything available."

"No, seriously, I'm scheduled to be in New York then," I replied. "Do you have time to get together?"

"Sure." We scheduled a meeting in his office.

After hanging up, I called Amtrak. I had lied—I had no travel plans. But Chalmers was a good contact. I needed to figure out how to get to New York with the little money I had.

The political unit was housed in a basement across from the flagship CBS News headquarters. I liked Chalmers right away. A longtime political operative, he had the smarts of a tough journalist but the demeanor of a good boss.

After about twenty minutes, he told me a job might open soon and invited me to stay in touch. I walked the mile and a half to Penn Station, where I caught a train back to Washington. I planned to call Chalmers every ten days—enough to make sure he didn't forget me, not so much that I would be annoying.

For the second time since graduation, I took several days off. One afternoon, I became aware I was sitting on my couch. MTV blared on a television in the corner. Time had passed, and I didn't know how much. But there had been no seizure. I had just been drifting, disconnected from everything around me. No one else was in the small house. My thoughts were blank.

Without warning, I burst into tears, and my weeping rapidly escalated into a wail. Despondency overwhelmed me, despondency over all my struggles, my concerns about being uninsured, the ever-present fear of injury, the barriers I faced because of my epilepsy that others might never imagine.

I want to shop in a grocery store by myself, I thought. I *ached* to shop for food by myself. The nearest store was more than a mile away. I had tried walking there a few times, but after one trip, I regained consciousness in an emergency room. I found my grocery receipt in my pocket; the food had been left wherever I had fallen. My meal budget was gone. *I can't even go grocery shopping, and I want to be a journalist?*

And I could die. *What if I died?* Weeks before, I'd awoken in a hospital, feeling weak and lost. A nurse told me I was in an Arlington orthopedic facility, which confused me more.* A doctor explained I had been found seizing and the convulsions wouldn't stop. An emergency crew had loaded me with IV Valium. He asked if I knew the meaning of status epilepticus. I did—a severe, long seizure that can end in death. He questioned whether I had been drinking or using drugs; I never did. Then he asked if I had missed my medicine. I didn't know. *I couldn't know.*

I rocked on my couch, covering my eyes with my palms as I sobbed. "Why did this happen to me?" I gasped. "Why me? *Why me?*"

This was the first time in my memory that I experienced unprovoked self-pity. I realized I was losing control. I stood.

"Stop it!" I yelled. "You're better! Get over it!"

I dug through my wallet and found the number for Talbot, my old rehabilitative psychologist. I had maintained contact with him for years, and I needed him now. He called back that same day. I explained that I had experienced an emotional breakdown without warning, over events that were months and years old. Okay, status epilepticus was a big deal. But losing my groceries?

"I'm so much better than I was when we met," I said. "Why am I falling apart now?"

"Because now you can," he replied. "You finally have a chance to take off your armor. And there are a lot of scars underneath you're only now beginning to face."

We spoke for an hour. By the end of our call, I understood that emotional pain I had buried for years was finally beginning to surface. That infuriated me; I didn't want that.

After four weeks of pestering, Chalmers called to let me know there was a one-month position available in the polling unit. I accepted the job before he told me the pay.

---

*I had been admitted to the National Hospital for Orthopaedics and Rehabilitation, which, despite its name, maintained an emergency room and treated a wide range of illnesses and chronic conditions.

This was real journalism. I just had to accept every assignment, every chore, leave the office last, and get there first. I knew people in Manhattan who would rent me an inexpensive room in a brownstone. There were dangers—the bedroom was on the fourth floor of the walk-up—but I couldn't let fear dictate my life.

I moved to New York in June. During my orientation, I was thrilled when a security officer handed me an identification card. For the first time, my name and photograph appeared on a record for a major national news organization. Then Chalmers escorted me to a dreary area that handled polling. Before he left, I asked if I could speak with him in his office.

He sat at his desk and put his arms behind his head. "What's up?"

I glanced at the desktop computer to his right, embarrassed. I felt like I had deceived him.

"Listen, if you want me to leave, it's okay," I said.

"Why would I want you to leave?"

"Well," I replied, "I have epilepsy, and my convulsions are not under control. There's a chance I could have one in the office, and maybe people won't be comfortable with that."

"What do we need to do if you have a seizure?"

I gave the usual instructions and assured him that, unless a seizure didn't stop, there was no need to call an ambulance.

He paused. "That's why you thought I'd want you to leave?"

"Well, yeah."

Chalmers rolled his eyes. "Get to work."

I don't remember my job with the polling unit because I received a promotion two days later. A group of journalists in the political unit were writing a handbook about the Democratic National Convention in San Francisco, and with the event just a month away, a lot of reporting and writing needed to be done quickly. Chalmers asked me to help.

He introduced me to the other writers, most of whom worked in a single large office. There was no room left there, so Chalmers posted me at a nearby cubicle. He cautioned: This was not a full-time job, just a one-month stint. After the Democratic Convention, I might be out.

Since now I would be interacting with the writers, Chalmers asked for permission to let others know about my seizures. He wanted them to have the same instructions I had given him and to let them know that they didn't need to be frightened. I thanked him for his consideration, and we went to the large office to discuss epilepsy with the staff; people asked plenty of questions, but no one seemed concerned.

I took on every assignment, staying nights and weekends to make myself seem irreplaceable. One Friday, I heard Chalmers sounding upset. He had forgotten to assign a book that was supposed to be a district-by-district analysis of voters, a huge project due in three days. Worse, that weekend was his daughter's fourth birthday, and the family had plans.

"Don't worry," I said. "I'll do the book."

"You don't even know where the data is. And this whole thing has to be pulled together by Monday."

"Show me the data and what needs to be done. I'll take care of it. Celebrate your daughter's birthday."

Chalmers thanked me for taking such a tedious assignment, having no idea I was bursting with excitement. As I learned when I helped the *Washington Monthly* editors by surrendering my byline, professionals remember favors. I doubted Chalmers would let me go in a few weeks after I'd gotten him out of this jam.

That night, I went home to grab my bottles of Dilantin and Mysoline and brought them back to the office. When I needed sleep, I saved travel time by sacking out on a couch. On Monday morning, I sent the digital version of the book to Chalmers's computer. I taped a note to his monitor telling him I had delivered the book and was taking the day off.

When the final copy of the Democratic National Convention handbook arrived at the CBS offices, I was sure my job was safe for another month. I wrote more than anyone else. At least one of my coworkers found my relentless eagerness annoying, but no matter. It was the only advantage I could use to offset my obstacles in the job market. As I'd hoped, Chalmers asked me to stay on through the election.

I enjoyed my colleagues' company, and we often grabbed lunch together at the CBS commissary. Major seizures occurred at the office

maybe once a month, but everyone learned to treat them as just a dis-
traction or even a source of humor. Once I awoke in a CBS health
center with another writer sitting beside me. He merrily told me the
news: I had experienced convulsions in the cafeteria and landed on
Lesley Stahl, then the host of *Face the Nation*, the highly rated Sunday
news show.

"Oh God," I slurred. "I fell on her?"

My friend laughed. "Close enough."

"Did I hurt her?"

"You didn't *really* land on her. Like I said, close enough."

"What did she do?" I almost didn't want to know.

"She was *totally* cool about it. She was talking with a bunch of people when it happened. They just picked up their table and moved it
out of the way, sat back down, and started talking again."

I covered my face with my hand. Then I laughed.

While working on the GOP convention handbook, I discovered Re-
publicans were dodging a potential showdown during the national
meeting. Quietly, they were assembling large parts of their party platform at town hall meetings around the country to avoid arguments
between different factions in front of the press. The story didn't strike
me as important, so I was surprised when Chalmers told me later that
it would have its own section in the handbook.

Shortly after the convention, I received a call from Martin Plissner,
the legendary CBS executive political director. He lavished praise on
my little scoop, then dropped a bombshell.

"I'd like you to come to Washington to be my assistant," he said.

Plissner explained that everyone who held that job went on to big
things at CBS; one of his former assistants was a producer on Capitol
Hill. I was taken aback. I had never planned for this. Plissner sounded
surprised when I asked if I could take a few days to think about it.

Chalmers heard about Plissner's call and dropped by to congratu-
late me. I thanked him but didn't mention my first inclination was to
reject the offer.

I replayed that night at Northwestern hospital. That person I'd
been—facing death, experiencing scores of seizures every month, un-

knowingly about to enter new battles—had set markers. There had been times he almost surrendered—considering suicide when facing the injuries, fear, and uncertainty—but he came back, dedicated to a vision of his life. He—I—had committed to becoming a newspaper reporter.

The person I was had made a promise, and my progress was due to his willingness to forge ahead despite the challenges. I had betrayed him once before by forgetting about everything in his plan other than my career. I was not going to do it again.

The next day, I telephoned Plissner. I told him I appreciated the offer but that I would have to pass. I wanted to work in newspapers.

Most of my CBS colleagues thought turning down Plissner had been foolish. There was no newspaper job waiting; so long as my seizures continued, I still had to start in a major metropolitan area with mass transit, a farfetched plan.

One of my coworkers, Joan Kelly, recognized that for me to have rejected Plissner, my commitment to newspapers had to be more than preference. Kelly had been supportive since we met and often encouraged me to submit an article to *The New York Times Magazine* about my experience living with epilepsy. A *Times* reporter named Nan Robertson had written a piece on her experiences with toxic shock syndrome and educated the country about that little-understood condition. I could do the same for epilepsy, Kelly said.

Repeatedly, I rejected her suggestion.

"Joan, if I announce this to the world, I might never work again," I said. "Not every company is like CBS."

One day, she offered a suggestion: She knew a senior editor at the *Times*. I could speak to him, explain my challenges, and ask for advice. He knew plenty of people, Kelly explained. Maybe he could guide me to a path that would lead to a reporter's job.

A week later, traffic clogged West Forty-third Street as I walked beside the Gothic building that housed the world's most famous newspaper. I entered through a revolving door and told security I was scheduled to meet with an editor. The guard made a phone call and told me to wait. Just standing in the lobby awed and intimidated me.

About ten minutes later, the editor arrived and escorted me to the elevators. He pushed the button for the fourth floor, disappointing me—I knew the main newsroom was on the third and had hoped to see it. He brought me to his desk and pulled up a chair for me. Then he sat and asked why I was there.

I explained that I wanted to work in newspapers but had been told many times I would have to start in a small town—an impossibility. I had poorly controlled epilepsy, which meant I couldn't drive. So I had to work in a city with mass transit, which meant starting at a major newspaper.

"That's it," I said. "Do you have any ideas how I can work around this?"

He leaned back and stared at the ceiling.

"Woof," he said. "That's a tough one." Quickly, he sat up. "I'd give up if I were you."

I didn't know how to respond. I kept my anger under control as we spoke for a few more minutes, then thanked him for his time. As I walked toward the elevator, I boiled.

Screw you! I thought. What if I was weak? What if I believed this man—a big name at a big publication—and gave up because my goals were tough to achieve?

A minute later, I pushed through the revolving door out onto Forty-third Street, vowing to prove this *Times* editor was wrong.

The next afternoon, the editor phoned me at CBS.

"I've been thinking," he said. "The *Times* has a writing program for clerks. It's a lousy job, but it can be a way onto the paper."

Lousy or not, I didn't care. "It sounds great."

"Actually, both Scotty Reston and Rick Smith have clerks in Washington, and the ones who work for them tend to get hired as reporters."

I recognized neither name. "I'm sorry, who?"

"James Reston and Hedrick Smith."

"Oh. Sorry." That was embarrassing. They were giants in journalism. Reston, a columnist, previously had been executive editor and

Washington bureau chief. Smith, the chief Washington correspondent, had also run the bureau. Each had won a Pulitzer Prize.

I tried to calculate the best approach. "Can I say you recommended I contact them?"

"Sure."

I sent letters to both men. I told Reston the truth about my health struggles, hoping to convey toughness. I decided not to gamble with Smith and sent a typical application.

Each granted me an interview. The Reston meeting was a disaster; my anxiety, coupled with discomfort about his knowledge of my epilepsy, undermined my attempts to appear strong and confident. I handled the interview with Smith much better, since he knew nothing about my health.

To my astonishment, Smith offered me the job a day later. I would be answering phones, opening mail, conducting research, and occasionally helping with reporting. In fact, he said, he wanted me to gather information from a government agency right away. I made a call from my bedroom.

"Hi," I began, "this is Kurt Eichenwald from *The New York Times*..."

I stopped for a second. I could not believe I had just uttered those words.

An audio diary from

KURT EICHENWALD, 1985

I don't . . . [pause]. How to start? I got the job. Rick Smith hired me. Give me a minute [pause]. I can't believe I'm still telling myself when I'm taking breaks. I should just turn off the recorder. Okay, I'm turning off the recorder for a second . . . Okay, back. I'm sorry. I keep moving between crying and screaming. Not upset screaming, excited. I just can't believe it. I have a chance. Some people never even get that. I have a chance.

An audio letter from

FRANZ PAASCHE, 1986

With that seizure at Mondale's, when I found out you still had my name on your medical card, it was kind of a funny awareness. In some ways, I feel like we're attached even though I'm not your roommate anymore. But it reminded me how constant it is for you, how your worries never really go away, and your responsibility for yourself and for the people around you is always there. It's kind of funny, but it's so bizarre that someone who has epilepsy has, beyond having to deal with this condition, all of a sudden has responsibility for all these other people because you don't want to freak them out, or scare them, or whatever. It's just so bizarre that you have to carry that responsibility at the same time.

CHAPTER TWENTY-SIX

Blood seeped through the back of my jeans, staining my sheets. I had awakened in my bedroom at a Northwest Washington shared house but couldn't recall how I got there. I remembered scattered images—nighttime, a bridge, a McDonald's sign, metallic-blue something. A man whose voice I didn't recognize putting me in a car. Pain, flashes, blackness. I assumed I had been taken to an emergency room, where someone had called a friend listed on my medical-alert card. But almost everything was blank.

I looked at my right palm. There was blood from the sheets I had touched. Panicked, I rubbed my left hand over the top and back of my head. No sticky wetness.

I turned in my bed and stood. I felt a spasm of soreness in my rectum. *Anus painus*, I thought. A stupid joke for myself. A good way to take my mind off of the wound I knew I was about to discover. I unsnapped and unzipped my jeans, then pushed them down along with my underwear. I stared at what I couldn't comprehend.

My underwear was soaked dark red. I touched my buttocks and the inside of my thigh. I felt the blood before I saw it on my hand.

Anus painus. Another twinge. Then I realized there was an ache that wasn't subsiding. The spasm just made it worse. I stepped out of my pants and walked to the bathroom. *I have to get clean.* I believed I was covered with blood everywhere, even though I knew that wasn't true. I wasn't thinking straight.

I filled the tub with a few inches of cool water. Baths were dangerous—I could drown if I had a seizure. But I didn't feel steady enough to stand for a shower, and I desperately wanted the blood washed away. I stripped off my shirt, stepped into the tub, and carefully sat down.

Clouds of red plumed off my body. I splashed them with my hand, then rubbed the spots on my skin where I saw blood. The water turned pink, but the darker clouds kept lolling and spinning from between my legs. That was the first moment I understood—I was bleeding from my rectum.

I drained the tub and filled it again. Sitting in watered-down blood repulsed me. When fresh water turned dark pink, I drained it and pushed the taps again. I don't know how many times it took, but eventually the red clouds slowed their swirling dance. The water wasn't so pink.

I may have sat there for hours. *Anus painus.* A spasm would subside, and I would return to my daze—awake but impassive. I didn't want to think about what caused this injury. I was afraid that, if I did, I would discover an answer I didn't want to know.

This is dangerous. I climbed out of the tub, wrapped a beach towel around myself, and headed to my bedroom. The sheets were bloody, and I wanted to sleep. I lay on the floor and dozed off.

When I woke, I was more clearheaded. I reached behind me to touch the towel. There was blood, but nothing like before. Still, my rectum hurt. The spasms were less intense, but they hadn't stopped.

I didn't want to go. I hated emergency rooms. I particularly didn't want to talk to some doctor about rectal bleeding. But ignoring what was happening would be crazy. I needed to go to the hospital.

An hour later, I was in the emergency room at George Washington University Hospital. As I waited for the doctor, I wondered why I had chosen this place. It was nowhere close to where I lived, and I didn't remember being there before. When I climbed into the taxi, I just said the name. Lying on the stretcher bed, I remembered Ronald Reagan had been rushed to this hospital when a gunman shot him in 1981. I wondered if I was in the same part of the emergency room where the president had been treated.

A doctor appeared, accompanied by a younger-looking man. *Probably a medical student,* I figured. After a few questions, the doctor instructed me to roll onto my stomach. The examination hurt. When he finished, he threw out his surgical gloves. "Are you sexually active?" he asked.

I knew where this was going. I knew, but I couldn't think it. "Not really," I replied. "Not for a long time."

"Have you ever had anal sex?"

Pleasestoppleasestoppleasestop. "No."

The doctor sat on a stool. I stared at it, wondering why I hadn't noticed the seat until that moment. He mentioned something—my name, I think. I looked at him. His face seemed angelic. I hadn't thought that before.

"Kurt," he said, "were you raped?"

Where had the stool come from? How was he just sitting on it all of a sudden?

"Kurt," he repeated, "were you raped?"

I chewed the inside of my lip, on the spot I bit during seizures. I tasted blood. It hurt. Why was I hurting myself?

"It's okay," the doctor said. "You're going to be okay. But you need to tell me. Were you raped?"

A tear ran down my cheek. "Was I?" I asked.

I refused everything. No, I didn't want to file a police report. What could I report? I didn't even know where it happened. A car, a bridge, a McDonald's sign. It meant nothing. There was a voice, but I didn't recognize it. And how did I know that was the guy?

The doctor urged me to let them conduct an ultrasound. No, I said, I was leaving. He told me I was making a mistake; they had to check for internal bleeding. They believed someone had put an object inside me, so there might be deeper damage. If there was an injury they couldn't see, it could be dangerous.

Stopitstopitstopit.

Finally, the doctor persuaded me. The scan showed no further injury to deeper organs. A woman in a multicolored smock spent time trying to convince me to allow them to call the police. I told her to get out.

An older doctor arrived. I heard the words "infectious disease." I glanced at the curtain drawn around the stretcher. This new doctor hadn't closed it completely.

They really should close the curtain. Why did they have a curtain if they weren't going to close it? I saw people walk by. I couldn't stop wondering about the curtain.

The doctor spoke my name in this odd tone that was both abrupt and kind. I looked back at him.

"No," I said. I knew his question even though I was certain I hadn't heard it.

I didn't have to discuss it today, he told me. I could wait until one of my follow-ups, but until then I should avoid sexual activity. The rape placed me in a risk category, and I should gain as much information as I could about all sexually transmitted diseases, including AIDS.

"No," I replied. I didn't want to know. AIDS meant death. People were already afraid of epilepsy; epilepsy *and* AIDS? I was at a breaking point. Emotional overload.

Nothing. I felt nothing.

He nodded, reminding me to discuss these matters with my doctor. He wrote a prescription for antibiotics to prevent an infection from the rectal injuries. Two doctors urged me to stay overnight for observation. I refused and signed a document saying I was rejecting their advice.

I left the hospital, hailed a cab, and headed home. It was dark. Had it been the previous night when I had the seizure? The night before? I didn't know. I went inside, walked upstairs to my room, and flicked on the light. Bloodstained sheets still covered the bed. I grabbed a pillow and lay on the floor, staring at the ceiling. I noticed chips in the paint and wondered how they got there. I fell asleep studying those spots, trying to see if they formed identifiable shapes like clouds do.

The next morning, I telephoned Rick Smith to let him know I would not be coming to work. I had been his assistant for several months, but we were no longer at the *Times*. He was taking time off to write a book about Washington and had asked me to stay on as his researcher. By then, Smith knew about my seizures and treated them as unimportant events with no bearing on my work.

Smith told me he had called the previous day when I failed to show up to the American Enterprise Institute, a think tank where we had set up shop. I apologized, explaining that I had been in the hospital because of a seizure. I then assured him that I would be well enough to return the next day.

After hanging up, I collected everything stained with blood—sheets, mattress pad, towel, jeans, underwear. I lived with a group of strangers who were all at work, so I carried the horrifying pile downstairs. In the kitchen, I stuffed it into a bag. Then I threw it in an outside garbage can. I never considered washing it. I wanted it all out of my life, forever.

I still felt nothing—no fear, no anger, no rage, no desire for revenge. I knew enough to recognize this emotional shutdown was destructive. I searched for the phone directory and called several psychiatrists until I located one in Northwest Washington willing to see me that week.

In our sessions, I reviewed my history, my fear of seizures, my experience being kicked out of school, my assault in Chicago. I often cried unexpectedly, sometimes over nothing. But I was unable to mention my rape to any counselor for years to come.

The pain in my shoulder was intense. At some point after the rape, I fell down the stairs outside of my bedroom and banged myself up. I suspected I had broken a bone and decided to get an X ray once I was more coherent. About an hour later, I hailed a cab and asked to go to the nearest hospital. Any doctor, I figured, could find a fracture. The cabby dropped me off at Capitol Hill Hospital.

I remember little that followed, but my father later told me what happened. Someone checked my blood sugar levels with a test strip. The person wrote down the results incorrectly, stating they came from a complete glucose test—involving drawing blood—rather than the finger stick that was performed. Mistake piled on mistake, and soon a doctor diagnosed pancreatic cancer. I may have gone into convulsions in the emergency room, and my planned short visit turned into a major hospitalization.

No one checked the MedicAlert medallion that hung around my neck, which disclosed my epilepsy and instructed medical teams to check my wallet for a card with my anticonvulsant schedule and emergency contact information. As a result, the hospital stopped providing my medication. For days, each time I went into convulsions, the staff infused IV Valium to stop the seizure. At one point, I opened my eyes and saw Neil Fisher, a friend from Swarthmore who worked in town, standing by me. I didn't know how he had ended up there, but I recognized I was in danger.

"Call my parents, and tell them to get here right now!" I begged him. "Tell them this is an emergency!"

Later that day, I was admitted to the intensive care unit.

I woke with someone stuffing pills into my mouth. I pushed up my tongue to block them from going down my throat, then spat them on the floor. I recognized the red bands around the white capsules; it was Dilantin, three times my normal dose.

A short, dark-haired man stood beside me.

"Get the fuck away!" I growled.

"You need your medicine," he said.

Right. In my sleep. At triple the dose.

"Get away from me, or I'll scream!"

I watched him leave the enclosed area and saw my parents in a main room. My father was confronting a doctor. They were too far away for me to hear the words, but I could tell Dad—who had plenty of experience brutalizing unprepared interns and residents—was ripping apart the other physician.

As staff members rushed about, producing records for my father, my mother saw I was awake and came to my bedside.

"Are you all right?" she asked.

I nodded. "Feel like I've been hit by a truck," I said. My tongue moved as if coated in molasses. "What happened?"

She told me I had been in the hospital for days and that the doctors had made one terrible gaffe after another. The medical team learned of my epilepsy only when my parents arrived. At first, the doctors insisted they had given me my medication, which set my father off: How the hell would they have known to provide me with my prescribed anticonvulsants if they didn't understand I had epilepsy? He called the doctor a liar to his face.

My father came in with my chart. He grabbed my arm. "Don't worry about how you feel; it's not because of something wrong with you. You're in intensive care. The doctors made a mistake with a blood sugar test and decided—but you don't!—they incorrectly decided you had pancreatic cancer."

"From *one* blood sugar test?" That was ridiculous.

My father shook his head. "Don't get me started."

"Why do I feel so awful?"

"They've been giving you IV Valium every time you had a seizure, and they've used too much. It settles in muscles and fatty tissue. Don't try to get out of bed. You'll fall."

Another man arrived who looked familiar. It was a former teacher from my high school who now worked as a Washington lawyer. He had picked up my parents at the airport and driven them to the hospital.

Soon after, Smith showed up. Assuming he would be panicked by my disappearance, my mother had notified him I was at the hospital in intensive care. When he saw me, his usual expression of calm assurance drained away, replaced by a look of shock.

The area around my bed was packed, with everyone listening to my father explain the gross incompetence of the physicians. At some point, a doctor burst in, angry about the number of visitors surrounding my ICU bed.

"Who are all you people?" the doctor barked.

My mother stepped forward, gesturing to each individual as she made the introductions. "I'm his mother, this is his father, this is his lawyer, and this is Hedrick Smith of *The New York Times*."

The four of them stared at the doctor in silence.

"Oh," he said. Then he scurried away.

———

Within the hour, I was transported to Georgetown University Hospital to recuperate from the damage caused at Capitol Hill Hospital. The doctors diagnosed a Valium overdose but also found that my anticonvulsant levels had dropped below the therapeutic level. When sufficient time had passed, a doctor told me they were going to infuse Dilantin. I asked what that meant.

"We're giving you a load of Dilantin directly into the bloodstream," he explained.

"You know I have a lot of Valium in me?"

I heard a voice. "They know." It was my father, who was beside my mother on the other side of the room. "They've been monitoring it, and it's okay now."

It's okay? Already? "How long have I been here?"

"Since yesterday," my father said. "You've been sleeping."

I remembered: *My shoulder.* It didn't hurt anymore.

"What happened to my shoulder?"

My mother spoke. "That was a dream. Nothing happened to your shoulder."

"No, it was real. That's why I went to the hospital. I fell down the stairs and hurt my shoulder. What did the X ray show?"

"*That's* why you were there?" my father asked. "We assumed you had been found on the street."

"So what did the X ray show?"

My father seethed. "They didn't take an X ray. They didn't do anything about your shoulder."

The doctor beside me asked how my shoulder felt now.

"It's fine," I said. "Guess I would have been safer if I had just stayed home."

Time detached from reality. There were moments of consciousness, then not. Hours, perhaps days, passed without my taking notice.

My next memory is of sitting up in my bed. A middle-aged doctor knocked on my door and asked for permission to speak with me. He walked in with a group of fresh-faced young people in lab coats, then introduced himself.

"These are medical students," he explained. "I'm visiting patients with them and was hoping you'd be willing to talk to them about why you're here today."

Damn straight I'll talk to them.

I chose my words carefully. "I'm here because a doctor at another hospital failed to take a proper medical history. The doctor—not a disease, not some chronic medical condition—injured me so badly I had to be brought here."

I gave an account not just of the latest near-fatal mistakes but also of the times over the years when doctors failed to ask questions, conduct follow-up, or listen. By shortchanging the importance of a patient's past, doctors could cause incalculable damage, I said.

I studied the students' faces. *Do they understand?*

"So someday, when you have a patient in front of you, remember me. Remember how bad I look right now," I said. "Remember this happened because a doctor didn't take a proper history. All the labs and machinery are *useless* if you don't talk to patients extensively.

"You need to ask about their health and about their medications. You need to look them up in the *Physicians' Desk Reference* to know if they're taking the right amounts or are on drugs that conflict. Don't let gadgets and drugs be your first thought. Ask questions. Write down the answers. Figure out why those answers are important and what they show."

I ended my lecture, and a few students tentatively asked questions. Then the doctor told them to head to the hallway.

"Thank you," he said to me. "I wish I had recorded that."

Six months. In six months, I would be off my parents' insurance. I thought back to Plissner's offer at CBS and cursed myself for turning it down. That job had insurance; it might not have been the right industry, but people like me didn't have the luxury of being choosy. My medication, my hospitalizations—group coverage was suddenly more important than my aspirations. After my success at CBS, I had grown arrogant and figured I would also climb the ladder quickly at the *Times*.

I told Smith I could no longer work on the book, that I needed a job with insurance right away. He introduced me to a senior editor at *National Journal*, who offered me a position at the Washington political magazine. I grabbed it—I had no choice. I hated the work, which mostly involved retyping press releases about people changing jobs in the city. I saw no future for myself there. I felt cheated, but at least I had insurance.

Or did I? After a few weeks on the job, I discovered the group policy contained a preexisting-condition clause. I had no choice. I resigned from *National Journal* so I could go back on my parents' insurance for the few weeks that remained until my birthday, when the company would kick me off the policy. Desperate, I told Smith about my predicament. I said I would take anything that offered immediate insurance with no preexisting-condition clause.

He telephoned the *Times* in New York and learned that they had some openings for what they called "copy kids." That was a full-time job, and the insurance benefits kicked in immediately. A senior editor agreed to meet with me, and my parents paid for a plane ticket so I could see him the next day.

I sat anxiously while the editor in charge of hiring clerks and copy kids studied my résumé.

"You're overqualified," he finally announced. "And why have you been jumping from job to job? What happened at CBS?"

"Nothing," I replied. "In fact, I was offered a promotion but turned it down. I can give you my old boss's contact information if you want to check."

"What was the promotion?"

"Assistant to the executive political director."

His expression was unreadable. "You turned that down? You would rather be here running wire copy?"

"No," I said. "I would rather have a chance at working for a newspaper. That's all I've ever wanted. As a copy boy, I have a chance to become a reporter through the writing program."

"Very few people are hired out of the writing program," he replied. "And it will take years."

"I know. I don't care. It's a chance."

"You could become a reporter right away by applying to small newspapers. Why not do that?"

Lie. Just lie. "Because I want to work at *The New York Times*, and I have a better chance of getting hired by starting here if people can see how I work."

He studied my résumé again.

"I promise you," I said. "If you hire me, you won't regret it. I'll work harder than anyone you've hired before."

He looked hard at me, sizing me up. "Okay. You can start in two weeks. But I think you're going to regret this decision."

He escorted me across the newsroom to a woman sitting at an isolated corner desk. "Marie," he said to her, "this is Kurt Eichenwald. We're hiring him as a copy boy."

I missed the deadline: For two weeks, I was uninsured. I turned twenty-five in June 1986, and on that day, the one that had terrified me for so long, my parents' policy no longer covered me. My start date at the *Times* hadn't arrived and the insurance at *National Journal* was still useless. I considered just staying in my house to avoid possible hospitalization, but instead decided to take a gamble and use that time for my move back to New York.

I shouldn't have taken the chance. Before my first day at the *Times*, I went into convulsions somewhere in Manhattan. An ambulance brought me to St. Luke's-Roosevelt Hospital Center in midtown, where emergency room doctors apparently checked my MedicAlert necklace, read that I had epilepsy, and left me to sleep it off. I received a bill for thousands of dollars a few weeks later, costs incurred for nothing.

Distraught, I telephoned my parents. My salary at the *Times* wasn't enough to pay the hospital and afford my living costs in New York. Ignoring the bill—hell, even delaying payment—would destroy my credit rating. Would I never be able to buy a house because of my epilepsy and this ridiculous insurance system? Why was I *forced* to jump from job to job in search of coverage? What if I had *wanted* to work at

National Journal but couldn't because of insurance? My panic escalated as I badgered my parents with questions before they could answer.

"I never told my new bosses about my seizures," I rambled in a tone of escalating dread. "I don't know if Rick Smith told them. What's going to happen when I tell them? And if I don't, what'll they do if I have a seizure in the newsroom? And what if I got pushed out of my job again? How would I afford my medicine? I can't pay this bill! How can *anyone* with epilepsy survive without insurance? Are we just supposed to go away and die somewhere?"

My parents, who were both on the line, urged me to calm down.

"Kurt, we'll pay the bill," my father said. "You're not alone. We're here to help."

My mother interrupted. "I promise, Kurt, I promise, you will have all of our financial and emotional support. No strings attached."

I wiped my eyes and took several deep breaths. "Thank you," I said softly. "Thank you so much."

A second passed, then I teared up again. "What about everybody else?" I asked. "What about other people with epilepsy who don't have someone to pay the bill for them? Do they all just die?"

My parents mentioned free clinics and other options, but eventually acknowledged that any uninsured person with epilepsy was at risk, and there were almost certainly others who stayed in jobs they hated simply for the insurance.

"So if I—so if any of us—ever lose our jobs, we could die?" I asked in disbelief. "What kind of world do we live in?"

"Slow down," another copy boy said as I rushed by with a pile of stories from AP and UPI. "They don't need everything so fast."

"I've got nothing better to do," I replied.

My work at the *Times* verged on the robotic. A row of machines in what was called "the wire room" printed stories on scrolls of paper. Men there ripped off each article before passing it through a hole in the wall to a senior copy kid on the other side. That person glanced at the story to see if it involved foreign, national, local, or other news and shoved the paper into the correct opening among more than a dozen slots. Then another copy kid would pull out the paper and take it to the proper desk.

Usually, the copy kids let articles pile up until they decided there were enough to justify carrying them to their final destinations. But I never stopped moving, walking in endless circles as I grabbed wire stories from the plastic slots and carried them to the correct news desks. I knew, once again, my overeager behavior annoyed some colleagues, but I didn't care.

Let them think I'm a jerk and a kiss up. With my approach, everyone in the newsroom saw me working all the time. It was a way to attract the attention I wanted. Copy kids in the writing program were all young entrepreneurs—striking up relationships with editors, pitching story ideas, offering to take any assignment, and handling the reporting and writing in the off hours. Our jobs were grunt work; we had to blaze our own paths to promotion by persuading someone at the paper to print our articles.

I quickly discovered that some editors in the high-stress newsroom considered copy kids and clerks to be objects for letting off steam, the moral equivalent of dogs to kick. I took a share of insults, quiet tirades, and nastiness from frustrated editors.

Members of the clerical staff often compared war stories, competing to see who experienced the worst ill-treatment. I joined in the grousing but rarely took it too seriously. No matter how nasty an editor might be, none could match the abuse I had endured over the past six years.

The lead of the first major *Times* article
written by copy boy

KURT EICHENWALD, 1986

LINDEN—*Fuzzy peach navel is the recommended drink at the Old Tavern Inn here, one of the latest and most unlikely ripple effects of the American auto industry's march toward high technology.*

CHAPTER TWENTY-SEVEN

Nan Robertson saved lives.

The thought struck me every few days. The article she had written for *The New York Times Magazine* about her experience with toxic shock raised national awareness of the condition. Joan Kelly, my friend from CBS, continued encouraging me to do the same for epilepsy. Now I was in the building; I could simply drop by the magazine office on the eighth floor and pitch the idea.

Still I resisted the impulse. This was hardly the time to reveal my health problems. I had worked at the *Times* for five months and been promoted from copy boy to national desk clerk. I knew I was terrible at the job—with my memory deficiencies, I often bungled the rapid demands of answering phone calls, taking messages, filling out forms, moving copy, and running for coffee. Fortunately, people thought I was just inattentive. Meanwhile, I wrote freelance articles for the paper and helped with "legwork"—covering events around New York for staff reporters. I'd had one seizure at the office, but I knew the newsroom was large enough that it had probably escaped senior editors' attention. If I announced my epilepsy in the magazine, I could derail my career. There were plenty of young people in the writing program;

once the top brass knew about my health, I was sure they would pass me over for someone without the baggage of chronic seizures.

Still. Out of millions of people with epilepsy, I could think of only one—Tony Coelho, a California congressman—who had publicly revealed his condition. A few years earlier, when I wanted to learn more about seizures, I found only one book, *Living with Epilepsy*. To avoid embarrassment, I had removed the jacket and covered the spine with tape so no one could see the title.

People like me lived in the shadows, afraid of losing jobs or friends or educational opportunities due to public ignorance. To reach them through the magazine, to educate the misinformed, a writer with epilepsy would have to disclose having the condition and know how to contact an editor. I fit every requirement except one: I wasn't willing to reveal my health problems.

One morning after my shower, I stared in the mirror. *Help others or protect myself?* I thought of the person I had been at Northwestern, trying to find purpose in life. *Helping others.* That thought had not occurred to him. *Helping others or being a newspaper reporter.* I knew what choice he would have made. If I could spare someone my pain, even though I might have to give up on a newspaper career, how could I stay silent?

The next day, I rode the elevator to the eighth floor. I identified myself and said I wanted to discuss a possible article. I was escorted to a magazine editor, who invited me to pull up a chair.

My fear of neurologists was unshakable, so I continued to travel to Dallas every six months to see Naarden, the only doctor I trusted. Now he was offering advice that alarmed me: My seizure control might improve if I changed anticonvulsants. The best choice all along had been Tegretol—the overdose that had almost killed me shouldn't bar us from trying it again, he said. I had never been at a good therapeutic dosage. At proper levels, it might work, and he promised to monitor my blood carefully.

"I have one question," I said. "If we make this switch, and the blood problem starts again, if we switch back, can you guarantee me I'll have the same control I do now?"

"You know nothing can ever be guaranteed with epilepsy."

A metaphor popped into my head. "Dr. Naarden, think of it like this: I wandered around on a foggy, frozen lake for years. I kept falling through the ice, getting so wet and cold I thought I would die. Then I found a thick piece of ice. It's still cold, but I can stand here and be sure I won't fall back into the water."

I could see he already understood where I was going. "Now I'm hearing a voice calling through the fog," I continued, "telling me if I just head toward him, I'll make it to land. But maybe I'll start falling through the ice again. And if I do, I might not be able to find my way back to the thick piece of ice where things aren't perfect, but at least I'm safe."

Naarden shook his head. "You're too smart for your own good," he said.

He increased my Dilantin dosage. Tegretol was off the table.

I wrote the epilepsy article for the magazine in a little-trafficked area called the recording room, one floor above where most reporters and editors worked. The process was torturous. I read and listened to some of my diaries, reviewing for the first time my own anguish from the worst moments. When I reached the tapes I made after my dismissal from Swarthmore, I couldn't play them. I did not want to immerse myself in that trauma again. I interviewed people who had been with me—my parents, Carl, Franz, and others—and used their information to fill in blanks. I had no records for the day I learned of my epilepsy, and on a tape where my mother recited her recollections, she cried when she reached that moment. It hurt too much to listen.

The final product seemed right. I was honest, at least as much as I could be at the time. There were hints about my memory problems, but that was one topic I would not openly address. If disclosing my epilepsy didn't destroy my future as a journalist, revealing my impaired ability to recall events might.

I reread the article and was intrigued to realize the most important paragraph was a quote from Carl:

If everybody in the world knew how to deal with epilepsy, if everybody in the world were not mystified by a seizure, if everybody in the world were willing to help out when they see a stranger have a seizure, then the lives of people with epilepsy would be infinitely easier. They would be able to go everywhere and do just about everything and not worry.

That was the reason I wrote the piece, the message I wanted the world to hear. I thought it fitting that it came from a person who had aided a friend with epilepsy rather than from someone with the condition.

I filed the article to the magazine, and a man I'd never met before edited it. When the piece was returned, I was horrified. It was maudlin, filled with a defeatism and drama that I had never expressed, attributing emotions to others that I had never heard. This would accomplish nothing—I would be revealing my epilepsy and portraying it as something to be pitied rather than a challenge to be overcome.

I was a clerk; this was an editor. How could I argue? I printed both copies and asked an older reporter I knew to read them. She complimented the original.

"What do you think of the edited version?" I asked.

"It reads like something out of *Redbook*."

A few seconds passed in silence. "I don't know what to do," I said.

She didn't miss a beat. "This is *your* story. Don't let them do this to you."

Her words gave me the courage to push back. The editor fought when I demanded the removal of made-up emotions attributed to others and me. Each time, I said loudly enough so others could hear, "But it's not true!" That led him to back down.

The Sunday magazine arrived in the newsroom each Wednesday, and I wanted to be out of New York when my article hit. That morning, I boarded the train to Washington. I'd decided to work in the bureau, far from where my story could be read.

As I typed at a desk, I saw Craig Whitney, the bureau chief, walking toward me with the magazine's next issue in his hand. I realized in horror—advance copies landed in the bureau the same day they reached the New York office. I wanted to run.

He reached my computer with a hand thrust forward to shake mine. "Congratulations," he said. "This is an incredible piece."

I nodded and uttered a soft "Thank you." He returned to his office, and I left the office. After a block, I leaned against a building, then slid down to sit on the sidewalk. I covered my eyes with one hand and cried.

I still dreaded the reaction in New York, particularly among senior editors. They rarely spoke to clerks, and I feared their true thoughts would be revealed only behind closed doors.

Those anxieties were put to rest in a very public way. The day I returned, I was at the national desk when someone tapped my shoulder. I looked around and almost fell off my seat. Abe Rosenthal, the *Times's* legendary and mercurial executive editor, stood beside me. I jumped up as I would have had the president suddenly appeared. I assumed he wanted me to handle some menial task. Instead, he shook my hand.

"That was an important and amazing article you wrote," he said. "It's an honor to have published it."

I mumbled my thanks.

"No," Rosenthal replied. "Thank *you*."

He returned to his office, and a number of people offered me congratulations; a compliment from Rosenthal was a rare thing. I excused myself and went to the men's room. I feared I was going to start hyperventilating.

Scores of letters arrived at the *Times* from people who had epilepsy or knew someone who did. Given that I had no desk, the correspondence stacked up in a wire basket in the mailroom. I read each one, but often felt emotionally unable to respond. So many of them expressed pain I could not salve, often from those with the condition who wrote to ask for my help in fighting discrimination they faced.

Only one letter contained a photograph. It spilled out onto the tabletop where I was opening the envelopes. The eyes of an old man sparkling behind thick glasses stared back at me from a Polaroid. I recognized him instantly and unfolded the note.

Dear Kurt: I have seen your byline several times and have wondered if you were the Kurt that I knew. When my daughter Lois sent me a copy of your epilepsy story, I knew that you were the young man with whom I shared a room at Northwestern Hospital in 1981—the young man I referred to as my ersatz grandson.

Memories flooded back of Irwin Henoch, my hospital roommate in Chicago who, with his wife, Florence, helped me to connect to my feelings again, to contemplate life and happiness, to set myself on the path that led to the very newsroom where I was standing. He told me that, when he was well on his way to recovery in 1982, Florence had died from a lung cancer discovered during a routine checkup. He was broken up by her death, he wrote, but was saved by the support of his children and through volunteer work. He remembered my mother, and always thought of her when he used the yellow pen she gave him, a pen that only recently had been replaced. The affection for this man I had known for only a few days came rushing back, and then I choked up as I reached the final words of his letter.

I am happy that you are making a name for yourself. I always knew that you were something special.

Best regards,
IRWIN H. HENOCH
Ersatz Grandfather

In the weeks after my magazine article appeared, life at the *Times* continued as it had. There were no stares or recriminations, no suggestions that my responsibilities be limited, no efforts to remove me from the writing program. I still received assignments for articles and legwork. And the next time I experienced a seizure in the newsroom, everyone knew what to do. I continued fumbling about in my job as a national desk clerk, still unwilling to reveal that my epilepsy caused severe memory loss. That led to an editor turning on me with a ferocity I had never experienced before.

My primary assignment was to move digital copies of newly filed articles from an electronic "in" basket to a directory used by the first team of editors, known as the backfield. Then, I filled out a piece of paper called a "buck slip" with the one-word name of the article and passed it to an editor who was infamous among clerks for her abusiveness.

One day, the article schedule included two stories with comparable names: "Immune" by Philip Boffey and "Virus" by Larry Altman. I don't know if the reporter mislabeled his piece or I mixed them up, but I filled out the slip as "Immune" by Altman.

The abrasive editor jumped on the error. "It's 'Immune' by Boffey and 'Virus' by Altman!" she snapped. "You can't be so sloppy in your job! Start paying attention!"

Another clerk had taught me never to apologize to this woman because it only made things worse, so I silently filled out a corrected buck slip and passed it to her.

She didn't stop the verbal assault. "It's one word and one writer! How hard is it to keep that straight?"

On and on she went, growing ever louder. She paused, and I saw a familiar expression of malign satisfaction. I knew she thought she had found the perfect insult.

"I didn't know epilepsy caused illiteracy!" she shouted.

Everything stopped—typing, talking, phone conversations. Editors and clerks stared at me. Nothing, not a sound or a motion, disturbed the moment as everyone braced for my reaction. In the silence, the angry editor realized she had gone over the line and turned away from me to stare blankly at her computer.

I knew from experience that I needed to say something, anything. Work would remain at a standstill until I did. At that moment, "Virus" by Altman appeared in the electronic "in" basket. I glanced across the news desk at Bill Dicke, the night editor.

"Bill," I said, "'Virus' by Altman just landed."

It was the equivalent of my saying, "Bill, the phone is ringing." But it was a signal to everyone that I was not going to respond to the comment just shouted at me.

"Oh, okay, thank you," Dicke stammered. "Can you move it to the backfield?"

Work resumed. Soon after, I was transferred from the toxic presence of the misanthropic editor to a better job in the third-floor newsroom. She moved to the fourth floor.

Everyone in the writing program had a deadline, a point when editors would decide if they would be promoted to reporter trainee. Mine arrived in early 1988. By then, I had written scores of articles. I had become the metro desk's go-to guy, accepting any legwork, even in the middle of the night. I had been awarded a one-month tryout as a reporter, and it could not have gone better—I asked to be assigned to the business desk to prove I could handle topics foreign to me. While I was there, the stock market crashed, and I threw myself into the coverage, sometimes filing several stories a day.

Editors and reporters told me my chances looked good, but then a hiccup. I heard from a friend that the editor in charge of the final decision had nixed me. I sat down at a desk and fished out a piece of paper I had prepared for any last-minute problems. I telephoned everyone at the *Times* who knew me or who owed me favors—Hedrick Smith, two editors in Washington, the assignment editor on the metro desk, and about a dozen others. I asked each of them to call on my behalf to the boss of the editor about to hand down the bad news. One ally, Rick Berke, reached me after his conversation.

"As soon as I started speaking, he said, 'Yes, I know. You're calling to recommend Kurt Eichenwald,'" Berke told me.

The next day, Warren Hoge, an assistant managing editor, summoned me to his office. He was on the phone when I arrived and waved for me to come in. My heart raced as he spoke in a foreign language I thought was Portuguese. He hung up, looked at me, and thrust out his right hand. My mind went blank as I stared at the silver bracelet on his wrist.

"Congratulations," he said. I finally took his hand. "You're a reporter trainee for *The New York Times*."

My beat was Wall Street. Based on my reporting during the market crash, the editors had concluded I must be a financial expert, though I actually didn't know the difference between a stock and a bond. I walked to a bookstore on Fifty-seventh Street and purchased business titles to help me learn the basics.

I marveled that a nobody like me suddenly was on the phone with power players in the world of finance—officials from the New York Stock Exchange, the Securities and Exchange Commission, Congress, major businesses. In one of the most surprising calls early on, Donald Trump contacted me to discuss a flattering profile about him from that day's *Times*. I had nothing to do with the article and tried to hide my confusion about why he had bothered to phone me to praise a piece about himself.

My strategy, for as long as I could get away with it, was to reveal my ignorance only to people I interviewed, a tactic I learned from another reporter. In one of my first days in my new job, I spoke to a man who told me he was an equities analyst.

"What's an equities analyst?" I asked.

The man ranted about my inexperience until I interrupted him. "Look, I can either look stupid to you now or pretend I know things I don't. That might make *you* look stupid in the paper tomorrow. Which do you prefer?"

He calmed down and answered my question.

When my trainee period ended, John Lee, an assistant managing editor, invited me to lunch at the fanciest restaurant I had patronized in years. We settled at a table near the back of the room, and he spent several minutes recalling his own experiences at the *Times*. Then on to me.

"Where did you learn about finance?" he asked.

I can't be fired. "On the job," I replied.

"Which job?"

"This one. Covering Wall Street for the paper."

If Lee had not been such a courtly southern gentleman, he might have spat out his drink. "You didn't know anything?"

"Not even the difference between a stock and a bond."

A wisp of anger crossed his face. "Don't you think you should have told us?"

"Let me ask," I responded. "You're told that you can be a *Times* reporter on an important beat. Would you try to convince the people offering you the job that they're making a mistake?"

He crinkled his forehead. "No," he said. "I suppose not."

As I settled into work, I decided finally to have doctors treat the physical damage inflicted by almost a decade of seizures. I visited an internist for a checkup. I asked about my ribs, which hadn't hurt for years; he told me the fractures had healed long ago. I also mentioned that my joints ached so badly I sometimes couldn't sleep. He looked at my knuckles and noticed a small growth under the skin on my right index finger.

"Has anyone ever examined that?" he asked.

"No."

"Have your knuckles always been this swollen?"

I glanced at my hands. They *were* swollen, terribly. "They haven't always been like this. I don't know when this started."

He recommended a rheumatologist, but before visiting with that doctor, I saw an oral surgeon. Years had passed since the fibrous mass had appeared in my mouth, caused by biting during seizures. With my drug levels fairly high, the doctor decided to use IV Valium rather than a stronger anesthetic while cutting out the growth. I vaguely remember watching unalarmed as blood spurted during the procedure.

During this round of doctor visits, I discovered I had found the strength to take control of my healthcare, ignoring poorly considered recommendations and always staying on the lookout for recklessness. In fact, I delighted in humiliating doctors for their gaffes, treating them as stand-ins for the medical specialists who had hurt me in the past.

At Naarden's suggestion, I sought out a New York neurologist. This new doctor was horrified that I still experienced convulsions every few weeks and recommended major medication changes.

"I'm not going to do that," I replied.

"Kurt," he said, "the most important thing is that we get control of these seizures."

I sat back in my chair. "Fine, give me a gun, and I'll blow my brains out."

His eyes widened. "What?" he gasped.

"That would take care of it, wouldn't it? That would stop the seizures."

"Are you . . ."

"No." I sighed. "I'm not suicidal. I'm making a point. You say controlling the seizures is the most important thing. Blowing my brains out would accomplish that. Clearly, that's a bad alternative."

He looked confused.

How can he not understand this? "The most important thing is having the life I want. If I'd rather have some seizures and fewer side effects, that's my choice. The decision of what's the most important thing is mine, not yours."

I never saw that neurologist again.

On to the rheumatologist. After an examination, he told me my anticonvulsants had probably damaged the soft tissue in my joints, which may have played a role in creating the lump on my finger. He recommended an anti-inflammatory to lessen the joint pain and started filling out the prescription.

"Excuse me," I said. "What effect will this drug have on my anticonvulsants?"

He kept writing. "I've never heard of it having any effect."

I've never heard of that as a side effect . . .

I looked on the credenza behind him. A copy of the *Physicians' Desk Reference* was lined up alongside other books.

"I didn't ask what you've *heard* of," I snapped. "I asked what's going to happen. Now, could you look it up in the *PDR?*"

The doctor stared at me with an expression of anger and disbelief, then grabbed the book, flipping through the pages. The fury in his face vanished before he spoke again.

"Well," he began slowly, "it might raise your Dilantin level. But that's not a big deal."

I was going to enjoy this.

"'Not a big deal,'" I repeated softly. "That's good to hear. 'Not a big deal.'"

I let a moment pass, then leaned forward. "Tell me," I said as I glared at him. "What's my Dilantin level?"

Silence, then a look of panic. He had no idea. "Well, I assume it's in the therapeutic range . . ."

"'I assume,'" I sneered, sarcastically mimicking his tone. "You *assume?* Are you *kidding?*"

I took a breath, trying to keep from screaming. "I'm at the *top* of the therapeutic level. And when you raise drugs to higher than therapeutic, they can become toxic. So this *is* a big deal."

I stood. "You're incompetent," I said. "And you're fired."

On New Year's Eve 1988, I wandered uncomfortably through an Upper East Side home stuffed with antique furniture, high-end glassware, and artwork. Each table held expensive decorative pieces, all of them breakable. A convulsion here could cause thousands of dollars in damage.

An array of well-dressed people bustled about, enjoying gourmet food and vintage wines. I had traveled to this party straight from the *Times* and felt utterly out of place. I was a newspaper scribbler, far from high-class. The owners of this home were the in-laws of my college roommate Franz, who lived in New York and had insisted I attend the party. The previous New Year's Eve, I had gone to South Street Seaport, where I had a seizure. I ended up in the hospital, and a nurse found my emergency contact information. That led to Franz being called away from a romantic evening with his wife so he could take me home. Not this New Year's Eve, Franz insisted. He would not walk out on his in-laws. If I had a seizure, he wanted me close by.

His demands were all a ruse. He knew that I would be uncomfortable in the fancy apartment, worried about expensive breakables and possibly about embarrassing him if I experienced convulsions. There was someone he wanted me to meet, and he didn't want to get into a debate with me about whether I would come. But he knew I would never refuse if he portrayed the invitation as being for *his* benefit. So he decided to trick me into joining the party.

I avoided food and drink to protect against dropping them on the rugs, which looked as if they would cost more to clean than I earned in a week. I wished I hadn't come; I could have avoided the chance of disrupting Franz's night by just staying in bed in my apartment.

Nearby, I saw a woman in a dark dress on a piano bench. She looked right at me and smiled. I immediately thought that her green eyes were stunning. She patted the spot next to her, inviting me to join her. I felt embarrassed; this woman was *way* out of my league. When she spoke, the words came out in an elegant accent I could not quite place, a mixture of British, French, and something else. She introduced herself as Theresa Pearse. She was loosely related to Franz; her older sister had married an older man who was the father of Franz's wife. I ran that through my head—Theresa was effectively Franz's aunt, though she appeared to be about my age.

We spent the evening talking. Usually I was nervous speaking to single women socially, but I felt relaxed, with none of my typical self-consciousness. She was flirtatious and intelligent and somehow made me forget my belief that I had been invited to keep me out of trouble. She mentioned that she was wearing a knee brace because she injured herself in a skiing accident. I glanced down; until that moment, I had been so captivated I somehow missed seeing the medical device wrapped around her leg.

She told me that she was halfway through a medical internship in Philadelphia and would be working as a resident in July. She had traveled to New York for the party and was staying with her parents, who lived nearby. I told her about my job and my background, but mentioned nothing about my health.

Unknown to me, she had already learned everything from her sister when Franz married into the family. For this evening, Franz had—without telling me—invited me as a blind date for Theresa after first making sure she understood how to react if I had a seizure.

As midnight approached, Theresa introduced me to her father, John Pearse. She took me aside. "Watch," she said. "Five minutes after midnight, he'll point at his watch and say, 'Well, Theresa, time to go.'"

Theresa told me this to give me time to think. At 12:05, she would leave unless I offered to walk her to her parents' house later. She did not know I worried about getting home by myself from empty streets where passersby would probably be drunk.

Midnight arrived, and just as she had predicted, five minutes later her father pointed at his watch. "Well, Theresa," he said, "time to go."

I stifled a laugh and made my decision. I offered to take her home if she stayed. She accepted. After thirty minutes or so, Theresa and I walked to her parents' brownstone. We kissed good night, and she headed inside.

Despite promising to stay in contact with her, I let two weeks pass without calling Theresa. Franz phoned me, annoyed I had broken my word. Theresa was his mother-in-law's sister, he said, and I couldn't be a jerk to her. My usual anxieties returned; I knew I owed it to Franz to call Theresa, but I feared she would shut me out once I told her about my health.

I made excuses until finally I phoned her in Philadelphia. We spoke every night over the weeks that followed, except for one Tuesday. We discussed my visiting, which I knew couldn't happen until I told her about my epilepsy. I brought it up hesitantly, and she interrupted to tell me the seizures were not an issue—Franz had told her everything long ago, she said. We set a date for my visit in late January, but pushed it off when the *Times* sent me to Chicago to cover a financial scandal. When I returned to New York in February, Theresa invited me to come see her.

I packed a bag and on the way out the door ran into my landlord, who asked where I was going.

"I'm headed for my first date with the woman I'm going to marry," I replied.

An audio letter from

THERESA EICHENWALD, 2017

The night I met Kurt, I was at my sister's on New Year's Eve, and I knew that we had essentially been set up on a blind date, and I was sitting in a dress that he actually remembers (and I didn't until he remembered it), and I had a brace on my leg because I had hurt my knee skiing. I remember sitting there at the piano thinking, I'm going to work my charms. I knew about his epilepsy from Franz, but I didn't think of it at all. It just never occurred to me that it would matter.

We really did get to know each other on the telephone, and I asked to hear the story of what he had gone through. More than having epilepsy, what struck me [was] the fortitude, and the ability to overcome obstacles without getting struck down. I had grown up in an environment where people would create obstacles that didn't exist, and here I was, talking to somebody who had real obstacles and overcame them.

Other than him answering my questions about his past, epilepsy really [wasn't the] focus at all in our conversations together. Then he finally did come down to meet me, and the only way that epilepsy ever really entered in the beginning of our relationship was that because of his medication, he could fall asleep just by closing his eyes, and was often deeply, deeply asleep and was hard to wake up in the morning. But so what?

CHAPTER TWENTY-EIGHT

Eight months later, Theresa and I stepped into a Manhattan restaurant hoping we had dressed appropriately for the evening. At a long table near the entrance, we saw a crowd surrounding Arthur Sulzberger, Jr., the heir apparent to the publisher of *The New York Times*. Recently anointed as the paper's second-in-command, Sulzberger had been inviting staff members—along with spouses or dates—for small get-togethers to establish a rapport with employees, and I had been tapped for this dinner.

I approached the table with customary "meal with the boss" anxiety. Without a word, Theresa stepped in front of me to take the seat directly across from our host. To anyone else, her move might have seemed like a nervy way to get face-to-face with one of New York's most powerful men. I knew better.

In our short time together, Theresa had learned how I assessed the dangers of my surroundings. In this situation, the chair where I was least likely to injure myself was to the left of where Theresa sat. The space around it was open, so if I went into convulsions, I wouldn't hit a hard surface other than the floor, and I wouldn't be trapped between the table and a wall. She also knew I would feel awkward sitting first in that spot; it would seem odd to take the seat catty-corner to Sulzberger, almost as if I were afraid to sit across from him. Theresa solved the problem, essentially blocking me into the spot she knew I wanted. I breathed a silent thanks to her, marveling at how lucky I had been to find her.

Things had moved fast for us. Theresa had planned to enter a residency program in Philadelphia but transferred to one at Beth Israel Medical Center in Manhattan seven months after we met. I had been nervous about moving in together so quickly, but we had little choice. Residencies begin in July, and if she continued training in Philadelphia, we would have been forced to live in separate cities for at least two years.

Even before she arrived in New York, my emotional barricades started to crumble. I had spent years focused on myself and my professional goals. Despite the outward signs of success, I lived in constant fear that a health setback or the revelation of my debilitated memory could destroy the life I had built. My dismissal from Swarthmore and my treatment by the Nader group left me believing I could lose everything in a matter of days, so I focused only on myself and keeping my employers happy.

All that changed with Theresa. The daughter of Polish Holocaust survivors, she grew up surrounded by the sadness and guilt that tore at her parents. Death loomed over the household; her father's family had all perished in the Warsaw Ghetto and the concentration camps, while her mother's youngest brother had sacrificed his life to save another sibling. Theresa's parents fled Poland to England, where she was born, then moved to the United States. But they were adrift in their lives— Jews who abandoned their faith out of anger at a God that allowed millions to die, Americans who never adapted to the culture of their new homeland. The disconnect between her cultural acclimation and her parents' alienation left Theresa torn between two worlds. When she tried to explain that growing up in the United States made her more American than the rest of the family, her mother responded, "Isn't that a pity?"

She possessed a happy, carefree side to her character and a sense of humor that matched my style, but Theresa was often shrouded in the gray sorrow of her upbringing. In our earliest months together, she offered me support in managing my feelings that stemmed from the constant threat of seizures, while I shared with her the lessons I had learned from a decade of health problems. I discussed finding the joy of each day, of escaping the emotional bonds of our past. We would sit talking on our bedroom floor, with me encouraging her to pursue her dream of becoming a clinician, rather than joining academic medicine as an homage to her father's goals that had been dashed by the war.

We became a mutual support system. For the first time, I told someone other than a counselor about my beating in Chicago. I no longer needed to record my thoughts in audio and written diaries; Theresa wanted to hear everything, whether from the past or from that day. My mindset changed from focusing on my own struggles to concern about helping the woman I loved to cultivate the humorous, daring, and joyful person submerged by her upbringing.

In short order, we also discovered our different upbringings could lead to hilarity. Born in Britain and raised in Manhattan, where she attended a French school with the children of diplomats, Theresa spoke in a way that sometimes left me confused. When she told me my shoes were in the cupboard, I headed for the kitchen, puzzled why she had put them in with the dishes; after a laugh, she let me know that "cupboard" was a word used by the British for "closet." Another time, she asked me to fetch my dressing gown. I stared at her for a moment, then said "American English, please?" She wanted me to get my robe.

The night at the deputy publisher's dinner was the first time I saw Theresa's true character on public display. The gathered reporters peppered Sulzberger with questions about the *Times*, his plans, and himself. When he learned Theresa was a doctor, he asked about her work. Sulzberger was fascinated by her description of problems caused by new city medical rules and invited her to write a piece for the *Times* about them.

Eventually, Tamar Lewin, a reporter sitting beside Sulzberger, asked a question. "How does it feel to be in a fishbowl, to know everyone is always watching everything you do?"

"Well," Sulzberger began, "I really don't feel like everybody's watching—"

At that instant, Theresa reached across the table and brushed Sulzberger's cheek.

"You have food on your face," she said.

The table went silent. Then Sulzberger and I broke out laughing. There was nothing on his face. Theresa was teasing one of the most powerful men in New York, someone she had just met. This was the woman I knew, one of confidence and daring humor. Serving as each other's anchor was changing us both.

Later that month, I kneeled in the small kitchen of our one-bedroom apartment, bagging garbage while Theresa washed dishes. Despite the humdrum nature of my chore, I considered staying in that narrow room to be an accomplishment; if I experienced a convulsion there, my head would hit the countertop. But Theresa had helped me set aside some of my worries. *Take the chance* was her attitude. I needed to walk into narrow rooms. There were too many to avoid them all.

As I tied the bag's drawstrings, Theresa interrupted my thoughts in the most dramatic way possible.

"So, when are you going to ask me to marry you?"

I looked up from the garbage. Theresa, I knew, was the woman I had envisioned years before when I planned my life at Northwestern. She was, as I had imagined, like the television character Laura Petrie—fun, funny, intelligent, supportive. I had feared my seizures would drive any woman away, but they bothered Theresa only to the extent they bothered me. I hadn't intended to make any big decisions while struggling with a Hefty bag, but I knew the answer to her question. Life was too short to delay.

"How about now?" I replied. "Want to get married?"

She said yes, and I apologized for not having a ring. After all, I hadn't expected to be asking that night. The next day, we visited Saks Fifth Avenue to purchase some earrings to commemorate our big day—we wanted to spend more time shopping for an engagement ring.

We planned the wedding for July 1990. For months, I silently pitied myself because my condition would rob me of some traditions. With my sugar restrictions and my knuckles swollen from medication, there would be no wedding cake or ring for me. To surprise me, Theresa quietly solved both problems: She contacted a jeweler, who manu-

factured a clasped ring, then arranged for the baker to make the top
tier of our wedding cake sugar-free. Those were the greatest gifts I
could have imagined.

The seizures remained part of our lives, but Theresa handled them
with aplomb. Once while she was on call at Beth Israel, a doctor from
Roosevelt Hospital phoned her. I had experienced a grand mal seizure
on the street, the doctor said, and had been brought to the ER. Someone needed to come for me. Theresa couldn't leave the hospital, so she
contacted Franz.

I awoke in the ER with no memory of what had happened. Whenever I found myself in a hospital alone, I checked my body for clues to
where I was when the seizure occurred. I dug into the pocket of my
jeans and found a ticket stub. I figured I must have been at a movie or
coming home from one when the convulsions struck. But knowing
that was no help—I remembered nothing. I read the stub.

Total Recall. The newly released Arnold Schwarzenegger movie. I
laughed—I had forgotten *Total Recall.*

A doctor who looked like Chuck Norris appeared. "What's so
funny?" he asked, sounding amused.

"Nothing," I said. "Hard to explain."

Franz showed up soon after. When the doctor stepped away, Franz
marveled at how much he looked like a G.I. Joe action figure. I didn't
disagree, but still thought he was more of a Chuck Norris type. Finally,
G.I. Norris gave me the all clear, and Franz took me to his apartment.
There, I slept off the seizure until Theresa arrived home the next day.

That seizure, which gave me a funny story to tell for decades, was
the last one I experienced as a bachelor.

After our marriage, Theresa felt more comfortable bringing up a subject that she knew, for me, was frightening: Should I try a new medical
treatment to control my epilepsy? She didn't understand why I was
still experiencing convulsions; she had little training in neurology and
believed that, if I received better care, they might stop. By then I was
seeing a neurologist in New York, Dr. Aaron Brachfeld, and he was
deliberate and methodical, never arguing when I told him I was too
frightened to accept his recommendations that I try new medications.

Even when he assured me that my severe joint pain could be a side effect of the Mysoline, he accepted my refusal to stop taking the drug.

My stubbornness angered Theresa. I had explained how my past made me resistant to change, but she thought my willingness to tolerate the situation was absurd. She did not want me to suffer from falls and fears out of obstinacy.

One day at Beth Israel, she attended a lecture by a neurologist, Dr. Douglas Pressa. Fascinated by the talk, she decided that he might be the neurologist who could help me. She returned to our apartment and urged me to make an appointment. We bickered until I finally caved, accepting her argument that I had allowed dread to overpower reason.

Knowing I was terrified, Theresa accompanied me to Pressa's office. I glanced around as we sat in the waiting room. Everyone was thin. *Everyone.* It was stunning. I wondered about the statistical probability that so many people in one room would appear almost anorexic. My anxiety level climbed.

A nurse summoned me, and I kissed Theresa before heading off. I was escorted to the EEG lab, where electrodes were once again attached to my scalp. I hated the test but felt relieved Pressa had not asked to inject electrodes through my jaw or slide them up my nose.

Once the technician finished, she picked up the fanfold of paper showing the tracings of the electrical firings in my brain. She carried it to Pressa's exam room as I followed, then laid it down near me.

I waited for several minutes until the door swung open and Pressa zipped in. His energetic demeanor was at once impressive and intimidating. We exchanged greetings. Then he walked to the table holding my EEG tracings. He ran his thumb up the side of the paper, turning pages rapidly as if he were studying an animation in a flip-book.

Is it really that easy to read an EEG? I thought.

He conducted a quick neurological exam—look here; squeeze this; push that.

"Okay," he said. "We need to change your medication."

So fast? All Pressa knew about me were vague details from a form I filled out. He had asked me nothing since coming into the room. He needed to slow down, I thought, so he could tell me about his thinking and learn about my background.

"Why do I need to change?" I asked.

"Because you're still having grand mal seizures. It's not safe. They have to be stopped."

I couldn't argue with that, but I also knew any attempt at achieving better control might fail. And what if new anticonvulsants caused problems that kept me out of work?

"I'm very uncomfortable changing drugs," I said. "I've had so many problems in the past—"

He interrupted. His tone was brusque, almost angry.

"Fine, do nothing," he said. "Let the seizures keep happening. Let yourself become demented in five years. You can sit in a chair, drooling in a corner, and never be able to hold your own kids. Is that really what you want?"

I felt as if a spear had pierced my chest. Was that my destiny? Was he lying? *Why hasn't Naarden told me I could become demented?*

"That could happen?" I asked.

"It *will* happen if you insist on doing nothing."

Confusion and anger overtook me. Craddock, the doctor who overdosed me, had told me everything was fine, and I believed in him. Then the doctor in Chicago exposed that the drugs were killing me. I believed in Naarden, but he had never mentioned my doomed future; Pressa had no reason to lie.

For years, I'd overruled neurologists, following Naarden's maxim that I was sole arbiter of whether the seizures outweighed side effects from a drug change. I never considered that, by letting seizures continue, I was destroying my brain. *How could he not have warned me?* I thought.

Resistance fell away. Pressa was my new savior. "So, what should I do?" I asked. "I really need to change medications?"

Absolutely, Pressa replied. "This has to stop."

I remembered Naarden had once recommended trying Tegretol again. I asked Pressa if that was a good option. No, he said. There was another medication he thought would be best.

"It's not available in the United States, but it's quite promising and could be very helpful," he said.

I was confused. "It's not available?"

"It hasn't been approved by the FDA, but it's showing good results."

Wait a minute. I knew what this meant from my own reporting about medical research. If the government had not approved this drug, it was experimental. That meant doctors were still testing it to determine if it was safe and effective; only neurologists cleared to conduct the studies could obtain the medication. Pressa had to be one of them. If he wanted me on this anticonvulsant, that meant he hadn't recruited enough patients to participate in the study. I would have to sign a document called an informed consent before he could add me to the pool of test subjects. He *did* have a motive to lie to me about my future. He needed patients for his research.

I feigned ignorance. "If it's not approved by the FDA, how can you get it?"

He smiled. "I'm one of the researchers in the clinical trials. So you're lucky, because there aren't many doctors who have access to the drug."

I swallowed my anger and continued to act oblivious. I no longer doubted that Pressa was trying to manipulate me, but I still feared his warnings about my future might be true.

"Does it have side effects?" I asked, knowing the answer was yes. All anticonvulsants did. I wanted to check his honesty.

"Nothing serious has turned up," he replied. "The most common one we're seeing is weight loss."

I thought back to the waiting room. I had marveled at the statistical improbability of so many people in one room being so underweight. This experimental drug caused weight loss.

He's pushed all of his patients into this clinical trial, I thought. I felt an urge to punch him.

"I'm going to give this some thought," I said calmly. "I don't want to make a decision right away."

"All right. But don't take too long. There's a limited number of patients who'll be allowed into the study."

I thanked him and strode briskly through the waiting room, desperately wanting out of that office, out of that building, out of that city. I saw Theresa chatting with a woman who appeared younger than me. An astonishingly thin woman.

"Theresa," I said curtly, "let's go."

I didn't wait for her. I needed to get away. My mind churned. Was I going to become demented? Was it all a lie so Pressa could have his test subjects? Would I never be able to hold my children? Was this experimental drug really my only hope?

I reached the elevator bank and pushed the button. Theresa caught up with me, annoyed that I had rushed off without waiting for her.

"How did it go?" she asked.

I stared up above the elevator door, anxiously waiting for the down light to flash on.

My voice was soft, my tone one of contained fury. "We're going to Dallas," I said. "I have to see Naarden right away."

I waited until we reached our apartment before recounting to Theresa what had happened with Pressa. My emotions were a jumble of anger and fear. I talked about my terror of becoming demented in my thirties, of being too feeble to be a father to our future children. But if it was all a lie, how could Pressa have done it? How could my well-being be less important than his research? Theresa then confirmed my belief—the thin woman I had seen in the waiting room had mentioned her treatment. She was taking the same experimental drug Pressa recommended for me.

I walked into the bathroom and climbed into our empty tub. That was a dangerous place, particularly given that my extreme stress could trigger a seizure. But I needed to feel contained, protected. I sobbed as I talked about my uncertain fate. In my mind's eye, I pictured my demented self in a chair, head lolling to the side, oblivious to children playing around me.

Theresa didn't know what to do. She had never seen the psychological collapse I experienced in moments of deep distress. She knew about my run-ins with neurologists, my dismissal from Swarthmore, my beating in Chicago, although I had held back on revealing the rape out of shame and embarrassment. While she felt empathy over these experiences, they were all tales from a far-off past. Now, for the first time, she was witnessing the magnitude of my despair firsthand.

She suffered an upwelling of guilt for having urged me to see Pressa, and she felt responsible for my emotional turmoil. She went into denial herself, pushing away the possibility that her new husband might soon descend into senility. She had been raised to discount severe upheaval, to adopt the cliché "stiff upper lip" of the British. She mentioned our dog.

"*The dog?*" I shouted. "Are you kidding me? You want to talk about the fucking dog?"

Effusive apologies. She didn't know what to do, she said. She didn't know what to say. She began blaming herself for my torment; she should have left things alone. "I didn't understand," she said.

"This is *not* your fault," I replied, words rushing out amid tears. "You wanted to help. Maybe you did. Maybe I am in danger of becoming demented. We don't know. That's why we have to go to Dallas."

Naarden, whom I had continued to consult and visit for checkups when I was in Dallas, agreed to an urgent appointment. Theresa and I flew to Texas; we both told our bosses we would not be coming to work because of a family emergency. At Naarden's office, I introduced him to Theresa, then instructed her to stay in the waiting room. I wanted him to hear only from me about Pressa's prediction. If Naarden confirmed it, I knew I would explode at him for having failed to warn me of the danger.

First, small talk. Naarden congratulated me on my work for *The New York Times*. I thanked him, then abruptly got to the point. I recounted Pressa's statement that if the seizures didn't stop, I would be demented in a few years.

"That is untrue," Naarden said. "There is *no* research showing epilepsy leads to early-onset dementia in adults. It's the other way around. The medical literature does suggest that elderly patients with Alzheimer's develop seizures. That has nothing to do with you."

Relief washed over me. "I think that answers my second question, but I need to ask. He said I would be so debilitated if I didn't stop the seizures that I wouldn't be able to hold my children, and I would just be drooling in a corner."

"That's *ridiculous*," Naarden said. "I have many patients who have grand mal seizures and are parents. You have to take some precautions, but there is no reason you can't be active in your children's lives."

Fears gave way, and fury took over. "You want to know why he told me this stuff? He's running a clinical trial," I said. "He told me these horrible things would happen to me if I didn't change medicines and that I should take the one he's researching."

Naarden didn't look surprised, which unnerved me. He asked if I remembered the name of the medication. I told him.

"This is outrageous," he fumed. "That's the problem for some of these doctors who run trials. They become entranced by the research and don't see the patient."

He said he wanted to report Pressa to his institutional review board, a hospital organization that supervises medical research to ensure it complies with ethical standards. What Pressa had done, Naarden said, violated those rules. Pressa had used his authority as a doctor in an attempt to manipulate me into signing up as a research subject.

"A person with your history should *never* be in a drug trial, unless it's targeted for patients with seizures that have been poorly controlled long-term," he said. "Particularly if all the standard treatments haven't been tried."

I bristled. I knew where this was going. Naarden once again suggested that I should change my medications. Nothing experimental, only well-understood drugs approved by the FDA. I was still taking Mysoline and Dilantin. He advised tapering off the Mysoline, then substituting another drug for the Dilantin. This shift to a new mix would be done slowly, he said. He assured me that he understood why I had refused in the past. But the time had come for me to rely on the best medical knowledge about treatments, he said, and not allow my anxieties to dictate my decisions.

I considered everything that had happened over the last few days: Theresa finding me a new doctor, arguing in an attempt to persuade me to consider treatment options, accompanying me to two appointments. Now the neurologist who saved me was saying I had been foolishly standing still, accepting my convulsions as just part of life, when I might be able to get better. I realized, once again, that I had been selfish. Whether I could deal with the seizures I experienced was no longer the issue. I had yet to include Theresa in the equation. I had no right to complicate her life simply because I was afraid. Plus, the pain in my joints that had been attributed to the Mysoline had been growing steadily worse.

I agreed. For the first time in a decade, I would allow him to change my anticonvulsants.

Years later, I wondered what had happened with the experimental drug Pressa had pushed on me. The FDA approved its usage, but it was quickly withdrawn after a number of patients developed a potentially fatal illness. The government eventually allowed the medication back on the market with severe restrictions. The manufacturer warned that it posed significant risks and advised using it only in extreme cases once safer medication had failed. In fact, doctors were forbidden from prescribing the anticonvulsant unless patients signed documents stating that they had been warned about the magnitude of the danger.

Patients prescribed the medication succumbed to aplastic anemia. Anyone taking the drug was one hundred times more likely to contract it. People like me, who had already experienced life-threatening bone marrow problems caused by an anticonvulsant, are most at risk of developing this potentially fatal disease. The package insert for the medication contains a black box stating that people with my medical history should never take the drug under any circumstances.

At the time Pressa pressed me to join the research, those perils had not yet come to light. Had he succeeded in manipulating me into the clinical trial through a false depiction of my bleak future, I could be dead today, a victim of the same blood disease I'd barely escaped a decade before.

THERESA EICHENWALD, 2017

Epilepsy was not something I thought about when we got engaged. Really, in our day-to-day lives, it didn't factor in. Kurt took medication, sometimes he had seizures. I was frightened about getting married in general, but that had nothing to do with his health. Besides, I was getting desperate. [laughs]

I'm not quite sure what to say. Kurt's asking me about memories of him and epilepsy, and how it affected our lives, and what I think of it. There's none of that to talk about. What there is to talk about is how much humor and wit and fun we have had.

There is something. One of the things that I found very, very difficult in the beginning was the feeling that he wasn't trying to fix this. I was trained in medicine, and when you're first starting off in medicine, you always feel that medicine can manage to fix everything and that things are simple. And Kurt's fears had made him very, very reluctant to seek medical attention. Rightfully so, he had only dealt with miserable experiences with doctors who had nearly killed him, and I didn't get it, and I really resented the fact that he wasn't trying to get better and get "fixed." I kept thinking that if he would only see a new neurologist or a better neurologist, that he would be fine. I still feel guilty about having hooked him up with a neurologist I heard talking, who made it sound like epilepsy was a simple thing to take care of. But it's not always a simple thing.

He was afraid, and there were lots of things I didn't understand about him being afraid, and I took a long time to get it. And when I did, I think he recognized that I got it, and he relaxed, and he started to be a little calmer when he was sick. It's all a question of people reading each other correctly and treating each other correctly. I think that that's true in every marriage and I think what happens in marriages that fall apart is people don't try to understand each other and don't try to figure out how the other one works. It is also very, very possible that the fact that he had epilepsy and the fact that I have my own baggage made us pay more attention to each other and recognize that we each need each other very, very much.

CHAPTER TWENTY-NINE

The late-morning sun bathed Manhattan's West Seventy-second Street as Theresa and I headed home. I scarcely noticed. An intense desire to tear off my skin invaded my thoughts, along with an agitated sense that something else was wrong, something I couldn't identify.

My glasses. They had bent. I was sure of it. I yanked them off my face and stopped in my tracks, twisting the frames to realign them until the metal snapped in my hands. Overwhelmed, I dropped to the sidewalk and sobbed as pedestrians stepped past us. Theresa kneeled beside me, quietly speaking while I aggressively rubbed my hands over my eyes. As if comforting a child, she assured me everything was fine, then coaxed me to stand. Gripping my arm, she led me the half-block to our apartment.

I was in withdrawal from my decade-long dependence on high doses of Mysoline, the barbiturate that was my second-line anticonvulsant after Dilantin. Until Naarden started weaning me off the drug, I hadn't known I was a legal addict. Obsessions stuck in my head, like the false certainty my glasses had bent. I exploded in anger and anxiety, and my forgetfulness worsened. Once, I took a friend to dinner and, during the meal, ranted irrationally about some inconsequential matter. I paid the bill and stormed out; seconds later, our waitress ran after me on the street and handed me twenty-five cents. "I don't need a tip like this," she said angrily. I apologized, told her I wasn't well, hadn't known I had left such an insulting sum, then handed her a twenty-dollar bill before rushing away like a madman.

Withdrawal struck in waves. Naarden, in consultation with Brachfeld, my New York neurologist, would cut the dosage. The irrationality would return, then subside, and soon after he would reduce the prescription again. Sleep transformed into hours of tossing and turning and popping out of bed to pace around the apartment.

Brachfeld prescribed Ativan to ease the symptoms. Even after purchasing the pills, I refused to take them. My brain was a mess, I figured; Ativan was another addictive medication. Better to suffer withdrawal, I thought, than to make things worse with more drugs.

Still, I always carried the bottle of Ativan in my pocket, just in case. One day, I was at my desk in a four-person cubicle when I realized I was sweating through my shirt. I wanted to punch someone. I glanced around and saw a reporter I considered a friend. I became angry for no reason.

You're going crazy, I thought. I took out the Ativan, struggled to unscrew the childproof cap, then swallowed the pill without water. About twenty minutes later, I felt better. I considered taking more than had been prescribed. *I have to get control of myself*, I thought. I put the bottle back in my pocket, then glanced toward a filthy window about forty feet away that overlooked West Forty-third Street. I knew that right outside, in Times Square, drug dealers were whispering to passersby that they were ready to sell.

A calm came over me. I thought about illegal drug users who kicked their addictions. I was coming off a prescription medication slowly, with medical assistance. In the past, I had dismissed addicts as people who only needed to sweat it out. Now I understood: They desperately required the care of professionals to help them wean themselves from their dependence. I developed enormous admiration for addicts who managed to get clean.

The process of tapering off seemed endless, until the day came when I finally took my last piece of a Mysoline pill ever. A milestone, but I dreaded the next step: About a month later, my doctors would start adding a new medication. When that drug was at full strength, I would slowly come off Dilantin.

Weeks passed. Then one afternoon at work, a thought: *When was my last grand mal seizure?* I couldn't remember having had one in a long time. I called Theresa and asked if she knew the date of my last convulsion. She told me none had occurred in more than a month.

I contacted Brachfeld, who sent me for a check of my drug levels. The Dilantin in my bloodstream had not changed—near the top of the therapeutic level, too high to increase the dosage. But something unforeseen had occurred: The amount of Dilantin unbound to protein had increased. This "free Dilantin" was the active portion of the medication. The doctor explained the situation until I understood: Removing Mysoline had decreased the stimulation of an enzyme, which apparently led to a higher concentration of free Dilantin. Even though my dosage had stayed the same, the therapeutic amount in my blood had increased. That combined with the elimination of the sleepiness associated with Mysoline—a side effect that could trigger seizures—led to better control.

I told my neurologists that I would not switch off Dilantin for a while; I wanted to wait and see what happened. A month passed. And another. No convulsions. I cautiously allowed myself to believe that, after twelve years, the grand mal seizures may have ended.

Smaller seizures began. With little warning, the muscles in my left shoulder would contract, leading to a sharp movement of my head. This could be accompanied with a high-pitched, uncontrolled vocalization that sounded like a bark. Once this happened in a store where Theresa and I were browsing, and a woman rushed out of the back room announcing she wanted to see the dog. I hesitated mentioning this to Brachfeld—I still feared how doctors would react to bizarre symptoms. When I told him, he was unfazed, saying these were myoclonic seizures and ictal barking.

"Seriously?" I replied. "It's actually called barking?"

"It sounds like barking, doesn't it?" he said.

I took to calling these small seizures "circuit breakers," imagining them as tiny bursts of electrical energy that shut down potential convulsions. This fantasy made me happy, since I could see each jerk as grand mal seizures I had dodged. These new episodes ended in a second. There was no postictal period, no confusion, no sleepiness.

For months, I still braced myself each day for convulsions that never came and was surprised that I experienced enormous trouble adjusting to this unexpected tranquility. Occasionally, I became convinced that a grand mal seizure was imminent, but nothing happened—each time, it was just panic born of my past.

Our lives calmed. No longer heavily sedated by Mysoline, I could go to bed and wake up refreshed, without having to drag myself from a drug-induced torpor. So it was that when Theresa came home from the hospital one weekend morning and jumped on the bed, I awakened instantly.

"Good morning, Daddy!" she said excitedly.

She was pregnant with our first child. And with the convulsions gone, I would be able to hold our baby without fear.

About a dozen expectant couples sat on chairs in a circle, listening as a Lamaze instructor discussed the miracle of childbirth. The opening monologue droned in treacly platitudes; she wasn't *teaching* us anything, except maybe how to write bad greeting cards. I knew Theresa, who was leaning against me, was having as much trouble as me keeping a straight face.

The instructor glanced around the circle. "Now I want each of you to tell me why you came today," she said to the men.

To learn Lamaze for childbirth so we can be there for our wives, I thought. *What other answer is there?*

A lot, apparently. The other men waxed on with saccharine fervor. Not one gave the obvious, simple answer that he just wanted to be taught about Lamaze. I thought the others were afraid to be honest, instead feeling compelled to rhapsodize disingenuously. Eventually, the instructor turned to me.

"So, Kurt," she said, "why did you come to this class?"

"I don't know." I shrugged. "To pick up chicks?"

The instructor and other couples looked at me in horror as Theresa broke out laughing, unable to stop until tears flowed from her eyes. She hugged me, and we both chuckled some more.

We knew our pasts made it difficult for us to take daily life too seriously. One of us had been immersed in the imminent threat of death for years, the other in the emotional remnants of genocide. We were loving, caring, and giving, but neither of us could tolerate mawkishness. We were never afraid to be matter of fact or to crack a joke at the expense of soppy, vainglorious emotionality. That was how we would raise our children.

Adam was born in 1992, and in the hospital, I noticed something alarming: When he slept, Adam trembled and twitched. We had been warned epilepsy had a genetic component, and the possibility I had passed on the condition terrified me. The doctors wanted to take him to the ICU for observation, but Theresa refused to send away our new baby. After we returned home, I filmed Adam as he slept, and we brought the video to a neurologist, who ordered an EEG. Afterward, she assured us Adam was fine and the twitches would stop. They did, about a month later.

Our second son, Ryan, was born in 1995, followed by Sam in 1997. As I had promised myself years before, I made family the centerpiece of my life. Everything else—jobs, prestige, whatever—was not even on the list. Theresa and I hugged our sons and told them we loved them multiple times a day, and I always sang to them after reading a bedtime story. We never listened to the radio while driving, instead using the time to talk. Although I had never been an athlete, I coached all of their sports teams.

Both Theresa and I made sure our sons knew they mattered more to us than our jobs. Once when I was in Houston covering a long-running criminal trial, I phoned the *Times* to say that someone needed to take over for a day; I was going home for Adam's tenth birthday. My boss replied that I was not allowed to leave Houston.

"We all have to miss things," he said.

I answered, "I don't." The *Times* could have a reporter there or not, I said, but I would not be absent during my boy's party. Having given him no choice, my boss caved and sent another reporter to take my place in Houston for two days.

In 2001, we abandoned our lives in New York to benefit our children. Commuting had robbed me of family dinners; the *Times* had tried to accommodate the situation by allowing me to work frequently at our home in nearby Westchester County. But it wasn't enough. Theresa and I were both unhappy about their schools. Worse, we realized that children in New York—even in the suburbs—needed sharp elbows and thick skin. Our boys had neither. When we heard my mother might be losing her eyesight, Theresa announced it was time to leave. We wanted our kids to grow up in Dallas. On previous trips there, Theresa had visited my school, St. Mark's, and we both thought they would flourish if they attended.

I approached one of my bosses, told him my family and I were planning to live in Dallas, and asked if I still could work at the paper. He responded that senior editors would have to confer about whether I would be allowed to transfer.

"You don't understand," I replied. "I'm not asking for permission. I'm going. The only question is whether you guys want me to continue to work for the *Times* when I'm there."

That night, as I lay in bed beside Theresa, I thought, *Who walks away from* The New York Times? I immediately knew the answer. Someone who understands what matters in life. Someone whose values have been shaped through suffering. A feeling I'd experienced in the past came roaring back, stronger than ever: I was glad I had been so sick. I was glad that I had confronted my own mortality, contemplated suicide, endured severe pain, been thrown out of school, been denied employment. It made me the person I had become. Without those experiences, I would have been a lawyer. While there is nothing wrong with the profession, I would have chosen law not out of interest but to dodge a fear of failure by taking a well-worn path. I loved my life. If I could go back in time, I wouldn't want to change a thing, because my trauma forced me to confront myself, to discover who I really am. To be happy.

We moved to Dallas in 2001. I continued at the *Times* as an investigative reporter, and Theresa opened a new medical practice.

No one in the family remembers when Theresa and I started discussing my epilepsy with the children—they all say they knew about it as far back as they can remember. I continued experiencing jerks and barks, and while Ryan feared for my well-being, he came to understand this was just part of my life and I would be fine.

We ate dinner together almost every night, spicing it up with boisterous laughter, chatter, and bizarre jokes. Often the boys and I took turns trying to shock Theresa or to make her fall into uncontrollable giggles. When the kids witnessed small seizures, they kidded about them, just as my college roommates had. Our boys' friends often dropped by uninvited to join in our raucous meals. Taking a cue from my sons, they reacted to my occasional severe twitches with disregard or jokes, not alarm.

We established a few major principles in the house—no emotional secrets; no one could be disciplined for admitting to misbehavior; and nothing would be punished more severely than lying, even through omission. However, we would also respect our children's privacy, never examining their computers, texts, or other communications with friends. The result of this expression of mutual trust was that the boys consulted us on deeply personal issues into their teenage years and beyond.

But I felt like a hypocrite. Despite our commitment to open communication, I kept a major secret, one that still tore at my psyche: I had never revealed to Theresa I had been raped in my midtwenties. I feared not only what she would think but also the impact on me from saying it out loud. When I'd first discussed what had happened with a psychologist years earlier, I hadn't been able to bring myself to utter "rape." Instead, I'd relied on the more abstract "sexual assault."

My decision to tell Theresa came as a sudden surprise to me. I hadn't planned on disclosing anything but suddenly felt a compulsion to reveal the truth. In our bedroom, I sat in an overstuffed chair and said I needed to discuss something important. Years before, after a grand mal seizure, I said, I had been raped. I winced at saying the word out loud and braced myself for her reaction.

"I know," she said gently.

I was stunned and asked how that was possible. There was no single answer, she said; an accumulation of things I had said and done over the years led to her recognition that, despite everything else I revealed, I was still holding back on something deeply traumatic. With an irrational and overwhelming sense of guilt, I asked what she thought of me. She replied that she felt nothing but pride, both because I had not allowed the rape to cripple me and because I had finally found the courage to tell her.

As life eased, I came to accept that my memory problems were worse than I had allowed myself to believe. I had known for years that I forgot names as well as events of little consequence. Long before, I developed compensation techniques for work to hide this part of my condition, especially from my bosses, who I feared might limit my assignments if they knew the truth. So, for work, I maintained extensive records, audiotaping or keeping notes on every conversation, whether with a source or an editor. I discovered writing notes by hand was nearly impossible; when I tried to focus on keeping the words legible and listening at the same time, I could not recall the second half of someone's statement after writing down the first. Typing interviews solved that problem—my hands hit the proper keys without my thinking. Sometimes compensating proved costly. Covering trials required handwritten notes, since reporters were forbidden from using tape recorders or computers. To get around the problem, I would ask court reporters if I could purchase a rough transcript the same afternoon as a hearing. I usually paid for those records myself to avoid questions from the paper about why I spent the money instead of just writing down testimony.

When I signed my first book contract in 1993, I recognized my memory problems might prevent me from keeping track of the volumes of documents and interviews such projects required. To compensate, I relied on intense organization. I adopted the narrative nonfiction style for my books, using time sequence as the basis for categorizing my reporting. My assistants transcribed interviews and sorted thousands of records by date. All of the documents, including interview transcripts, were placed in binders, color-coded, and labeled to identify the types of information they contained. Then we reviewed every piece of paper, scouring transcripts and documents for events and entering them into a massive time line. Each entry cited where I could find the information using coded identifiers. Running hundreds of pages, the chronologies served not only as virtual outlines of each book but also as an artificial memory so I would never overlook information I had obtained.

I no longer kept such records in my personal life, and as my children grew, the severity of my memory impairment became apparent. While in the car one day, I suddenly felt regret for never having fished with the boys, a typical son-dad experience. Maybe they would have enjoyed the experience or just spending time with their dad.

"Guys, I've been thinking," I said. "I owe you all an apology. I've never taken you fishing. I think that would have been fun. I'm really sorry. Maybe we can go soon?"

The boys were silent for a moment. "Dad," Ryan said, "you took me fishing."

"Me too," Sam said.

"You've taken all of us fishing," Adam said.

I felt certain they were mistaken. "No," I said as we pulled up to our house. "I never took you fishing."

Everyone climbed out of the car. Adam walked to a corner of the garage and called me over. "Look at this," he said, pointing at shelves against the wall.

I stared in disbelief. Four fishing poles and tackle boxes. I opened one and saw lures, line, weights, and bobbers. They were dirty, and the box smelled like it had been used many times.

"You took each of us fishing," Adam said. "That's why these are here."

I still remember nothing about these trips. Later, I looked at photographs and found an image of the boys peering out of an icehouse. I tried to recollect where this had been; no luck. Theresa told me the photo was from our vacation to Lake Louise in Canada. Not only had I been there, but I took the picture. The memory either hadn't been stored in my brain or could not be retrieved.

The dam of truth opened. Theresa told me I forgot far more than I realized. She would tell me a story, and a week later I would remember nothing about it. I could watch the same television show repeatedly, not knowing I had seen it before.

I reverted to old habits and tried to push the problem aside. Instead, it loomed even larger—in 2007, a failure to remember an event in my personal life caused serious problems at work. I was plagued by uncertainty; I wondered, how did experiences unremembered differ from those that never occurred?

Naarden had retired from his practice by then, although he still played a role overseeing research at Medical City. My new neurologist, Dr. Robert Leroy, had—like Naarden and others before him—urged me to switch from Dilantin in hopes of stopping the twitching and barking, but I adamantly refused. Now, distressed by my memory problems, I accompanied Theresa to Naarden's office.

I told him I wanted to discuss forgetfulness. "If I changed medication, would I recover lost memories?"

Unlikely, he replied. "It might help with your memory going forward," he said, "but you know that we can't tell you beforehand what will happen."

Before I asked the next question, Naarden changed the subject. "I've been speaking to Theresa," he said. "You're in denial about how bad things are with your seizures."

I looked at Theresa. "It's true," she said. "I've been trying to tell you. You're too afraid to hear it."

I didn't understand. I wasn't having grand mal seizures.

Theresa told me I was wrong. I had experienced a major seizure at home while on the phone with a friend. No one had seen what happened, but the friend called her at the office, saying I had dropped the phone and wasn't picking up. Theresa telephoned Adam, who was in the house, and he found me on the floor. At fifteen, he already knew how to handle the situation.

"Dilantin is not the best medication for you," Naarden said. "You need to change."

From there, Theresa brought me to see Leroy. This, I realized, was a triple tag team—Naarden, Theresa, and Leroy had planned an intervention.

Leroy repeated the message that I was in denial about the poor state of my health and that the time to switch anticonvulsants had long passed. I asked again if changing would help me recover old memories or at least improve my ability to recollect events in the future. He repeated Naarden's assessment: Possible but unpredictable.

Leroy prescribed Lamictal to replace Dilantin. The switch proved complicated and unpleasant. The shoulder and head movements as well as the barks stopped, replaced by a severe left arm jerk. That spasm was so strong and abrupt that, if I rested my arm on a dining table, I could suddenly knock everything onto the floor. I avoided carrying drinks in my left hand after splashing Theresa when I had a sudden jerk. Worse, I experienced severe tremors and sleepiness. I took Dilantin only before bedtime but Lamictal was three times a day. I carried the medication everywhere but still messed up the schedule. At interviews, I shut off the phone alarms I used to remind me when to take the drug—if the chime sounded at an inconvenient moment, the discussion might be derailed. Afterward, I often forgot to take my medication or to turn the alarms back on.

The tremors were terrible. When I traveled to England to interview a lawyer for one of my books, I could not control my hands well enough to flip over a cassette; I was forced to ask the attorney to manage my tape recorder for me. On my return to the United States, customs officials pulled me out of line and demanded I explain why my hands were quivering so much.

Because I'm a terrorist! I wanted to yell. I was furious at being forced to give details of what was obviously a health problem to strangers, who then compelled me to answer personal questions unrelated to their jobs. This had nothing to do with protecting America—they obviously just wanted to satisfy their curiosity.

Eventually came the day when Theresa and I were sitting on bleachers for the final assembly at St. Mark's, an annual event attended by students, parents, and faculty. I watched my hands tremble. We were sitting in a spot where, if my left arm jerked, I would not disturb anyone. A terrible thought struck me: I had been in these same stands for the same ceremony a year before, experiencing the same problems. I could not believe how much time had passed, how long I had been dealing with these side effects. When the assembly ended, we went to the car. I remember saying that I couldn't put up with this anymore, that I would rather be on Dilantin than continue shaking and jerking.

I saw Leroy that week, and he prescribed a new medication, Lamictal XR. This was a long-acting dosage that kept a stable blood level. I would no longer have to remember a three-times-a-day schedule, just once before bedtime. After weeks of dosage adjustment, the trembling stopped, and the violent arm jerks dropped significantly in number and intensity.

The new drug released me from a fog. I realized I had separated myself from my children over the past year, playing less of a role in their lives, because of both my impaired cognition and my concern that the tremors would embarrass them in front of their friends. When I mentioned this, they each scolded me. Anyone troubled by my health, my sons said, was no friend of theirs.

Once my head cleared, I again took up the role of active father. Despite their assurances, I worried about how my recent year of troubles had affected my sons. Were seizures now a source of fear and anxiety for them? Or did they still view epilepsy as just part of my life, part of their lives, something that they could continue to treat as simply an unavoidable bother?

The answer came in 2009. Adam would graduate the following spring, and we were chatting about possible questions he might face in college interviews. We looked online for examples, some of which struck us as juvenile, such as "If you could be any animal, which would it be?" But many related to family life. One of us mentioned there was a chance a question might lead him to discuss my seizures. How would he answer, I asked, if someone inquired about how the family dealt with my epilepsy?

"I'd say, 'Mostly we just laugh at him,'" he replied with a smile.

For minutes, we roared at the joke and teased each other. But his words meant far more to me than a moment of levity. I left his room minutes later secure in the knowledge that my family remained comfortable and calm about my health.

Audio letters from my sons, 2018

RYAN EICHENWALD

I was always really, really proud that I had a dad that had been through hell and spat in its face and said, "Not today." That had nearly died more than once and had resolved to live as hard as he possibly could. Knowing that I was the product of that is one of the things that I take more pride in than anything else, knowing that you fought your own brain and knowing that you survived all of that, and to a small degree knowing that it was for us.

SAM EICHENWALD

We dealt with Dad's epilepsy in stride. We got used to it. Sometimes, it got kind of tough, but I personally grew to respect him more because of it, because on a day-to-day basis he had minor things he would struggle with but it really didn't affect him more than that.

Yes, he has a disability, but I honestly do believe that he used it as fuel to motivate him more to succeed in every aspect of his life. It's almost weird to say it, but knowing that and knowing how it inspires each and every person in our family, I think having epilepsy might have made him into a better man today than he would have been. He's faced countless struggles, not simply because of the epilepsy itself but because of people invalidating him and him going out and proving those people wrong. He helped impart the lesson to me of, if you work as hard as possible, then it doesn't matter who else is in your field, who else has what advantage over you, you can succeed, as long as you work hard. I have been endlessly inspired by this.

ADAM EICHENWALD

Even though you had seizures sometimes, epilepsy didn't define our lives. It wasn't really even a part of our lives, but the lessons learned from epilepsy not only drove our family but set me on the path for who I became. You learned life lessons from having epilepsy and then you turned around and instilled them in us.

People shouldn't have to go through a near-death experience to understand that there are things in life they can control and things they can't control, that their lives matter, that even when the world's against you, you don't stop fighting. It's hard to remember when you've been beaten down over and over again. But you hit back when you're knocked to the ropes, you've got to get up and get back in there. Sometimes you fail, and sometimes you fail over and over again, but you can't give up. I think that's the biggest lesson that we learned from you and your past: Once you give up, it's over. So you can't give up.

CHAPTER THIRTY

Almost every year, someone from Swarthmore phoned me seeking a donation. And, as I had promised a school administrator just before my graduation, each time I refused. I had committed to deducting ten dollars a year from the college's debt to my family, the semester's tuition it kept after throwing me out of school. Perhaps, I often joked, if I lived for the hundreds of years it would take to balance the books, I might start contributing.

While working on one of my books, I received another call from a Swarthmore fundraiser. This time, after I refused to give, she asked why. She seemed to detect that there was more than disinterest in my snub and wanted to know the details.

"I don't think you want to hear this whole story," I said.

"No, please," she replied. "Did something happen to you?"

I paused. This woman was a stranger. My connection to Swarthmore was limited to reunions of Sixteen Feet—the a cappella group still lived on decades after Carl and I founded it. I maintained no other connection to the school. The indignity of my dismissal—being treated as a frightening oddity impeding other students' education, my disbelief at the falsehoods I had to defeat to gain readmission, my inability to forgive—had warped part of me. My anger lay dormant until someone asked me about the school. Then the memories and rage would flood back.

As a term of readmission, Swarthmore had required me to keep silent about my dismissal and return, so I rarely discussed the ugly details with anyone outside the family, even in my *Times* magazine article. But what could they do now, take away my diploma? So I spoke. For twenty minutes, I recounted the turmoil and solitude of those terrible months, the times when I thought I would lose my treatment, the fear of choosing between abandoning my school or possibly losing any chance for an education. I knew this woman should return to calling other alums, but for the first time, from a position of strength, I could tell the tale to someone affiliated with the school. I needed to talk.

"Oh my God, I am so sorry," she said at the end of my monologue.

"Thank you, and I hate to say this, but that doesn't mean much. The school never apologized. I succeeded in my life when they could have destroyed me out of their fears or stupidity about epilepsy. All of my accomplishments have been despite Swarthmore, not because of it, and until the school acknowledges that what they did was wrong, I want nothing to do with it."

"I understand," she said. "But I *am* sorry that happened."

Days later, my office phone rang. On the line was Stephen Bayer, Swarthmore's vice president for development and alumni relations. Apparently, news of my conversation with the fundraiser had reached him, and he hoped I would speak with him.

"Yours is a terrible story," he said. "I want to assure you, nothing like that would ever happen now. The president personally and Swarthmore as a whole have a strong commitment to providing support to people with disabilities."

The president. I realized I didn't know who held the job. It might still be David Fraser, who took the post in my senior year.

"I'm sorry. I haven't kept up. Who's the president?"

"He was a professor, I think, during your time. Al Bloom."

I couldn't believe it. "Are you kidding? Al Bloom is president of

Swarthmore? He was the most supportive person there when I was dealing with my health problems."

"That's good to hear," Bayer replied.

Al Bloom. My mind reeled. The man whose wife, Peggi, had epilepsy, who met with me at their home when I was a freshman struggling with seizures, who encouraged me to participate in school activities. He was the professor who told me to ignore my grades, advice that helped me graduate with my class. When I fired my first neurologist, I ran to their home in search of support, and they tried to connect me with a new doctor.

Bayer told me that the school was taking my concerns seriously. He and Al Bloom wanted to travel to Dallas for a face-to-face discussion with me about what had happened during my years at Swarthmore.

Theresa and I agreed to meet with Bloom and Bayer for dinner at Mi Piaci, a favorite local restaurant. When they arrived, I gave Bloom a hug. I knew it probably took him by surprise, but my response to seeing him was almost involuntary. His support decades before had set me on a trajectory that allowed me to make my way from freshman year to graduation.

A waiter escorted us to a table where we could see ducks swimming in a pond outside the restaurant's picture windows. After about ten minutes of preliminary conversation, I thanked Bloom again for everything he had done for me.

"You have no idea how important you and your wife were," I said. "I seriously don't know where I would be right now if you hadn't helped me."

Bloom seemed to remember little about our encounters. I marveled that people could have such huge impacts on other individuals' lives, and not even realize what they had done.

From there, it was on to recounting the events that led to my dismissal. Theresa had coached me ahead of time, urging me not to become bogged down in details. She knew from hearing the story herself that I could ramble about what had happened endlessly, shifting from narrative to fury to outrage to depression and back again.

Bloom and Bayer listened as I expressed my almost unquenchable anger about my experiences. I had prepared for our meeting by reviewing some of my records and occasionally laid out some details that seemed to make both men wince.

After I finished, Bloom spoke. "What can we do to repair your relationship with Swarthmore?"

I considered the question. Bloom was one of the good guys. Still, the young man who had been forced to fight the school needed official recognition that the college's treatment had been wrong, that the impact had been terrible. Throughout my career, I had never been able to shake the dread that everything could suddenly be taken away without warning. That was why I worked myself to exhaustion, refusing assignments only if they conflicted with the needs of my family: I feared that turning down a project could cause me to lose my job and my health insurance. Then there were the nightmares that still haunted my sleep about the night I was thrown out, the pleading as I tried to convince the administration that my treatment and life could end as a result of what they were doing.

"I need an apology," I said. "I need someone to tell me, officially, that this never should have happened. And I want back the tuition that was stolen from my family."

Bloom nodded. But he made no commitments.

The letter from Swarthmore arrived at our home shortly afterward. Usually, I threw away the school's correspondence, assuming it was a request for money or an announcement of a rah-rah alumni celebration. But this letter looked different, like something personal. I opened the envelope and unfolded the single sheet of paper. It was from Bloom, writing in his official capacity as the president of Swarthmore. The words struck me hard: After more than two decades, this was the school's official apology for illegally kicking me out.

"Theresa!" I called. "Come look at this!"

Soon after, Bayer called. The administration wanted me to return to Swarthmore and speak about my work as a journalist. This was no ordinary talk but part of a series of special annual addresses often delivered by prominent alumni.

"You'll be receiving an honorarium for the lecture," Bayer said. The amount: equal to the tuition I had told him my family lost for the semester I was forced out.

I laughed. "You guys are very, very smart."

An apology and a tuition reimbursement. For the first time, I felt like Swarthmore actually *was* my alma mater, not just a place that had handed me an undergraduate degree.

I told Bayer I would be delighted to deliver the lecture. Then, after I spoke to Theresa, we agreed to contribute the honorarium to the school and pledge twenty thousand dollars more. My decades of freezing out Swarthmore were over.

A stately beech tree spread its limbs over the porch wrapping the Second Empire house reserved for Swarthmore's president. As I approached the doors, I marveled at the heavy moldings and bounteous windows decorating the residence. In my years at the school, I had never visited the home, but on this evening, I had been invited to join Bloom there for dinner before delivering my lecture.

The meal was delicious, and Bloom and I spent some time discussing the changes at Swarthmore since the eighties. We chatted about the letter he had sent, and I commented how odd it struck me that the official apology came from someone who had offered so much support. The person who really owed me an apology, I said, was Whitaker, the school psychologist.

"He doesn't work here anymore," Bloom said. "In fact, he was pretty much driven out of Swarthmore."

Years after my graduation, Bloom said, Whitaker had set off school-wide controversy. He had been behind an effort to push another student out of the school after he decided she was suicidal, then fought to prevent her return. There had also been complaints that he told a woman being abused by her boyfriend that she bore responsibility for his behavior. After dozens of students launched a campaign to have him removed, accusing Whitaker of unprofessional and abusive practices, Bloom had agreed to assemble a team of outside experts to evaluate the students' claims. Whitaker resigned rather than allow his activities to be reviewed.

"Good," I grumbled. "But it would have been better if he was fired."

One of the best experiences of my life was taking college tours with my sons. The first time was in 2009 with my oldest, Adam. At that point, I could drive. The medication change that had begun two years earlier in my fruitless effort to regain memories had been brutal, but the side effects had lessened and the seizures abated when I switched from regular Lamictal to the extended-release form of the drug.

With a schedule of colleges and universities to visit, we drove across the East Coast without ever turning on the radio. Instead, we talked for hours about everything and nothing, about secrets and dreams, about goofy jokes and serious concerns; it was the same experience I would later share with my younger two boys when the time came for their college visits.

We arrived at Swarthmore after touring a half dozen other schools. Adam had expressed uncertainty regarding my thoughts about the college: Would I want him to attend or be opposed? I told him, even if I hadn't already made my peace with Swarthmore, his choice of college had nothing to do with me. The decision was his; I would not pressure him toward any conclusion.

We finished the official tour for prospective students and were walking up the path from Sharples Dining Hall. I could see the spot where I had fallen on my face in the gravel during a convulsion; fortunately, I remembered nothing of that experience, and it never turned up in any frightening dreams.

I saw a man jogging toward us in sports attire that suggested this was a routine exercise for him. As he approached, his eyes lit up in recognition. I instantly identified him too—Allen Schneider, the psychology professor who was the first official at Swarthmore to witness one of my seizures. He had helped after that convulsion in a hallway, met with me to offer his support, and ultimately led me to Al Bloom.

"Professor Schneider?"

"Kurt!"

He wrapped his arms around me in a tight embrace.

"I am so proud of you," he said. "I didn't think you'd make it."

I was amazed. Not only did Schneider remember me, not only did he remember the magnitude of my health problems, but he also remembered fearing for my well-being. Nearly three decades had passed since he saw my seizure, but our experiences still resonated in his mind.

I introduced Adam to Schneider, and we spent a few minutes catching up. Then he resumed his run. Bumping into Schneider reminded me, Swarthmore was not just a place of nightmares. Yes, there had been trauma, but there had also been much kindness and support. Carl, Franz, Schneider, Bloom, and so many others made sacrifices that brought me to this moment with my son. I had borrowed their strength, and that blossomed, allowing me to confront years of challenges. Some people at Swarthmore almost destroyed me, but the community saved me. I could never allow myself to forget that again.

Adam and I resumed our wandering, heading toward Clothier Hall, where I had directed *Pippin*. He stopped on the pathway.

"Where did you get buried in the snow, Dad?"

I had always been open with the boys about my experiences, holding back only on disclosing my rape. I finally told them about that while working on this book, asking if the revelation of my sexual assault would embarrass them in front of their friends; each replied that anyone who thought less of me or of them because of the attack was not worth their time.

But on the day we toured the campus, Adam knew that the night of the blizzard remained my most frequent nightmare. He had noticed that, when I discussed my seizures, I rubbed the inside of my right palm, the spot I had scraped along the ground repeatedly, forcing myself to stay awake as I crawled through the snow. Now he wanted me to show him where that horrible experience had occurred. I couldn't go back.

"It's far away from here," I lied. "We don't need to go there."

He shook his head. "No," he said. "We do."

This wasn't curiosity. He wanted to force me to confront a major source of my fears. The enormity of that spot in my psyche had overwhelmed me for much of my life. And now Adam wanted to drag me back there, to see it again?

"No," I insisted. "There's no reason to go."

Adam stopped walking. "We're going. I'm not moving until you agree to take me there."

I knew Adam was stubborn enough that this standoff could last all day, so I agreed. We walked toward Wharton dormitory until we reached the site. I pointed out everything to him. That's where I fell into the tennis court fence. That's the lamppost I saw. Those are the stairs I climbed. Those are the windows where I could see students, the ones who couldn't hear my cries for help. That's where the student football player found me. That's the door he carried me through.

Adam said, "Okay, now look around, Dad."

I did.

"Dad," he said, "it's just a place. Something bad happened here. But it's just a place. See it for what it is."

I stared at this monstrous location. Grass, trees, a fence, a building. These were the sights of a thousand other spots on a thousand other college campuses.

"It can't hurt you, Dad," Adam said. "It's just a place."

It's just a place. It's just a place. Nothing more. I had surrendered part of myself to this space of grass and asphalt. I had allowed it to control me, to haunt my dreams. But Adam was right. It was just a place.

I turned and hugged my son. And then I thanked him.

On the evening of March 25, 2011, Theresa and I walked across North Broadway in Los Angeles toward a windowless building. I told her this couldn't be the right place; with its shabby, dark blue façade, the place looked more like an abandoned warehouse than the site for an important party.

An employee opened the front door, and we stepped inside. The rooms were gorgeous and well-appointed, at the opposite end of the spectrum from the building's outside appearance. We were escorted to a back room where crowds milled about. A goat's head hung on a brick wall, a decoration that struck me as an oddity for Los Angeles. I glanced around for faces I might recognize. No luck.

Someone called out that the guest of honor would arrive momentarily, so everyone stopped talking. Minutes later, a tall man appeared in the entryway accompanied by his wife.

"Surprise!" the crowd yelled. My college roommate Carl Moor looked stunned to see so many people gathered to celebrate his fiftieth birthday. He made his way around the room, greeting everyone. When he saw me, we hugged as he thanked Theresa and me for flying in from Dallas for the party. I saw Franz, who had flown from New York for the party, and we also embraced.

Carl, Franz, and I had stayed close since our final year in college. We visited one another occasionally, spoke by phone and email. My ties with Franz would undoubtedly be lifelong. In a strange twist, he was now my sort-of nephew, since his wife's stepmother was Theresa's sister.

I chatted with Carl's wife, Ann, whom I had known for many years, and met his two children. Then I resumed looking through the crowd for anyone I had met during that terrible summer in Chicago. I saw Tom, one of Carl's two friends who had been staples of our social life during those months, and we spoke for a few minutes. Then I ran into Carl's brothers, Peter and A.J., and we discussed family, jobs, and stories from the thirty-odd years since we had last seen one another.

The distance I had traveled from desperately ill college student occasionally came up in the conversations with party-goers who had seen me at my worst. Some congratulated me on obtaining my goal of working in newspapers, particularly given that they had heard that years ago I'd been named one of the youngest senior writers ever at *The New York Times*. Others told me they had read my books, congratulated me on being a *New York Times* bestselling author, or mentioned they had seen the Matt Damon movie based on my second nonfiction work, *The Informant*. When asked, I told them I was working on my fourth book, about terrorism and national security after 9/11.

Eventually, I noticed an older couple across the room and recognized them as Carl's parents, Lynne and Donell Moor. I thought about their kindness to me in that dreadful time. During spring break of junior year, they also had let me stay in their home while I searched for a summer job. I remembered being touched when Donell told me that he was proud I'd had the courage to travel alone on Amtrak from Philadelphia to Chicago. We all knew that if I'd experienced a grand mal seizure on the train, I would have been taken off at the next stop and brought to a strange hospital in an unknown city, and then I would have had to find my way back home without friends or family to guide me.

I brought Theresa over to meet the Moors. Hugs and introductions followed. Theresa and I talked about our kids, our work, our lives.

"How are things with your health?" Donell asked.

Theresa replied first. "Not well—" she began.

"Wait!" I interrupted. She was coming at this from a different context, I told her. What the Moors had seen and what she experienced were so dissimilar, the standards of good or bad from the two perspectives were unrelated.

"I'm doing really, really well," I told the Moors.

One last promise to keep.

On a summer day in 2015, my children and I arranged to meet on F Street in Washington, D.C., one block from Union Station. Adam, who had graduated from Bowdoin College the previous year, drove from Baltimore, where he was working as an environmental scientist. Our youngest, Sam, was with me on his college tour, and he was being recruited by the University of Pennsylvania for his skills as a photographer. The three of us stood near a green awning, chatting as we waited on my middle son, Ryan; he was a student at Duke University and had been meeting with New York publishing houses in hopes of a career in that industry. Theresa had wanted to come but couldn't leave her medical practice for the one-day trip.

Ryan's train arrived, and he walked down Massachusetts Avenue to where we were waiting. I hadn't seen my sons together since Christmas, but I knew everything happening in their lives. They kept Theresa and me updated; having raised them knowing they could speak to us about anything kept open a flow of conversation. We spoke multiple times a week.

Crowds wandered past as I looked at my three boys, successful young men who never would have existed if I had given up when my challenges seemed insurmountable. They were my reward, the personification of why I had struggled. Now I needed to take that last step, to honor the person I had been, the one who had made a commitment so many decades before that helped me achieve my dreams.

Small seizures had continued, but I mostly ignored them. After my fourth book was published in 2012, I joined *Vanity Fair* as a contributing editor and then also took a job at *Newsweek* as a senior writer. I believed things were good until Theresa and my neurologist intervened to once again tell me I did not have as much control as I believed. The doctor added another medication, called Onfi, and I struggled with the side effects as he adjusted the dosage. My boss at *Newsweek*, Jim Impoco, was supportive and allowed me to take a day or two off whenever I was struggling with the fine-tuning of the treatment. My control improved but was not perfect. My neurologist told me for the first time in 2014 that I had what was known as refractory epilepsy. I did not know what that meant.

"It's intractable epilepsy," he said. "It means it's very difficult to treat. We'll probably never achieve total control."

No matter. Naarden always advised me to find the balance between seizures, side effects, and an acceptable life. By that standard, I was satisfied. I found the balance. I achieved the life I wanted, and it all led to this moment on F Street with my sons.

Throughout college, Adam had asked, "When will we be going to Washington?" They all knew of the promise I had made to myself.

"Soon," I always replied; it wasn't time until after he graduated. The other two griped that they would be left out for part of this experience, but I had no choice. I explained that I had to abide by the commitment I made based on a fantasy about my future. Only one, the firstborn.

I told the boys to wait outside and pulled open the bright red door at the entrance of The Dubliner. I glanced around the dining room with dismay—they had rearranged the tables from how they had been decades before. I needed to honor the promise precisely. I owed that to the person I had been.

A hostess asked me if I wanted a table for one.

"No, actually I have something really strange to ask you," I replied. She gave me a perplexed smile. "Okay . . ." she said hesitantly.

"Many years ago, in the early 1980s, I was in this restaurant at a time when I was very sick. Every day it took a lot of energy and effort to fight. Sometimes I didn't know if I could keep going."

Her confusion gave way to fascination.

"I was here having lunch, and I gave myself a goal. I wasn't married and didn't have any kids. But I promised myself that someday I would come back here with my future son, and sit at the same table, and tell him I was proud of him. I've come here today with him to keep that commitment."

The hostess's eyes moistened. "That's so incredible," she said. "Which table was it?"

"That's the problem. It's not there anymore. The tables have been moved to different places. So I was wondering if we could move a two-person table to the same spot where it was when I made that promise."

She nodded. "Absolutely. Let me get the manager."

After she explained the story to her boss, the two asked me to show them where the table had been. I walked to a window that looked out onto F Street.

"Right here," I said.

Each of them hunted the room for a table they could move. As they searched, I studied the furniture. It might have been replaced over the years, but it looked exactly as I remembered.

The hostess returned. "There aren't any two-person tables free right now. Would you be able to wait?"

I laughed. "I've waited more than thirty years. I can wait a little longer." I told her I would be outside with my sons.

Adam fetched a hard apple cider from the bar, then rejoined us outside. My sons and I talked for about thirty minutes until the hostess appeared.

"All set," she said.

I looked at Ryan and Sam. "I'm sorry, but it has to be exactly as I promised. Only the oldest. Maybe just go for a walk in the train station, but come back in twenty minutes."

"Okay," Sam said.

Adam and I stepped inside. A table had been moved to where I had sat in 1984. I took the same seat, with the window on my right. Adam sat opposite me. I ordered a diet soda.

I stared across the table at my oldest son. He was healthy, strong, built like a marine. I was stunned to realize that he was almost exactly the person I envisioned so many years before.

I tried to speak, but the moment overwhelmed me. Finally I pulled myself together and looked him in the eyes.

"Adam," I said, "I'm proud of you."

I'd fulfilled the final promise, and my tears spilled forth. Adam took my hands.

"Dad," he replied, "I'm proud of you too."

I wept for a short bit, then dried my eyes. I asked the manager if we could move, this time to a spot for four people. The hostess brought us outside to a metal table alongside the black guardrail. Soon I saw Ryan and Sam walking back to the restaurant. They joined us, and we ordered lunch.

I watched my three beloved boys eat and talk, then glanced up at the clear blue sky, translucent and serene. Realization washed over me. The period of pain and fighting had passed; the commitments to the young man I had been, the one who had struggled for so long, had all been kept.

A new era in my life had begun.

A note to readers from

SCOTT THORNTON, 2018

My PTSD psychologist

Despite his successes, post-traumatic stress symptoms associated with decades-old events prompted Kurt to get into psychotherapy a number of years ago. In that context, I've had the privilege of bearing witness to Kurt's painful, triumphant ongoing story. It offers both inspiration and practical guidance, not only for those who have epilepsy, but for anyone affected by trauma or abuse.

For each of us, there can come a moment when we must take stock of our circumstances, acknowledge what we desire, and then take responsibility for attaining those things. There will be setbacks, and there might be debilitating symptoms for which we must seek help. Grit and perseverance, delayed gratification, and the tools of stress management can be developed, and will be needed. The shift from survival to thriving entails balancing this fierceness with large doses of humility and extending ourselves to others. Also remember, like Kurt, to be grateful along the way. Take nothing for granted. Accept that the process of authentic living never ends, and that at any moment our world can be shaken.

AFTERWORD

Dr. Allan Naarden retired from clinical practice. He now chairs the institutional review board that oversees research at Medical City, where Theresa also has admitting privileges. The two of them frequently lunch together at the hospital doctors' lounge.

Elva Eichenwald died in 2016 at the age of eighty-five. She lived in a retirement home that was walking distance from our house, and we saw each other frequently. We had numerous conversations in the year before her passing about the events in this book, which she eagerly wanted published. In those talks, she told me about experiences I did not remember, as well as things she had never disclosed for fear of the emotional impact they might carry for me. Months before her death, St. Mark's named the nurse's office for her, posting a bronze plaque that said she was being honored for "the care and love she dispensed." In the presentation of the plaque, which she attended, the headmaster of the school described her as "the consummate Florence Nightingale."

Heinz Eichenwald died in 2011, also at the age of eighty-five. My forgiveness for his errors in the earliest years of my convulsions never wavered. After his 1986 taping of his recollections of those events and his apology to me, we did not discuss those times again. I did not want to stir up any guilt or regrets for him. However, he often asked for details about the state of my health. After his death, the flags at University of Texas Southwestern Medical School, where he had worked for seventeen years, were flown at half-mast.

Eric Eichenwald graduated from Harvard Medical School and is now chief of the Division of Neonatology at Children's Hospital of Philadelphia and holder of the Thomas Frederick McNair Scott Endowed Chair. He and his wife, Caryn, have three boys in their twenties and thirties.

Carl Moor was named an associate justice on the California Court of Appeal by Governor Jerry Brown. He lives with his wife, Ann, and his two children are now in their twenties.

Franz Paasche is senior vice president of corporate affairs at PayPal, the worldwide online payment company. He is married to my surprise sort-of niece, Alison. Their three daughters are now in their twenties.

Adam Eichenwald graduated from Bowdoin College, obtained his master's degree at Yale University, and is currently pursuing a doctorate in environmental science. His fiancée, Lauren, is studying to become a physician at the same medical school that Theresa attended.

Ryan Eichenwald graduated from Duke University and is working in New York in the publishing industry. In his spare time, he has become a superb musician, playing both piano and guitar.

Sam Eichenwald is attending the University of Pennsylvania, pursuing his interest in visual media. His work has won scores of awards in photography contests worldwide.

Dr. Charles Nicholson, [*] my first neurologist, is chief executive of a small, little-known company that advocates the use of food additives

---

[*] Pseudonym used.

for the treatment of Alzheimer's disease, depression, and chronic alcoholism.

Dr. Milton Craddock,[*] who pushed my medications into the toxic range without checking my blood levels, has abandoned the practice of neurology and now works solely as a psychiatrist.

Dr. Matthew Strauss,[*] my Chicago neurologist, died a number of years ago. After the summer of 1981, I never spoke with him again. Except for the blood work and related diagnoses, the medical records generated from his interactions with me have consistently been disregarded by my subsequent neurologists.

Dr. Richard Roskos, the psychiatrist I saw after my expulsion from Swarthmore, continues practicing in Dallas. After my return to college, I never saw him again in a professional capacity.

Dr. Leighton Whitaker resigned from Swarthmore in 1994 after the college assembled outside experts to hear and evaluate students' grievances against him. A group of thirty students, called the Coalition for Improved Psychological Services, claimed to have "uncovered a psychological service system which had not only engaged in unprofessional and abusive practices, but had effectively immunized itself from accountability." Melanie Wertz, the leader of the effort, spoke to me in 2017. She said her group discovered that Whitaker refused to give students referrals for psychiatric help and falsely told patients that antidepressants were addictive and would "flatline" their personalities. Moreover, Wertz said, students had complained that if they revealed depression to Whitaker, they could find themselves placed on involuntary leave. "By reputation, Whitaker loved getting students thrown out of school," she told me. "Everyone took it as a warning: Be careful not to say you are having gloomy thoughts, or he would get you kicked out." The motives for this puzzling behavior became apparent when I located a 2002 essay Whitaker wrote called "Mental Health Issues in College Health." Whitaker focuses much of his analysis on minimiz-

---

[*] Pseudonym used.

ing lawsuits and on how to protect psychologists from criticism. Rarely does he comment on the welfare of individual patients. On the contrary, he states, in the context of discussing required discharges of students, "Campus mental health staff have a definite obligation for the well-being of the community as a whole and not just to certain individuals." He disparages deans who "may not relish" dismissing students for fear of losing popularity and says school psychologists must conduct their work "with a view to the benefits and hazards that might accrue to their particular institutions." He belittles "new, uninformed and untested college presidents and deans" who fail to protect the mental health centers. According to his family, Dr. Whitaker could not respond to my questions regarding the information in this book because of health problems.

Janet Dickerson, the new dean of Swarthmore at the time of my dismissal, joined Princeton University as the vice president for campus life in 2000 and retired in 2010. During my reporting for this book, she learned for the first time the full story of the events surrounding my dismissal from Swarthmore. After I reached out to her regarding this book, and told her the whole story of my dismissal from Swarthmore, she reacted with shock. She sent me a touching apology, much of which is cited in this book. I forgive her and wish her only the best.

ACKNOWLEDGMENTS

I have written acknowledgments in a number of books, but I'm struggling with how to start these. This time, I am not just giving thanks to the people who played a role in the writing and publication of this book. This is also about expressing my gratitude for those who helped me survive and thrive.

What words can be used to capture the depth of my appreciation toward people who saved my life, who loaned me their strength, who made it possible for me to have a family, to achieve my professional goals, to write any books at all? Every phrase seems inadequate. Every phrase *is* inadequate. Even for a writer, language does not provide sufficient tools to express the magnitude of my emotions and my thankfulness. But language is all I have.

The names of many of the people who have my lifelong gratitude are evident in this book. My mother, Elva Eichenwald, found a grit she never knew she possessed in order to fight for me. I know that the experience caused her emotional scars; her tape-recorded diaries to me from the early 1980s make that clear. But from those depths, she was able to recover to heights as she watched her three children blossom and her seven grandchildren make their marks on the world. My brother, Eric Eichenwald, provided an important support to my mother and my father, according to their taped diaries. He was also there for me.

Of course, I owe deep thanks to Dr. Allan Naarden, the neurologist who finally provided the correct diagnosis and brought me back to functionality. He never knew until he read the manuscript for this book how close I was to giving up on the day I met him. As I told him recently, if he hadn't been the great doctor he is, one who knows how to speak to patients, I likely would have died that week. I know there are many wonderful neurologists; I have been treated by several after Naarden retired. But he untangled the mess I had become by the day I arrived in his office.

Then there are Carl Moor and Franz Paasche. As young men, they were presented with a medically struggling roommate, someone they barely knew. I believe many people that age, and in that situation, would have walked away. But both of them took on enormous emotional and physical challenges to help me. They stood by me even when our relationship was rife with tension. They have been my friends for decades, and always will be.

I also must thank Jason Kinchen, Mari Cossaboom, and Errington Thompson, three dear friends who stood by me during the nightmarish months after I was dismissed from school and had to fight back against fictions. Each of them listened to me, each of them supported me, and all continue to be important people in my life.

Others played significant roles in helping me during bad times, but I haven't been able to delve into many details in this book. Some of the events involving them did not appear in my diaries, and so I could not reconstruct them. I did not obtain (or if I did, I did not subsequently find) tape recordings from them. But all of them should be acknowledged. Dave Robbins, the fourth roommate in our suite in sophomore year, has remained my friend from that day until now; he assumed a lot of responsibilities when I was getting particularly sick. Pat Cronin was there for me in my freshman year. Harry Schulz, Neil Fisher, Jocelyn Roberts, Karen Searle, Joelle Moreno, Julia Cutler, and many others were more of my heroes.

After I graduated from college, a lot of great people hired me despite knowing about my seizures. Hedrick Smith, Ross Brown, and Wally Chalmers treated me not only like any other employee, but also like a friend. At the *Washington Monthly*, Tim Noah and Jonathan Rowe were always kind, supportive, and encouraging. At CBS News, Joan Kelly, Eugenia Harvey, and Steve Manning were great colleagues who were sometimes called upon to deal with the consequences of my seizures and who offered me advice on career and life.

At *The New York Times*, I was always treated like everyone else. Alison Leigh Cowen and Susan Keller both dealt with a few seizures and discussed the issues surrounding them with me. I have no idea who else to thank at the *Times* because my epilepsy did not take center stage for anyone there.

The book itself could never have been written if not for the encouragement and support of Andrew Wylie and Jeff Posternak, the greatest literary agents in the business. Neither knew of my past, and some in the publishing world expressed concern that telling my story could damage my "brand." From the first minute I told them of this project, Andrew and Jeff were strong advocates for it, and cheerleaders who helped me through some difficult times in the process.

I can't say enough about Pamela Cannon, executive editor—and my editor—at Ballantine Books. Pamela championed this book from the beginning, sometimes understanding my goals better than I did. She offered major contributions that made this book better, and she also stood by me when the emotions of writing this book got tough.

As he has with so many of my books, Brent Bowers once again sprinkled his magic throughout these pages, giving me an invaluable second edit (with the first being from my wife). My friends David Michel, Jim Nadalini, and Ray Balestri provided important input as the readers of the first version of the manuscript. Jim Impoco—my editor at *The New York Times*, *Portfolio*, and *Newsweek*—not only provided great thoughts, but also has been an enormous professional support for me when medication changes were slowing me down.

The rest of the team at Ballantine were simply jaw-dropping in their talent. Kara Welsh, the publisher, pushed for me to make certain changes to the book that improved it immensely. Matthew Martin, who handled the legal review for Penguin Random House, had his hands full with me as sometimes we drifted into emotionally difficult issues, but he handled it with aplomb. Loren Noveck, production editor, and Katie Herman, copy editor, are easily the most brilliant people

I have ever encountered on proper grammar; their work was astonishing. Rachel Ake and Paolo Pepe handled the beautiful jacket design. And there are so many others to thank: Kim Hovey, associate publisher; Susan Corcoran, director of publicity; Melanie DeNardo, associate director of publicity; and Quinne Rogers, deputy manager of marketing. Pamela's editorial assistant, Hanna Gibeau, was endlessly helpful, and, as I often joked with her, seemed to always make it into the office despite the worst of snowstorms.

Most important of all are my wife and kids. Theresa and the boys—Adam, Ryan, and Sam—encouraged me to write this book, consoled me when some of the memories proved overwhelming, and accepted ugly details of my past with nothing but love and support. More than once, I walked away from my keyboard in tears, and Theresa was always there as my support, my shoulder to cry on. They have also lived through my medication changes, health setbacks, and improvements with the humor, laughter, and attentive disregard that have made my life a charmed one. I love you all more than I can express.

RESOURCES

If you, a family member, or a friend needs help in dealing with epilepsy, or if you want to learn more about the condition, go to:
>The Epilepsy Foundation: **epilepsy.com**
>Citizens United for Research in Epilepsy: **cureepilepsy.org**

Please contribute to these wonderful groups, which are not only fighting so people with epilepsy can live full and complete lives but are also searching for a cure.
>Donate at:
>>The Epilepsy Foundation: **epilepsyfoundation.givenow**
>>**.stratuslive.com/donate**
>>Citizens United for Research in Epilepsy: **cureepilepsy.org/**
>>**get-involved/donate**

If you or someone you know has been the victim of sexual assault, RAINN is a fantastic antisexual violence organization that offers numerous resources. For help, go to: **rainn.org.**

If you or someone you know is struggling with post-traumatic stress disorder, PTSD Alliance deals with the broad spectrum of psychological and healthcare issues. For help, go to: **ptsdalliance.org.**

ABOUT THE AUTHOR

Kurt Eichenwald is a *New York Times* bestselling author of four previous nonfiction books. His second, *The Informant*, was made into a movie starring Matt Damon and directed by Steven Soderbergh. In addition to his distinguished work as a senior writer at *Newsweek* and a contributing editor at *Vanity Fair*, Eichenwald spent two decades as a senior writer at *The New York Times*, where he was a two-time finalist for the Pulitzer Prize and a two-time winner of the George Polk Award, as well as the winner of the Payne Award for Ethics in Journalism and an Emmy Award nominee. He lives in Dallas with his family.

kurteichenwald.com
Facebook.com/KurtEichenwald
Twitter: @kurteichenwald

ABOUT THE TYPE

This book was set in Jenson, one of the earliest print typefaces. After hearing of the invention of printing in 1458, Charles VII of France sent coin engraver Nicolas Jenson (c. 1420–80) to study this new art. Not long afterward, Jenson started a new career in Venice in letter-founding and printing. In 1471, Jenson was the first to present the form and proportion of this roman font that bears his name.

More than five centuries later, Robert Slimbach, developing fonts for the Adobe Originals program, created Adobe Jenson based on Nicolas Jenson's Venetian Renaissance typeface. It is a dignified font with graceful and balanced strokes.